ALASKA RAW

BY BOB LACHER

ISBN: 978-1-57833-721-7
Library of Congress Control Number: 2019936097
First printing April 2019

Printed through **Alaska Print Brokers**, Anchorage, Alaska

Book Design: Crystal Burrell, 𝕿𝖔𝖉𝖉 𝕮𝖔𝖒𝖒𝖚𝖓𝖎𝖈𝖆𝖙𝖎𝖔𝖓𝖘
The body typeface for this book was set in Bookman Old Style

Published by:

Arctic Nomad Press
PMB 249 3060 N. Lazy Eight Court #2
Wasilla, AK 99564

Distributed by:

𝕿𝖔𝖉𝖉 𝕮𝖔𝖒𝖒𝖚𝖓𝖎𝖈𝖆𝖙𝖎𝖔𝖓𝖘
611 E. 12th Ave. • Anchorage, Alaska 99501-4603
(907) 274-8633 (TODD) • Fax: (907) 929-5550
with other offices in Juneau and Fairbanks, Alaska
sales@toddcom.com • WWW.ALASKABOOKSANDCALENDARS.COM

Table of Contents

Introduction 4

Chapter 1 - The First Aleutian - Unimak Island (2004) 5

Chapter 2 - Fall on the Alaska Peninsula (2003) 31

Chapter 3 - Winter (2006) 55

Chapter 4 - Soiled Dreams (2006) 74

Chapter 5 - Killing Machines (2008) 90

Chapter 6 - The Odds Were Never Worse (2003) 120

Chapter 7 - One Miracle Per Customer (2010) 134

Chapter 8 - Sheepzilla in the Brooks (2007) 165

Chapter 9 - The Wrong Side of the Edge (2010) 191

A Final Word 200

Introduction

Living in a way you can be certain that every decision and every move holds urgency and purpose...is being alone at 30 below zero and looking out over a blowing snow scape where the horizon has disappeared and the dimming light is replaced by a shifting, fluid cruelty of whiteness, where you cannot tell where the earth ends and the sky begins and, right then...you feed yourself into it. It's a spiritual place of such enormous wonder and intensity because you can't be sure how things will go. And it is because nothing is certain, that so much more is possible.

I have spent much of my life flying and hunting in some of Alaska's most remote parts, and in some of the most brutal conditions it could serve up. Hunting for many of us is cultural. When I was a young boy it was more than that. Hunting was connected by a straight line to eating and therefore it was important to become good at it.

My motivation in writing about these experiences was to share a place and time that few of us will ever get exposed to or can even imagine. Alaska is unique by virtue of its extremes of topography, of climate and often...its people. Growing up in Alaska was a world removed from the pedestrian proofed, asphalt framed cities that too many of us blindly suffer. Urban life, as it has evolved, brings with it a dullness of routine that acts on some of us as a slow poison. This is a book about cutting your own trail. It is my antidote.

I have always believed that if you surround yourself with familiar accoutrements, and you retreat into a cluster of the likeminded, and on the weekends you do what they do, and you read what they read, and you chant when they chant, and you nod in agreement when they nod...something of you has vanished. We all get but a single stab at this thing. If we are fortunate, we find a few precious moments of pure authenticity.

I'd rather be at 7,000 feet on a snowmobile trying to plot a route through glacier crevasses, or pioneering a crude landing strip high on the spine of a foreboding mountain so I can hike a peak that's never had a man's boot on it. To understand some of this book, it helps to understand that for a few of us, happiness comes from the uneasiness of the unknown rather than the comfort of the familiar.

This is a book about living those rare moments of authenticity. It's a book about how small we really are, with stories laced with the sharp edges of risk and unknowable external influences. For a good part of my life that has been my oxygen and I want to share some of it with you now.

Chapter 1

The First Aleutian - Unimak Island (2004)

As my father trailed behind me just a couple of paces, I noticed when I glanced behind to check his progress that his head was down and it looked as though he was trying to neatly trace my footsteps as we picked our way across the heavily undulating tundra. There was a small herd of caribou about 1,000 yards distant and one of the several bulls was big. Of all the possible thoughts I could have had during that moment of a final stalk, of tactics, strategy, stealth and focus, my mind instead went to a much earlier time when I was a small boy of ten or twelve, moose hunting with my father.

I remembered practicing being as quiet as possible, by shadowing his exact boot print as I set each foot down right where he had, staring at little else beyond his tall legs filling my field of view. I mimicked how he picked a spot to land his foot and then moved ahead carefully, softly. I would do anything to avoid earning a scowl from him by mis-stepping and snapping a twig, or crunching some dry leaves, or just heel striking too loudly, at which time my father would stop, turn his head backward to me, and give me "the look". Of course he never really needed to give me the look, my teeth being gritted in self disgust the instant the offending sound came off my boot...holding my breath...as though that would reel back in something of the sound, or cause him to notice it less.

Those times when I had been sloppy and committed the noisy deed, I cringed inside and just waited for his legs to stop moving, his head to pivot backward and then down to me, his message delivered once again, loud and clear, with one strained rogue eyebrow and scrunching of crow's feet framing his eyes. But back then a mistake was a big deal as it may have meant a missed opportunity that was connected to how well we would eat that winter. He was a serious man on a serious mission. I did the best I could, always looking for his approval.

As we stalked the caribou this time, the significance of this role reversal was hard to avoid. My father was trying hard to follow exactly where I had made trail, not so much to maintain stealth in this case, as the Aleutian wind was blowing off the ocean at a steady 40 MPH masking every bit of our noise - but simply for his own security. His 70 year old body sensing that if I stepped there, he could too, and without the risk of an unrecognized hole or rolling an ankle off an unstable wad of tundra. It was tough walking that day, but wherever I led he followed.

This caribou hunt was especially memorable for me for many reasons. It has some twists, turns and diversions as you will see. It begins with a plan to hunt Unimak caribou in late September. Frank, one of my hunting partners, was along with me on a trip I had planned specifically for my father. Frank owns and flies a Maul, a four place aircraft. I would be making the trip in a Super Cub which seats two. Both aircraft are high performance "Bush" planes and both can carry big loads of fuel and gear.

Our destination was the first island on the Aleutian Chain, called Unimak, a trip that is 750 miles from my home in South Central Alaska.

To give an idea of the scope of this flight, it is 100 miles less than Anchorage to Prudhoe Bay, or about the same as Orlando to Washington DC, or from the California/Oregon border all the way to Mexico. It's no small undertaking in a small aircraft. There are no Jiffy Marts on the way to Unimak.

There are a couple of places to ditch for the night, if you really wanted to, and fuel can be had at the villages of Iliamna and King Salmon near the halfway point. Our trip could not be made straight line, at least not made safely, since it would take us over too much ocean with no place to land in the event of problems. The route was a familiar one that I had flown on other hunting trips many times before - two hours gets you through the jaw-dropping peaks tightly lining Lake Clark Pass and down the lake's glorious, deep aquamarine blue length. Swing the compass left slightly and continue towards Lake Iliamna where the towering mountains begin to diminish and melt into the rolling tundra. From there it's onward to the small and isolated aboriginal villages of Iguigig and Nondalton.

The next enclave coming into view through the windscreen is King Salmon, the usual place for a piss break after three and a half hours in the skinny, thinly padded Super Cub seat. That's a good time to check the oil and look for nuts and bolts that rattled themselves off the airframe. King Salmon is home to the twenty five dollar hamburger, a bargain that cheerfully sinks in as you take on a load of seven-dollar-a-gallon aviation fuel. Our two aircraft held over 130 gallons in the four wings so to fill them up there you better have a pocket full of Ben Franklins and no aversion to shedding them as though they were cappuccino change. Food and fuel at this midpoint can run a cool $1,000.

Things were going well. We had a 20 MPH headwind coming through Lake Clark Pass that changed to a stiffer 30 MPH westerly crosswind as we lifted off from King Salmon with fat tanks of gas and better legs. The head wind slowed everything down and added another hour to the plan but it was a steady, predictable wind you just put your shoulder into, dial up a little more throttle and settle in for the grind.

It was much better than the thrill-ride blows that can come in from either the Pacific or the Bering side of this forbidding stretch of volcanic coastline that stretches nearly to Russia. The type of wind that can be experienced on "The Chain" requires serious skill from the pilot to keep the airplane top side up.

Dad was riding shotgun in Frank's plane, a more comfortable and spacious bird than the Cub. This gave me more room to pack camping gear for the three of us. Lifting off from King Salmon I always prefer to track more west than the direct plotted route south/southwest. I want to get to that awesome Western Alaska coastline as soon as possible and begin one of my all-time favorite pastimes, beachcombing for dead things.

Departing King Salmon we angled over the barren tundra for 20 minutes to the coastline, met it, and then turned more southerly. We dropped down on the deck and flew low along the breaking waves of the Pacific. Nowhere else on earth can you fly along a black sand beach for 400 miles at 75 feet off the water, scouting for dead walrus ivory and whale bones.

The pilot's entire journey down the Alaska Peninsula can be hugely stressful in different places. It's not for everybody. The passes are often wracked by high wind; the ceilings are most often low and spitting rain. Fog to the ground can have you flying by braille, looking for the worm holes to advance a half mile at a time.

We had some of all of that. But when you hit the coast just past King Salmon, the pall of continuous mental heavy lifting usually eases somewhat. Nearly the entire 400 mile coast is your runway, if you had to put it down, or if you simply wanted to stop the clock for a while and take in a trek. Land anywhere, eat, drink, rest, listen to the breakers crashing, fill your lungs with the salt air and decomposing kelp and sea grass, watch the birds, the pods of seals or observe huddles of walrus.

You have arrived at one of the most breathtaking marine environments anywhere in the world, and you have hundreds of miles of it all to yourself, and I do mean all to yourself. You will see no one else.

You are as infinitely mobile as an eagle and your full accommodations for camping are all packed tightly in the back seat and the trunk. The sense of freedom and discovery is off-the-charts.

That day our two aircraft were flying paired up fairly close, slipping down the beach, lazy as she goes, two notches of flaps to dirty up the slipstream, throttled back to 55 percent power, the tail a bit low and dragging through air, bumping along in an easy chair with wings and without a worry in the world. We flew past Pilot Point and on to Port Heiden.

Large pods of seals speckled the sandbars surrounded by endless crisp white breakers as far as the eye could reach. I brought the airplane up a few hundred feet to give the seals a break from the propeller noise we were about to greet them with. The seals noticed us but just rolled on their sides in the sand unbothered. We pushed on down the coast taking it all in, straining our vision onto the beach, moving past in relative slow motion to hopefully detect a whale vertebrae or skull or a walrus carcass.

Wind was still fairly brisk coming onshore at about 30 and causing a heavy crabbing attitude of the planes to keep them flying straight down the beach. Sitting in the pilot seat the view straight ahead in the cockpit appeared to be about a 35 degree angle heading hard out to sea, when in fact the path of travel was straight down the beach. It was an oddly cocked but steady and predictable gait that had your vision focused continually through the left window with a crooked neck.

Far ahead I started to make out another of the large chunks of tundra and dirt bluff sections that periodically break off the shore bank and are pushed by the tides and wave action to the middle of the beach. From a half mile away, the size of a small car, they often look like a potential walrus carcass, same size, same color, same profile, which is to say a lifeless brown blob. One can hope. After approaching and then passing many of the giant teasing dirt mounds, half buried in the sand, disturbed only by the breaking surf, I tried to continue to pay attention.

The one coming up was unusual in a telling way. An eagle lifted off of it as our aircraft got nearer. An eagle is not interested in dirt for dinner. It was a great looking walrus carcass! As I zipped by at 65 miles an hour I could look down and see part of one ivory tusk. Bingo! I banked the plane up on one wing and came around for another look. Frank and my father dropped in behind and followed my pattern around.

As we turned the wind became a quartering tail instead of quartering head. The downwind run had the aircraft going about 95 or 100 MPH, too fast to see detail of what the beast really had for tusks and if it was worth risking a beach landing in the crosswind. The quartering upwind passes were where we got a decent look, making several sweeps around it to finally decide we were going in.

I set up full flaps and attached my vision to a section of sand that pointed as correctly into the wind as I could get and not risk an overrun into the surf if I could not get stopped on the steeply sloped sand.

The first section of the landing zone sloped somewhat less for perhaps 200 feet, while the remaining 200 feet was heading down the bank at a stiffer 15 degree slope, terminating in the crashing waves... if you somehow failed to get it stopped in time. There were rocks at one end and a couple of root balls blocking the other which forced the angled landing headed toward the water. It was not great, but with the quartering headwind component it should have been a pretty good bet to get it done in the first two hundred feet.

I dropped a wing low on the windward side, slipping and crabbing the bird down toward the spot of sand I wanted to hit. Slowed to the limit of stall, I made first contact with the windward side tire.

In a single, coordinated, fluid motion I immediately kicked the tail up wind and fully straight to my direction of landing, chopped the throttle to zero, dumped all the flaps, and smashed all of the brakes the sand would allow. I was stopped in the first 200 feet. I pulled forward out of the way and shut down. It was Frank's turn.

My wingman circled a few more times to see just what the zone looked like with a plane parked on it. This is a good visual reference where there may be no other. It's a way to put distances and angles and slopes in perspective. The second guy in usually has the easier time of it. It's mental if nothing else. Frank lined up just as I had and descended toward the sandy sweet spot well marked by my first tire impact. He had been flying in that same crosswind for the last two hundred miles so that was no issue. He just needed to be right on his toes, and to slow the airplane up well, work the left rudder to the firewall when called for...then once everything is squared away and looking good, to get on the brakes hard before the salt water did the braking for you.

There was nothing to it, especially for Frank who had thousands of flight hours and a long career as an Air Force aviator. Frank's approach looked great. I could see both him and my father sitting side by side, eyes wide open, locked in on the ground they soon wished to be walking on.

The crab angle looked good, the appropriate wing tipped into the wind perfectly. Flaps at full, steady...steady... and...contact. The touchdown was nice and slow, perhaps 45 MPH. Then, for some reason, Frank thought he was done with that particular landing. He thought he could relax, that with all those perfectly made moves during the approach...that it was a sure thing. His mind may have already moved on to the grand prize, the walrus, the ivory booty, or maybe the stories of harvesting it that he would tell his grandchildren. The Maul settled in perfectly, spot on and with both wheels initially pointing directly down the strip.

At this point is exactly when the sharp wind blowing from your right will want to push your tail hard left, thereby pointing your nose at the breaking waves coming up fast on your right.

It is at this point that you also must jam the left rudder to the floor with your boot with roughly the same determination and full commitment that it takes to kill a crocodile by stomping on its neck. And if that crocodile don't die under your boot, you stomp a bunch of left brake to help out the left rudder. You force everything the airplane will do to make the nose go left and stay out of the water, and you do it instantly. You do it by pure reflex.

As I watched the beginning of a perfect touchdown I thought it odd that Frank allowed the tail to swing with the wind a little wide, then....wider. He was allowing the plane to roll out as though there was no crosswind. The jack boot to the left rudder never came. It looked like things might get salty.

The airship was headed for the water. This was not at all amusing, mostly since my father was at some risk, being over 70 and unable to swim a lick. My dad, like many Alaskans who have never learned to swim because it's so damn cold here all the time, is not a big fan of ocean water. Moreover, he has only one hand which is paired with a much less handy stump due to an electrical accident that happened in his mid- thirties. Ice-fucking-cold-ocean has a nut-shriveling effect which I was certain my dad was not looking forward to.

Just then I could see sand shooting off the left outboard wheel, the brakes coming on hard (finally), and that sent the plane into a ground loop to the right, toward the water, but the left wing tilted down so hard it impacted into the sand. The effect of all the skidding, ground looping and heavy breaking was just a little better than going into the drink.

Frank and my father came to a stop just short of the final down slope heading to the breakers. In slow motion the plane tilted up onto its left tire and struck the left wingtip, threatening to flip altogether, but rocked back down on its three wheels. Not great, but it could have been so much worse. I asked myself: Now how far away from help are we? It was time for a walk around and some deep breaths.

Dad bailed out. Frank fired up a Camel and checked his panties for shit stains.

It was a challenging but perfectly landable set up. Frank is a good pilot, with a full suite of skills. He did all the hard parts and then checked out. He cooked a perfect seven course meal, then took a nap in the recliner and, forgetting the oven was still on, burned the house down. I had a few emotions of my own, selfish certainly, all surrounding our ability to continue the trip to Unimak and find a big caribou for my father.

Our first concern was if the Maul was flyable, or if it could be repaired. If yes... could it be done on the beach, if yes...could we do it with the tools we had onboard. The actual damage was not severe.

No buckled landing gear, but the final two feet of the wing was well bent upwards as was the aileron. We jaw boned the "what ifs" of the landing, took turns gawking and pawing at the bent parts, and generally opining on how "this or that" amount of force "here or there" may cause some miracle of aeronautical metallurgy to occur.

After some time collecting Frank's rattled ego and focusing on the problem, we got out all the tools we thought necessary to do the required body work. We did not have many.

It takes some amount of resolve to finally decide you are going to attack a near new 125 thousand dollar aircraft with a Leatherman, a crescent wrench, a small sledge hammer (brought to drive tent stakes) and an ax. But once it had been decided...we went to work like a cluster of Bangladeshi rickshaw repairmen. Soon we had the offending sheet metal hacked off, the bent tip surfaces hammered into rough shape, and space freed up for the aileron to move up and down again.

The aileron was bent up about 30 degrees and kinked. Once we made space for it to move within the wing, it was still crippled because of the range limitations and interferences caused by the kink.

The big hammer was just bouncing off the bound up metal. The noises from each blow sent shudders rippling through what was left of Frank's bruised disposition. There was nothing left to do but perhaps get up on top of the wing and jump on it. That seemed rude. I finally tried a chin up, grabbing the end of the aluminum section and reefing down with all my weight. It finally started to come into shape. A few more reps of that and we were able to swing it through the full range of motion. We face checked each other for full approval and satisfaction.

In flight it clearly would pull to the left, but we all agreed it should fly. In fact it might fly reasonably well. After another cigarette and more jaw jacking about how fortunate we were, the conversation finally got back to the dead walrus that was half in the water, half out, just a hundred yards away. We were for sure going to cut its head off.

Nothing would be more humiliating than wrecking an airplane and getting nothing. The act of beheading would begin the man-healing process. We rounded up the tools for the task, big ax, bone saw, serrated long bladed Cutco knife, rubber gloves, hip boots and long rain jackets to shield us from the putrid splatter of magnificently rotten walrus goo.

Our trip plans were seeing some daylight again. The plane looked airworthy and the walrus was about to receive serious neck surgery. Given all of that, it seemed like it was about the right time to drag out into the open the notion we had all been thinking about since the Great Mistake: If the plane flew reasonably well, did Frank have the appetite for limping on down to Unimak and completing the trip?

What was unthinkable several hours ago was now thinkable, at least to me. I threw it out there. My father's response was to give me his best confused and disoriented look like he misunderstood what I said, like maybe if he ignored the crazy street person who was smelling of urine and asking for spare change....he would eventually escape his piercing stare.

Frank, apparently all jacked up on the fetid fumes of the nearby rotten walrus, did not take long to agree, at least to the concept. With an introspective tilt of his head he mumbled something about "if it flew, why not finish what we started?" This would be easy. If it pulled to the left, just steer more to the right, like a car with a low tire. The structural analysis was completed with confidence and, even more amazingly, without any beer. Nods of affirmation were being exchanged and re-exchanged all around. Let's do this!

All further issues would be worked out during the test drive.

Dad was slowly coming around to our position to keep the venture on schedule and we set about soothing disrupted feelings and jangled nerves by acting normal and beheading the walrus.

It was a dandy. Half of the animal's head had been buried in the sand and the tusks were bigger than previously scouted from the air. It was an hour and a half long job since Frank wanted the entire skull to clean and mount, rather than just the tusks.

Incoming tidal breakers were rolling the 3,000 pound carcass up and down the inclined beach like a massive beach ball caught in the surf. We'd make a few cuts in the three inch thick neck hide while standing in three foot deep water, trying to time the waves so we could run back up the bank each time a big one came in and swamped the operation.

Back and forth, cut, slash, hack, chop, hack...outrun the incoming wave...follow the outgoing sea back out, jump on it again and repeat. The blood and snotty decomposed flesh swirled in fetid pools around us. Thigh deep in the cold surf and bathing in the revolting stench, we cannibalized the huge head off the body and drug the prize up on shore. We felt back in charge.

Both airplanes were loaded to near capacity given the fuel we still had, so we decided to stash the head well up the bank in some tall grass, marking it with a GPS and brightly colored flagging to allow retrieval on the home bound trip. Frank and I cleaned up and sacked and sealed our bloody, rancid clothes and gloves in big garbage bags and loaded for the flight further south. After liftoff, some back and forth on the radio between us confirmed the Maul was flying well enough. It would be a couple hundred more miles to get to Unimak and I was hoping to get another walrus head, or even better, a couple more.

We got back into the low level, throttled-back flight pattern along the ocean's edge and picked our way down the beach at just 100 feet elevation.

Though we did not find another walrus head to harvest we did find a spot where several hundred walrus were hauled up on a sandy shore to build up some body heat and take a break. There was a beach area several hundred yards away that appeared flat enough to get the planes landed on and we decided to stop and take a closer look. These were a batch of mature bulls and weighed 2,500 to 3,000 pounds. Stacked shoulder to tail, flashing long ivory tusks. They clearly did not see us as predators and didn't get the least bit agitated about getting visitors.

The smell made our eyes water and throats burn, the bitter fumes of ammonia in their excrement was not just really unpleasant as in a humid, confined chicken coop or the worst corner of a dirty barn, it was physically overpowering, seizing your lungs if you got a big hit of it straight in.

After a good half hour break and a snack and taking a round of pictures, we walked back up the beach to the airplanes and continued on. The next stop would be Cold Bay, a place to regroup, fuel up and possibly stay overnight. The wind was picking up. What had been 25 to 30 MPH was now 35 to 40 and spitting rain harder than when we began.

It's difficult to keep a small aircraft parked and stationary in wind over 35 MPH unless you can find a washed up log or heavy brush to tie it down to or unless you drive your own earth anchors, which we carried with us but were a pain to install and remove. If it did not slow down we thought it may be best to overnight in Cold Bay and see what the next day brought. Mile after mile of black sand came and went. The winds continued sharply.

When we finally arrived in Cold Bay there was no question the best plan would involve finding a tie down and waiting out the weather. A quick check revealed the winds were to slow to 25 or 30 MPH by the next morning and stay that way for at least one day.

Cold Bay is an interesting place. It rests on a narrow piece of volcanic real estate in the middle of nowhere. It's also unusual in that it is a Caucasian rather than aboriginal community. Originally a WWII Air Force outpost, the NOAA weather station and Federal Aviation runway maintenance employees are mixed with a handful of PenAir employees along with a few U.S. postal employees to make a tiny town. The Izembeck National Wildlife Refuge staffs a small office there also. Ten to twelve children in school keep a single teacher occupied. A steady flow of migrant cannery workers head to Dutch Harbor or King Cove by going through the town during the fishing seasons.

The town also comes alive, in relative terms, during the spring and fall when hunters from all over the planet drop in for the world class waterfowl or to chase brown bears as large as any in the world. There is a small hotel and bar with a few rooms and a pay phone.

The low roof, plywood wrapped, wind beaten structure also holds the town's only grocery store, an establishment with mostly dried, canned or frozen food, whatever can be made consumable with a microwave or a hotplate.

Frank, dad and I fought against the wind to tie down our birds and then lugged some gear the couple blocks from the runway to the "hotel". We rented a couple of 80 dollar cubbies in the bunkhouse and headed for a room down the narrow hallway that was the makeshift grocery store.

Our big treat for the night would be microwave cuisine, some Hot Pockets and something that resembled pot pie with white cheese and chicken-bits-come-back-to-life. I resisted buying a can of Spam and dicing it up into a can of SpaghettiOs but it was tempting.

My final choices were determined entirely by what mixed well with Budweiser. I tried to visualize if the SpaghettiOs would sink in Budweiser or float. In the end I knew that for it to sink, it had to be greasy, so I went with cheesy chicken pot pie. My only complaint was the frozen goo billed as the dough on the bottom never cooked and it took a little extra beer to swill the pasty globs down. I determined the heavy dough in the bottom of the pot pie to be a conspiracy, an extra thick filler snuck into the recipe to economize on both cheese and chicken bits.

The next day broke with less wind but still enough to make the plywood "hotel" creak and groan. After some instant coffee and a weather check we headed out to continue our excellent adventure. There was to be a temporary lull in the wind, down for most of the day, then back up to 40 plus by early evening. In this part of Alaska if you waited for a windless day you may wait months. We'd take the somewhat quiet weather-window and try to fly the next 60 miles to Unimak and find some cover, behind a hill or in a draw, and set some good earth anchors, or fill some empty sand bags that we carry for the occasional tie down. We also had lift spoiling wing covers that could be pulled on the wings like stockings to help them from acting like a kite in a storm.

We crossed the scenic channel of ocean at False Pass after just a few minutes of flight time and made the shoreline again on the edge of Unimak and continued on. This channel is the first place going south that the Bering Sea meets and mixes with the Pacific Ocean. The views were magnificent. To our left some long shallow gorges, remnants of an old volcano being eroded, each lined with low green foliage interspersed with scree slopes of black volcanic rock. Straight ahead lay open plains with spotty high alder.

Repetitive small streams cut left to right, spilling off of the higher volcanic inclines and each heading to the ocean shores which dominated our view off to the right which was now the Bering Sea. The airplanes droned along in tandem, idle chatter on the radio, back and forth, pointing out this or that interesting landmark or topographical anomaly.

That weather window we hoped to squeak through must have been narrowing because the farther we went southwest the harder it seemed to be blowing. Within 30 minutes after liftoff we were almost to our planned destination but the gusts were mixing things up and causing some worry. We were flying a crosswind course but I banked the cub right and directly into the wind for a quick and accurate check of the GPS ground speed verses indicated airspeed.

The difference of the two numbers provided true wind speed and allowed us to determine what sorts of issues we may incur when trying to set down. It was again cranking

35 with gusts to 45. Clearly we need to find cover to be able to set up any sort of tent camp and to be sure the airplanes could be safely anchored.

As we headed away from the volcanic foothills, the terrain was a mixed array of black sand blows, many long enough to land on, interspersed with rutted, undulating, vegetated flats.

Frank and I spat observations back and forth on the radio, discussing the pros and cons of each long sand blow we found, cranking our birds around, swooping low to look over the dips and gullies and the banks formed upwind of the landing spots that may provide cover. With each gust that slammed into the airplanes, and each heavy handed maneuver required to keep them flying true, the conversation became incrementally more serious.

It is often a fine line in such deteriorating situations, balancing the urgency to get the plane on the ground with the mental absolution that the place you have picked to finally put a noose on the madness is a good one. A quick consensus came together over the radios of which spots may be flat enough to land on, with cover, and within reasonable proximity to fresh water, something that is also necessary to have close to camp.

We picked a long and mostly smooth volcanic sand blow that was tucked in next to a large hill and ridge feature that spanned lengthwise on the windward side of the landing zone. It should have afforded a good wind block and it also had the bonus of a random, large volcanic boulder the size of a pick-up truck sitting half buried in the sand right where we wanted to park and set up camp. With luck we could find a way to anchor the airplanes and the tent to the rock.

Setting up for landing squarely into the 40 MPH wind, the groundspeed was near zero at touchdown. Easing down like helicopters, both of us landed capably and taxied carefully over nearer to the boulder. We taxied with our tails high by pushing forward stick thereby forcing the big wing airfoils neutral to the wind.

The wind speed was right at a tipping point. If you set your parking brakes and jumped out, you had better be doing so with ropes in hand and trying to instantly get a wing snagged and then tied off to something stationary. Failing that, the aircraft would be trying to fly without you, alternately lifting one wing or another and bumping backward against the locked parking brakes. My Super Cub was more difficult to ground handle than the Maul since it took a little less wind to make it fly.

I had taxied in first and hogged the boulder, the only tie down, while my father and Frank took a position just behind me. I looked back and they were instantly out of the plane and furiously digging the Maul's tires into the soft volcanic sand to lower the wind profile of the wings. Frank also readied some Duckbill earth anchors and a short sledge hammer to drive them.

Holding the airplane door tightly, I shoved it open into a howling gale delivering up a face full of blowing grit. I had sat in the airplane for a few moments to plan my moves and left it running just in case I had to gun it and lift off again, if the plane was going to resist being ground handled and tied off. My plan was to jump out with a fistful of ropes in hand and to quickly circle one all the way around the base of the big boulder and come off of that with a lead line for the right wing which I had pointed more windward than the other.

The left wing and tail would be handled by digging the tire in and then a couple of driven earth anchors. The only close call came when I was trying to make the first tie for the right wing, from the looped rock to the wing strut. A forceful and sustained gust swept through and lifted the left wing three feet into the air and held it there, levitated as if by a magic trick. What that meant was the entire aircraft was ready to go missing if the other wing got just a whiff more wind at the right angle.

I ran to the high side to throw my weight onto the wing strut and yelled for help. I could hardly hear myself yell into the wind let alone expect Frank and my father to react, 75 feet behind me. Fortunately my father was watching the gyrations of the Cub as he helped Frank finish digging the last tire in on the Maul. Having secured the Maul momentarily, they both jumped forward and grabbed on to the left strut of the Cub which allowed me to finish tying to the boulder and quickly grab the shovel and dig a hole for the free flying left tire and then pound in an anchor just forward of the left wing.

There were no wasted motions. The wind just kept steadily building. The three of us beat back the wind demons attacking the Cub and secured it one limb at a time. We then immediately ran back to the wildly bouncing and shifting Maul to affect its final exorcism. Already this was not working out as planned. The hill we parked up against was chosen to give us cover. The big rock was a bonus.

Alaska Raw

But the wind direction had shifted in the fifteen minutes or so we had taken to fly several patterns and inspect the site, confer on the radio, and then get the planes on the ground. Once on the ground it became obvious that the wind was gushing over and around the hill like water in a stream moving around a pebble.

We were not much better off than being in the wide open, with the exception of the big rock which proved to be priceless. After all, the winds are notoriously wicked and unpredictable on the Aleutians. This fall storm could have easily built to 80 or 100 MPH and the rock was the only immovable protrusion from the landscape for miles.   No trees, no brush, just rolling tundra and sand.

Moreover, we were stuck there until the winds tapered off enough to re-launch, something that was not going to happen before nightfall. We started prying out the tents and bags and trying to divine a clever method of erecting a tent in what was now a steady 50 MPH blow.

After a couple of attempts we got the four man "Bomb Shelter" tent standing tight up against the backside of the boulder with tie lines going every which way, reaching back to driven stakes and tied to various parts of the Cub which seemed to be holding its own.

After getting enough of camp established to be able to overnight, and after spending some time scraping the sand out of our ears, teeth and eyes, we settled into the tent to listen to the power of the warring meteorological gods. The tent's door position allowed me to peek at the Super Cub from time to time, to see if my $100,000 investment was going to be slowly deconstructed and rendered to scrap.

Our tent was square in the lee of the rock but was still getting hammered and by now it was leaning away from the wind at increasing angles, straining against all its tethers with each new pummeling. Inside, on one cot and two folding stools, the three of us had positioned ourselves so that the force of the wind shoved the tent against our bodies to provide more of an immovable anchor, a human hedge against the raging furry on the other side of the 6 mill nylon. Dad was on the cot. Frank and I manned the stools.

I continually maximized my anxiety by unzipping the tent door six inches and peeking out at the airplane. I felt like a tightly wound dope fiend all spun up and looking through a crack in the drapes for invading spooks that had no shape, and about which absolutely nothing could be done. In some ways, and for reasons unknown, this is the stress some of us live for. There is a lot at risk and you wear the lump in your throat for hours on end until it feels like a new body part.

Each big gust that slammed the tent bent the aluminum poles a little further downwind. It was still building. During one particular gust that got everyone's complete attention, I looked over at my father lying prone on his cot, jammed tight against the heaving wall. The shrieking blast lifted the tent wall and its attached floor section which, in turn, had lifted his entire cot off the ground several inches with him in it. The Cub was now fairly regularly hovering hard against its tethers, literally levitating in its parking stall a few inches off the ground.

A big gust would hit and I would look out and see the tires jerk up out of the depressions we dug and the airplane would strain against its ropes, the tail would raise and it would fly until that gust bled off enough for it to settle back to the ground. This is when you know you are close to losing an airplane. Besides the visuals of your expensive toy flying without you, the roar in your ears is unrelenting, and the tent is being held up only by a community effort of our backs being pressed hard into service on the windward side. In those moments you hope for just a little something to go your way.

On one of our several high velocity trips outside the tent, which we made to check and tighten ropes, we actually took some video. Frank crawled in the cockpit of the Maul which was shielded somewhat from the wind since it was parked just behind the Cub and the rock and the tent. Video from inside the Maul showed the airspeed indicator hitting 55 MPH in the few short moments he was in the plane filming.

I estimate some of the larger gusts in the middle of the night were over 70 MPH. Incredibly, there would be no break. The chaos continued all night and into the next day until around noon. It was a night of zero sleep and long faces. We lost nothing but I did have to replace the set of tent poles on the Bomb Shelter, a brand of tent made to hold up to just about any weather that anyone would want to camp out in.

That next afternoon, after the wind died off to about half, we dosed heavily with coffee, broke our temporary camp, and launched a spotting mission to try and find some big bull caribou.

Just south of Urilia Bay there are some great feeding areas for caribou and we weren't in the air 15 minutes before several small, scattered groups of cows and bulls were logged into the GPS for locating during the next day's hunt. Another hour of flying further south and east did not result in finding much else, only a few stray groups of small bulls with cows and a few really nice bulls that were too high in the hills for my father to hike to.

We circled back to a location several miles square that was in the crux of the several groups we had selected and began the same systematic check, looking for a smooth landing spot with wind cover that was close to fresh water. Finding exactly what we were looking for after just a few big circles, we set the airplanes down and taxied up against a steep cut bank that was again to be a fortress wall, deflecting the wind now coming generally out of the north. All hands began to unload and give shape to base camp. Walking just behind the cut bank delivered you to a twenty foot wide stream, shin deep but clear and running with purpose.

As Frank and I admired the stream for a moment, a well fed nine foot brown bear emerged from the low brush that was lining the bank to the right. It appeared to be a boar, square nosed and dark toned. It was at 75 yards and slowly closing the distance, walking in the middle of the streambed, fishing for salmon, head down, oblivious to us and upwind. The current rippled with fish trying to outmaneuver the bear's determined prospecting. The bear was probably 800 pounds.

He did not see us and we did not linger, but slid back around the cut bank quietly retracing the 100 yards to the airplanes, hoping the brown would just move on by and not take an interest in the cooking we were planning later in the evening. We never saw it again.

The winds had softened to 20 with just occasional and short lived spikes. We welcomed the dramatic change. Sun was showing in fits and starts for the first time of the entire trip, stabbing columns of light onto the darkly greened hills in the distance, shifting, disappearing and recasting through tight holes in the low clouds. The weather was better but reminding us constantly of how very unsettled Aleutian weather is in general.

Good spirits were pushing aside the stress of the last 24 hours spent on a high wire. Banter flowed easily without the need to out-yell the wind with a worn out throat during the simplest of exchanges. Stories emerged about who thought this or that about the previous day's eroding conditions, about contingency plans that were never shared, let alone put to a vote, about the ferocity of this or that series of gusts, about living the oppressive thrill throughout the night, one hour at a time, caged like an animal.

Gear sorting and the pitching of camp pattered along unhurried, rhythmically, in perfect step to our relaxed surroundings, in a shared solitude, in communion with everything and nothing at all, taking more time than any task needed, and much more than that if you wanted it to, or if the lightweight tool or toy in your hand held a particular interest for you just then, and you were deciding if it would be useful enough to make the cut...and actually make it into your day pack that would sustain next day's hunt, stalk and kill.

Fattened up by a good meal and in shrinking evening light we walked to some higher points within a hundred yards of camp to do some glassing. Caribou were in every quadrant radiating out from our stoop.

We saw lots of cows grazing and cavorting with medium size bulls, other bulls with horns mated up, in slow motion pushing contests that were establishing not much of anything by way of dominance as far as I could tell. It appeared far too casual to be definitive, like play wresting amongst best friends. We also saw a small group of cows with one real champ of a bull to our southwest, out about half a mile. We watched it for as long as we could, until our eyes watered so heavily and continually from the wind that it was wearing to continually clear them.

The group had four or five smaller bulls with it but the dominant bull was for sure the ball smasher of this harem. Double shovels, large bases, bejeweled with thick tines in quantity like overdone Christmas tree decorations. In the morning, providing the group had not moved very far, we'd go after that one. We retreated to camp. Everyone was excited about our good fortune and hopeful that the weather would hold and allow a successful hunt. After not getting any rest during the gale the night before, sleep came easily. I had hardly crawled in my bag and a symphony of snoring rose from Frank and my father.

Normally my strategy is to beat the snorers to sleep. Even the jowl flogging and tongue snagging noises were nothing compared to the wind racket that had worn me so thin the night before, so falling asleep was a snap.

Closing my eyes, I allowed myself a final mental walkthrough of how in the morning we would move up on that herd bull with, unfortunately, zero cover between us and them, and give the big daddy a one-way ticket to Wasilla. I was halfway through the perfect stalk, making my way in a super-stealthy commando belly crawl when my lights blinkered out.

On the Aleutians one thing is certain; there is zero possibility of waking up to the sound of birds tweeting, say, or a bubbling brook. No. It is always the ever present slapping of tent fabric, the invisible forces tearing at the small structure, reporting to your ears as though surrounded by an army of antagonists snapping wet towels about your head. And so we rose, rubbed our gritty eyes clear, and stretched and yawned our way into another day of 35 to 40 mph wind. Of course all anyone was thinking about was if the herd had moved, or how far.

Skipping even the morning coffee, we layered up and headed for the close high ground just a hundred yards from the tent and then got on the field glasses to try to find them. The group we wanted had moved, but just rotated around our camp about 90 degrees, and we were still quite close, about half a mile, and at a direct crosswind to them. They were relaxed and grazing.

Given how relaxed these caribou were, I found it odd that through the night, nearly every other small group and even stragglers had migrated outward from our position, as though our landing and camping registered with nearly all the caribou, as though we were the Big Bang and they were planets and stars accelerating ever so slowly away from our epicenter. Every group except the one we wanted was now two to three miles out. It was a lucky break. My father would hold up better with a shorter stalk.

Dad can walk just fine for miles under normal conditions. But this tundra looked like a field of four foot beach balls crammed together with a thin green blanket draped loosely over them.

It was a brutal up and down "high stepping" and the surface itself was mushy and grossly uneven underfoot. Difficult when sober but impossible after three beers describes it pretty well.

We hung tight to the ground in labored crouches and closed the distance to the group. The wind was nearly a direct cross, howling and masking any amount of noise we could possibly make. The only cover we had was the lumpy terrain. When the three of us got within 175 yards there was a final depression allowing slightly more cover before it flattened out to an open plain of sand and low grasses that the group of caribou was cavorting and grazing in. Up closer the big bull looked to be all we'd thought it was as we made a final appraisal. My father wasted no time getting to prone and building a rest out of my rucksack full of game bags.

Once a couple of cows moved out from in front of the bull my father had a steady rest and a clear shot and so he aimed carefully, took a deep breath...and let one fly. The crack from the gun barrel disrupted the relative quiet but the noise was quickly swept away by the crosswind. Nothing at all happened. Some nervous glances in about every direction came from the several caribou.

They were now alert.

I thought perhaps my dad had hit a lung and the beast would bleed out and topple over shortly. I watched in the glasses for blood. Nothing. It was a clean miss...and my father is a good shot.

This surprised me. He chambered another, made doubly sure of his well cradled aim... and sent the 180 grain .300 Win Mag bullet to flight. Nothing was falling. We were both stumped.

He racked up another. My father had been aiming for a neck shot, the same shot he always takes on big game. About this time we both thought for a minute about how hard the wind was blowing in a direct cross, still 35 to 45. We both had an "ah ha" moment and talked about the conditions, deciding to put the crosshairs on the absolute leading edge of its chest hoping the wind would carry the round back 16 inches and punch the lungs, a bigger target. He let fly round number three. The bull flinched visibly through my glasses but looked generally unruffled.

On a hunch I thought it may have been a gut shot. Maybe the wind and the lead required was much greater than we had thought, and the bullet pushed all the way back past the lungs. It had. After some rapid strategizing we both agreed that maybe aiming a foot in front of the animal would be just the thing.

But the wind was gusting and very hard to gauge. By this time most of the cows and the smaller bulls were dashing around and smelling trouble, looking for an exit but they had no idea where the shots were coming from. My heart was racing and I was thinking for sure we were going to fuck this up. The bull stood fast, stunned, with a gut shot stomach.

Dad took careful aim and sent round number four down the barrel. In the glasses I saw the big bull finally sacked to the dirt with a little puff of red mist coiling above its back and then settling over it. It was a lung shot, catching just a little shoulder on the far side, blowing out a bit of bone which provided more knockdown shock than pure lung would.

Oddly enough, as much as we hunt, neither my father nor I had ever tried to work a bullet to its mark in that heavy of a direct crosswind. The numbers were off our mental charts. We may take crosswind or quartering wind shots in 10 or 15 mph autumn breezes out shooting at moose or sheep... sure. But nothing that ever required this geometry.

I looked over and saw my father begin to breathe again. He had been more and more pissed off with each squeeze of the trigger, cursing his marksmanship and being way too hard on himself. Getting repeatedly horse kicked by the big gun did him no good either, his bones being a little less resilient than at a younger time. It was a great father- son moment, rich in memories that will be with me long after he is gone.

After the congratulatory exchanges the three of us hustled over to see just how nice the bull was. We would perform the "Ground Check" a term we try to utter without the smug chuckle of success, but can't seem to manage without the gloating. The cameras came out, as did the ear to ear smiles. Everyone busted their best antler poses several times and then a few extra. We laid down some proofs of finally being in control of something in this world, which is especially rewarding since one usually has so little control of anything. Knives followed the cameras as they always do.

The smell of blood soon hit our nostrils, a universal signal to the primal synapses of hunters that it was time to let down, time to come off high alert, time to allow the big fat pulse in your neck to tuck itself back into your chest.

It's the smell of success, and if there were a ceremonial chant or song or dance to be laid down, or a shaman to summon for blessings, now would be the time to conjure whatever spirits made such bounty possible and give thanks to the Meat God.

One caribou was enough for us even though we had tags for three. Our cargo load was bloated as it was, given how much extra support gear and fuel we like to have along when going to high risk, far off areas like Unimak. One of us also needs to save room for a very large walrus head that weighed as much as a hind quarter of caribou. The next morning we broke down camp and piled both birds chock full of gear, meat and antlers.

Unimak is not a place to lounge around after you get what you came for. I had briefly thought about hiking into a hot springs that was several miles to the south of our camp, and there was also an incredible waterfall close by that needed further exploration from the ground, but beating a path ahead of the next weather front trumped all of that. To the northeast the weather looked manageable and we set off for Cold Bay to refuel and do some flight planning for home. We made the 40 minute flight to Cold Bay with the gorgeous green rolling hills and plains of Unimak fading behind us. We regretted every minute of retreat. I wondered if I would ever see such a unique landscape again.

With the fueling done and our wallets thinned we pointed back up the beach, plugging away low and slow for two hundred miles back to where the walrus head was stashed. As we approached the GPS coordinate, we sized up the wind direction and made a couple of low passes over the windswept tire marks we had left there just a few days before. Getting the airplanes down this time was simple. Everyone was paying sharp attention. We located the stashed walrus head and carefully wrapped and double wrapped it in large garbage bags to try to seal in the stench.

I moved some gear behind my seat and made a spot for the one hundred plus pound head and tusks and we loaded and re-launched. It was afternoon and we had enough time to make it back home, but it would be getting dark toward the end. We wanted to clear the mountain passes with some light in case the ceilings were low or it was raining or snowing in the mountains.

On the way back I was really hoping to find another walrus. The wind had been blowing onshore for several days making the chances much better. Anything dead and floating comes ashore eventually. Another hour and another 80 miles up the coast I spotted a big brown lump grounded just above the receding tide. As our aircrafts approached closer I could see in the distance something was moving in the mass. It was a walrus alright, with one long tusk intact and the other a broken off stump just barely showing color.

The walrus was dead...the movement among the mass was a big brown bear. I could see the bear clearly now, its face a bloody mess all the way back to its neck. It was busy eating its way past the front flipper and into the shoulder of the walrus. I slowed the airplane up as I went past thinking for sure the bear would move off.

Frank and my father were in contact by radio and pulled up to a higher altitude and began circling. They were not keen on landing given the fading light and wanted to keep moving. We talked back and forth a bit about letting the bear have this one and the shortness of time.

Just about convinced, I thought once more about how seldom this sort of opportunity presents itself and decided to take a closer look. Frank decided the opposite and made a few more circles above, agreeing to wait and see if I got the plane down OK and what the bear was going to do. The scene had all the makings of a Quentin Tarantino slasher movie so it was hard to resist watching from above.

Since both airplanes had been flying fairly low coming down the beach, I expected to look back and see the bear shagging off in a hurry. Instead, the intrusion appeared to have made him more possessive. The hulking bear took up a guarded position hunched over top the walrus and snapping and popping its jaws. The whole deal was starting to look challenging, fitting my style perfectly. I thought the ivory should be negotiable. My generous offer would be the bear could have the entire carcass but he needed to make room for me at the table for just an hour or so. But he didn't see it that way.

With time short and the bear uncooperative, I needed a plan B. I decided to land just down the beach and taxi up nearer to it and see what would happen. As I taxied up I would keep my spinning prop between me and the bear and see how big its balls were. Once I landed the game of chicken began. As the airplane got within 100 feet, the bear started to move off, but only retreated 50 feet before stopping. That seemed like progress so I moved a little closer, spooling up the engine to taxi ahead.

The bear was not small. In the high eight foot or low nine range, it probably weighed 700 pounds. He paced around just 50 feet away from the carcass, moving out then back, lurking, not wanting to give it up. I kept easing the airplane forward and slowly closing the distance. With 100 hundred feet between us and a walrus directly in the middle, we were at a standoff.

He was not eager to move all the way off the carcass and I was reluctant to get the airplane fully into a shutdown position where he could charge it. There was no telling what might happen, he could have enough sense to avoid the prop and attack the fuselage or tail. I did not want him to charge the propeller either, of course. If that happened there would be no winners. With the bear seriously hoarding his kill, I thought hard about the next move.

I inched the plane ahead slowly and gunned the engine a few times trying to establish some dominance. The bear finally decided he was out matched and moved off further, heading up the incline of the beach to the cut bank...but he was still only 150 yards away.

He initially sat down and stared at the idling plane, then within a minute had rose again and started pacing back and forth, but at a distance. I stayed put in the front seat and stared back, hoping he would entirely abandon the kill. My father and Frank were still circling above and no doubt shaking their heads. It was getting darker by the minute.

This was obviously not developing into a situation where I could take an hour or more to debone and cleanly cut the head off the walrus. If I wanted the tusk I had to get innovative and whatever I did would have to be quick.

The bear was still watching, swinging his head from side to side in an agitated, aggressive posture but never getting any closer than 150 yards. I let a couple of minutes pass and remained sitting in my cockpit, engine running, hoping his pacing and nervousness would chill out a little. But it didn't.

At this point, seeing nothing was changing, I was close to calling the whole thing off. I could not be sure what would happen once I jumped out of the airplane and physically exposed myself...and provoked the bear by taking over the carcass. But it was now or never. The plane was still running and was by then about 20 feet from the carcass.

Remembering that I had a .44 mag revolver stashed behind the seat, I reached for it and put it in my lap thinking about how I might be able to use it as a dental extraction device. I left the engine running at idle, locking the parking brakes so it wouldn't pull itself ahead.

I opened the door and jumped out, revolver in hand, and never taking my eyes off the bear. If he decided to challenge me I thought I would fire a few rounds into the air and dive back in the airplane.

Stepping carefully around the spinning prop, I took several big and rapid strides to the walrus and pulled his single tusk upward, freeing its half buried skull from the sand. My genius plan was to fire a .44 mag round (or rounds) into the gum line and hopefully dislodge the three foot long chunk of ivory. I knew that when I fired the gun I wanted to be several feet away at minimum, and with my head turned away to help avoid any bone and flesh blowback.

Crouching to my knees and aiming first from a distance of five feet, I could not seem to hold a point of aim steady enough in the exact spot I needed to be certain to hit the root cavity. It needed to be perfect. All the while I'm keeping my eye peeled for the bear to come charging in. I'm a ball of nerves and sweating buckets.

I could see the problem with my set up from five feet was that my aim deteriorated the instant I tried to turn my head sideways and shut my eyes before pulling the trigger. It was not going to work. To make sure to hit the sweet spot I really had to do this execution style. I had to be much closer. I had to be point blank.

The bear was now intently focused on the fact that I was out of the plane and probably that I no longer looked so big and threatening. I could feel his eyes on me and knew he could be on me in just a couple of seconds. All of my senses told me that time had run out.

I quickly stepped in close to the walrus and put the nose of the Smith and Wesson .44 revolver three inches from its head, aiming for a spot about four inches up the gum line precisely above the top of the tusk. Turning my head hard left to try to avoid any flack, I closed my eyes and let loose the carnage. Kaboom! Bits of hide, goo and bone flew everywhere. The right side of my cheek and ear and a couple of knuckles were immediately on fire with little slivers of bone embedded in my skin in several places. My right hand and coat sleeve were spattered to the shoulder with bloody chunks of rotten walrus gums and dental cavity bits.

The hydraulic shock and bone busting power of the .44 round loosened and partially ejected the tusk out of its socket. It was loosened well enough that a couple rapid ninja kicks fully freed it. Surprisingly the bear never reacted to the gunshot but stood staring, head hung low, body crouched and looking for his opening to lurch. In seconds I salvaged the tusk and hustled the few steps back to the running airplane, jumped into the front seat, slapped shut the door, throttled up and took off. Making one more circle over the carcass in the shrinking light I saw the bear was already back feeding on it.

We had our caribou, we had our ivory. We had slipped in and out of a part of the world almost no one gets to see. And we did it without breaking too much hardware. The flight back was indeed made in the dark and not at all comfortable. Lake Clark Pass is nothing to be toyed with on a heavily overcast evening late in September. But it worked out.

By the way dad, this story is for you. I will always remember how good it felt to have you along to share some raw Alaskan adventure. And thanks for never second guessing your guide. I'm amazed that you always trust me 110 percent even in some really sketchy circumstances. It occurred to me, old man, that you must mistake my commanding self confidence in the field with actual capability. Don't be fooled. I'm never too far away from shitting my own pants over something going sideways... I just hide it well.

Chapter 2

Fall on the Alaska Peninsula (2003)

When I start thinking about putting together a brown bear hunt, everything else becomes background noise. I enjoy the building anticipation that seems to never let up from the time you start initially mapping it out...to finally crawling out of the tent that first morning and being in the zone. And when I finally get to go, it feels not so much like a departure as it is an unleashing.

I was again with my wingman Frank and we had decided to block out some time in early October and make our way once again to Cold Bay, the epicenter of some of the world's biggest bruins. The simple act of setting aside a week for bear hunting, months in advance of the season, kicked my carnivore instincts into overdrive. We hatched a plan. But this time we would fly on a commercial airline and then hire a boat to drop us off. It would be a simple and relaxing hunt, without any worry of bad weather destroying an airplane.

Logistics are a continual puzzle down south on the Alaska Peninsula given the lack of infrastructure. There are no roads and no way other than boat or airplane to get where you need to go. The logistics of this trip were planned around a local bird hunting guide, the sole human in the town with a skiff for hire that could ferry us across Cold Bay and drop us off nearer some prime ground. Our chosen hunting spot circled a lagoon which was attached to the main bay by a small channel. Frank and I also had a boat, but it was more like a toy.

The boat was an 11 foot Zodiac with a 3 HP Johnson outboard motor that would extend our reach deep into some long and shallow side lagoons that the guide's 18 foot aluminum skiff could not navigate. The inflatable would also make it easier to carry a bear hide out to the main bay for a later pick up by the guide.

Our Zodiac was newer and in great shape. The motor was borrowed from my father. It was old and firmly antique. It was a single cylinder two stroke that held about a third of a gallon of fuel in a built-in tank that sat atop the power head.

I'm thinking Norman Rockwell was the original owner, but then he wanted to update to something newer. It ran reliably enough, and generated about the same amount of power and frantic noises as a modern weed whacker. At full throttle, with two people aboard but empty of gear, it propelled the boat along at four miles an hour. In our original scheme, this boat and motor set up was needed only to move us around within the well protected lagoons. It seemed up to the task. We had a couple of folding paddles also, further assuring nothing could stop us.

The inflatable boat was selected and procured on account of its light weight. It was broken down into two pieces, with a roll-up pressurized floor and then the main hull structure. The two pieces were 90 pounds together. But separated they came in under the U.S. Postal Service's weight limit of 60 pounds per parcel and could be shipped, via U.S. Third Class Mail...for dirt cheap.

The 40 pound motor was drained of fuel, dried out well, and also mailed to the Cold Bay Post Office. We mailed all of our gear and dried food, taking only our guns and optics on the commercial flight from Anchorage. You see, common air freight was three or four times the cost of U.S. Mail and beating the system, any system, is a useful hobby of mine. I love a good shoestring safari. It's no secret that almost anyone with $20,000 and a Cabela's gift card can kill an Alaskan brown bear.

They can probably even have a Jacuzzi that evening while their guide grills them a rib eye. But the bragging rights to a brown bear hunt that is totally crushed for a cool $1,500 bucks.... now that's something else altogether. That's real hunting and a neat trick I could crow about for months.

Once we landed in Cold Bay the first order was to walk across the street from the ramshackle airport terminal to the post office and check the general delivery mail to see if the packages I had shipped ten days before had actually made it. They had. We took possession of our gear, stacked it outside the door of the Post Office in a heap, and took off on foot to track down our bird guide who lived just a few blocks away at the end of "town". For purposes of this story his name shall be Dick.

Dick's place was the last habitable structure on the dead end of main-street which was a gravel road. At four in the afternoon we were on his porch and knocking on his fabulously weathered wooden door. After a couple rounds of knocking we heard noises inside. Another slow minute passed and the outlines of a face appeared in the filthy glass panes of the door. It appeared that Dick had just woke up, his eyes dark and set back. He looked to be a man trying to collect himself in one pile and recover from what presented suspiciously like a week-long bender.

He waved us into his clapboard hut of a house. It was likely a WWII relic left from the original infrastructure of the outpost during that war. Paint-less on the outside, sparse on the inside, weathered, without frills and neglected throughout, the home was a perfect reflection of its owner.

Standing in the doorway, not sure if we should go in or if it was best for all if he just came out, I started in on the final negotiations for the $800 total round trip, the fee for him to haul us the eight miles across the bay, a price we had haggled over by phone but not quite put a final closing to. As we talked, Dick was distracted and dodgy. He was shuffling around in his bare feet on the cracked and buckled sixties vintage red and yellow linoleum as he searched for something he had lost.

I was thinking he had a note scribbled someplace that he wanted to find and refer to, maybe to refresh his poached mind as to who was scheduled to appear at his door on this day, or what he had promised these strangers, or to buttress his future negotiating point that the fare was really supposed to be a bigger number.

If Dick's mouth were a little more turned up at the corners and his hair pulled up and captured in a bandana, he would pass as a more elegantly wasted version of the Rolling Stones' lead guitarist Keith Richards. I swear they could dress each other and for sure they used the same personal trainer.

Dick anxiously pawed his black hair backwards from his eyes and wandered the back of the room while talking with his back mostly to us. He was mumbling in what sounded like the lost language of the Guinean mountain people. He fiddled to light a cigarette. Dick was either avoiding talking about price or he had never actually registered my bringing up the topic. Just then he quit slithering around the room and became silent. He had found his socks on the kitchen table under several days of domestic rubble. A relieved look settled over his face. He was solving the afternoon's problems one crisis at a time.

I brought the conversation back around to price and we soon agreed that it was in fact a firm $800 for the venture. Frank and I were still standing half in and half out of the doorway. With his sock hand he waived us in again. We entered. To the smell of yesterday's coffee rewarming on the propane stove we took up chairs and looked at the map we brought. We made certain our captain was clear on where we wanted to go.

Dick was coming around nicely, his tall skinny frame gathering momentum as the coffee kicked in and he moved about the small room, slumping less and less, eyes swollen but the fatty pockets under them looking more and more like they belonged on his face, relocating and reorganizing personal items he had misplaced in the fog of the lost days.

Dick found his pickup keys first, then relocated spark plugs he said were needed to fix his boat engine which he thought, at the end of his diagnosis a week earlier, had really only quit running because of water in the fuel, but maybe not, maybe it was bad spark. He was pretty sure... of very little. The boat was sitting out front of his shack on a trailer. I soon went to work replacing the spark plugs.

It was coming up on five in the evening. Dick told us there was not enough light to make the trip, even if he was able to get the boat running well enough. This was a real disappointment to us since the wind was down and it rarely stayed that way for long. It was only a twenty minute run in the skiff but there was the loading and unloading to consider and everything takes longer than it should to get secure and ready. We agreed to give it up for the day. He offered to run up to the Post Office with us to get our gear and, if we liked, we could stay overnight at his place...adding that modest donations were always appreciated.

Dick found his shoes but by then had misplaced his socks again. He was glancing around the room with a defeated look on his face that Frank and I feigned not to see, saving him a measure of dignity. Finally, a shoed but sockless Dick headed out the door.

His worn, rusted 80s model Chevy pickup had a worthy patina of saltwater cancer that was worse at the back end, no doubt the result of repeatedly launching the skiff in saltwater.

The smell of damp, moldy sofa took over as soon as we jumped in the truck. Dick fired up the engine. Once underway, he brought to our attention that the heater worked excellently. We all nodded approvingly. Sure enough. In just a few minutes we had collected our gear from the front stoop of the Post Office, returned to the shack and settled in for the evening. Before we could get to sleep the wind kicked up enough to rattle the single pane windows throughout the place and make a whistle come down the stack of the oil furnace.

The blow was out of the southeast and would build some waves, pushing them from the Gulf of Alaska into the wide open end of the bay that we had to cross. Unless it changed, the wind would ruin our plans for an early morning launch. Luckily for us Dick was a little light on duck and goose hunting clients and he was fully focused on the $800 and getting the deed done.

We all hung out at his place, jawboning and reading, looking at the maps again and again, peering out the window every half hour and listening to Dick remind us to turn the single light bulbs off every moment we weren't using them since electricity cost 43 cents a kilowatt hour, or something like that, which surely would eat into his soup and cigarette money if not properly managed.

Our host was getting edgy, or more likely thirsty, not wanting to crack the bottle as long as there was a chance to get us delivered in the skiff early the next morning.

That night he did spend quite a bit of time outside working on his boat by flashlight, draining and replacing fuel in the lines and pulling and replacing a spark plug or two that I had already installed hours earlier. Reassuring sounds came from behind the house when he got the 40 HP Johnson to fire and run for a few moments.

Frank was winding down his evening by reading a paperback with only his headlamp, and saving 40 watts, just to make sure that if Dick popped back inside he would know we were all on the team. My bag and pad were rolled out on the floor of the front room. Even over the steady howl of the wind I dozed off quickly.

At morning we all drove out to the water's edge to see whitecaps, the wind smartly snapping off the tops of five foot surf. And so it goes.

This was a violent part of the Pacific Ocean and it could kill you after the smallest misstep. We went back to Dick's plywood palace and killed the time, bullshitting all day about past hunts that worked and some that didn't, re-marking too repetitively about how each gust hitting the house was an indication that it was either building or eas-ing, as though the wind had to be doing one or the other to allow more talk of it. Hour by hour, we waited out day number two.

As we came up on four in the afternoon we were be-coming hardened to the near certainty of spending another dimly lit night moving among the shadows of Dick's place. But just about then, when hope was slipping away, the wind started to lay off, the rattling windows telegraphing a slightly lower amplitude vibration. Everything had been loaded into the skiff in waterproof bags the night before and we were beyond ready.

The frequency between gusts spread out enough that we decided to jump in the truck again, drive down and take a quick check from the boat launch area. The waves had come in half, just about what we needed to make sure the low sides on the aluminum boat would not be breached.

We hurriedly drove the couple blocks back to Dick's to hitch up the boat on its trailer and then returned to the ramp. Raingear, rubber boots and life jackets went on and Dick launched the boat off the trailer while Frank and I parked the truck.

The wind continued to die off and things could not have looked better. We had time, but it was getting dark with heavy overcast bringing a uniform grey flatness as far as the eye could see, towards our target lagoon, and across the ocean in every direction. It was a bitter 40 degrees. Running eight miles across the ocean in waves that were near the safe limit of the fully loaded boat and in approach-ing darkness is not a trip to be taken casually. In this tiny village of 150 people there is not another boat in the water or even pulled up on the gravel shoreline. None.

It is not a fishing village. It's a drinking village. There is no recreational boat dock to even tie a boat to. The handful of aluminum skiffs in town are stashed in people's back yards in various states of disrepair. A mayday call would take hours to answer...if our handheld radio even worked after a dunking. If the skiff failed us and we swamped it in the waves, hypothermia would have us dead in 40 minutes tops. Our pal Keith Richards would be the first to go, he being of such sturdy health and all.

Alaska Raw

With the 40 horse Johnson outboard engine humming along smoothly we were making about 18 or 20 miles an hour in choppy seas. We had accomplished most of the trip across the Bay after fifteen minutes. We had taken a few wave tops over the bow, enough to soak everything but nothing that we weren't prepared for. We bailed a little water now and then with cut off milk jugs and never missed a beat. Approaching the far shore, the water was getting shallow. Looking down through the water we could vaguely begin to visually register the sea bottom moving briskly under the boat.

Just then, out of nowhere, the boat severely and almost instantly decelerated from 20 miles an hour to zero, throwing all of us out of our seats and to the floor. Gear was dislodged and surged forward but all of it stayed in. It was as though we had rammed something hidden and solid in the water but we were missing the huge crunching noise of an actual impact.

At the same time we slammed forward, the outboard's propeller violently jerked up out of the water and was over revving in a cringing fit of racket before Dick could switch it off. Once we all picked ourselves up off the floor of the boat, looking back at the engine it was easy to see the cause of all the distress. A thick rope attached to a sunken, abandoned commercial crab pot had been floating in our path but invisible in the poor light. It had caught the motor as we sped by nearly ripping it from the transom when the slack pulled tight.

The crab pot weighed several hundred pounds and was half sunk in the sandy mud bottom making it as immovable as a truckload of bricks. We were very lucky to not have been pitched out the front and into the water. The rope was wadded round the prop in a magnificent gob and this snag had kicked the engine upward in the mount. And there we were, dead in the water, each wave hitting near the top of the gunnels...with evening setting in.

After half an hour of cutting the rope mess loose from the lower unit we tried to get the motor started again but could not. It absolutely defied logic that after we freed the prop, and the motor pulled through with the rope starter easily, that it would not start again. Another half an hour spent messing with it and it never did run again.

Dick, the forward thinking captain that he was, had a seven horse kicker on the transom as a back-up. What thinking! It was open ocean to the east. Without the little spare motor, a light west wind could have pushed us to

British Columbia, or at least as far as the first big wave that swamped the little boat.

We used the kicker to limp back to Cold Bay in darkness. After putting the boat on the trailer we retreated to the house and spent the rest of the evening trying to get the 40 horse running again. It never came back to life. It is still a mystery to me and I'm among the mechanically inclined. The mission had to go on of course, and Dick had a contingency plan...another well used skiff back at his house.

Though smaller and unsuited for open ocean, it had another outboard motor that we robbed and installed on the larger skiff that evening. It was to be another night at Dick's crib, our welcome wearing thinner as his alcohol deprived brain recoiled at the thought of strangers again using some of his precious electricity. I have to hand it to him. He was no doubt in heavy withdrawal and really having to work for his money. The cool $800 was within his reach even though the idea of the payday was beginning to take on mirage like qualities.

Morning came and as if a miracle, the wind was again manageable! With averted eyes and little conversation beyond a few grunts of acknowledgment of one another occupying a mutual space, we again headed for the boat launch and put the plan in motion. To no event we crossed the bay and found a good sandy spot to ease the skiff in close to shore. We tilted up the engine, beached the skiff and unloaded the gear, including the packaged Zodiac with its tiny, antique outboard motor straight out of a Sears Roebuck catalog. After handing Dick four hundred dollars for the twenty minute ride, the agreed one-way portion of the fare, he left without saying much of anything.

Frank and I immersed ourselves in unwrapping and setting out our kit in purposeful little piles on the beach and blowing up the inflatable boat.

We had been dropped at the mouth of a large lagoon that was joined to the much larger Cold Bay by a single narrow channel. The lagoon was so shallow it could only be entered and then traversed at high tide. In just a couple of hours the leading edge of incoming tide would rush rapidly into the lagoon's narrow entrance and propel us on the pulse of the current, with the little outboard motor running or not.

In the land of ten foot tides the moon's power is a thing to behold. We were loaded like the last outbound Mogadishu refugee bus, with our belongings heaped to overflowing, mounded into the 11 foot Zodiac and spilling out over the bumpers. It took some strategic loading to make two small holes that were open to the floor so we each had a place to fit our hip booted legs while sitting on the side pontoon.

With everything still secure in waterproof bags, we positioned the tiny overstuffed boat squarely in the jugular that fed and drained the lagoon. We waited as the rush of lunar gravity began. The tide built speed sweeping us into the center of the water body and several miles down its length toward our destination.

When the tide finally ebbed after a couple of hours, I gave a couple of tugs on the pull cord of the outboard and it sputtered to life, propelling us for an hour down the remainder of the lagoon and then to the chosen beach. At long last, we were in!

We set up camp directly up the bank from where we beached the boat and then took a quick look around. A few salmon were still running up the small tributaries that fed the lagoon. This was a really good sign. By October first, the start of the bear season, the fish are often spawned out and gone. If it is a late run, the few left over fish keep the bears attention and concentrate them around the easy food source. We hunted that evening in a stiff wind and intermittent spasms of rain.

It was cold, still in the low forties. With the wind and humidity, it was tough to stay warm. Our preferred field of view faced directly into the driving rain and wind making glassing out of the question. If you couldn't see it with your naked eye, you wouldn't be stalking anything. Nothing much could dampen our excitement, but I can say it was physically miserable. We ignored it and hunted, savoring the pure state of being in the zone after all the boat trouble.

The 25 to 30 mile an hour wind and lateral rain kept steady all night. After coffee and some oatmeal the next morning we again packed our rucksacks with carry food, a few extra clothes and the necessary tools of the trade. We set out for a day of hunting. The hunting method here consists largely of walking to the best high vantage point and sitting and glassing. Spreading your smell all over by covering a lot of ground is counterproductive. If a brown bear crosses your scent, it will split, never to be seen again.

It is hard to keep this in mind when over each hill is another hill that could offer another wide panorama. The best way to make a kill is to find the best view over the best food source. You stake it out and wait and stay on the glasses every moment you can. There are no trees and very little brush so you can see a long way from a smartly chosen high point.

Just halfway through the second day, still in the driving rain, we caught the briefest flash of a heavy bear moving way out to our left.

The bear was nearly a mile away and we saw him for only a couple seconds as he passed from behind one distant hill, through a clearing, and then disappeared behind another low hill.

We had the glasses on it long enough to see that it was dark, probably a boar, and mature. It was moving directly sideways to us and we would have to get in a foot race to ever have a chance to get a shot. We picked a hypothetical angle ahead of its path and started humping that direction.

Knowing we could not keep up a dead run in hip boots and full rain gear in the uneven soft muskeg, we alternately shuffled, fast walked and jogged, breaking into a run at times and going as hard as our lungs would allow.

The terrain was wide open, low rolling hills and as we closed the distance we were cautious about topping each rise thinking that at any moment we would be catching sight of the bear. After ten minutes of all out sweat-soaked labor, our legs and lungs were burning. We hustled fast around the left side of an almond shaped rise that was no more than 50 yards high.

As we rounded the end of the rise we caught a flash of the back end of the bear. It was ahead of us and quartering away, ambling up a short valley 300 yards distant. We continued to close the gap trying to get within 200 yards.

The bear was continuing to move away at a deliberate pace, about the speed of a fast walk for us. It had no idea we were stalking. We were now totally exposed with not even a twig between us and the bear. With the wind blowing hard and the correct direction for us, and rain still pounding down in horizontal gobs, we had excellent scent and noise cover.

Frank and I had both taken a few seconds at various points to put the glasses on the bear and size him up. It looked like a boar with a very dark hide and a big boxy head.

The head was smaller in relation to the body which is a good sign that it was a big one. It appeared to be in the low nine foot range. Fortunately, the bear finally slowed and started pawing around in a berry patch in the draw it was moving through. As it rooted around, head down, we continued stealthily to close the gap.

The jig was up when it swung its head back towards us once while feeding. The bear caught our motion and stopped cold.

We had hit the ground and froze the same instant we saw its big body begin to turn towards us. Confused, the bear just stood there motionless for a moment, trying to sort out what we were.

The distance was about 240 yards. Frank had a .338 Ultra Mag that could deliver plenty of hot smack out that far. Frank was already lying prone. He shouldered his rifle, flipped open his scope covers and fed the big brown into the crosshairs. Round one, krack-boom! The bear did a little spin as though he either heard the round hit the dirt beside him or was himself slightly hit. If he was hurt it was not instantly clear.

Frank jacked in another round and sent the lead downrange, krack-boom! That one landed better apparently and sent the bear spinning and clawing at his side, angry and snapping his jaws as though insulted by a cattle prod to his soft parts. Going down was not in the program for this bear. He continued moving away, looking back at us, lurching around and swiping at the bushes beside him.

Krack-boom! Frank let round number three go and we heard that bullet slap on impact. The bear reacted by spinning and jumping backwards, acting as though the offending blows were coming from in front of him. He then did a couple of gymnastic rolls that led us to believe it was almost over. Then, against the odds, the bear collected itself, shook it off, and started to run up the shallow draw. What a display. The bear ran like it was fresh! Amazing.

My partner chambered his final shell as he yelled to me "shoot"! I was happy to help and dispatched a couple quick .300 Win Mag loads of my own, the second of which I heard hit with a splat. The bear was now still upright, pawing and gnashing a hole in the tundra as if the very ground was its tormentor. Krack-boom! Frank let number four go from the big Ultra Mag. That round also hit with an audible thud. The bear's front legs finally gave out then five seconds later it rolled on its side in waist high brush.

We held tight and I watched the bear as Frank reloaded his magazine in a rush. The brush continued to move for another minute before a stillness came over the kill site. We were both physically toast. Sweated out and fully spent. You don't really know how exhausted you are until the adrenalin tapers off. It was time for a few deep breaths.

After letting the bear bleed out for a few more minutes we approached it cautiously.

It was a hefty boar that squared eight foot ten with a perfectly dark coffee colored hide. It was thickly muscled from eating and shitting fifty pounds of salmon a day for the last two months.

The head was unusually boxy and short snouted, quite distinctive and unlike any skull shape I had ever seen. When skinned, there were two lung shots that hit perfectly in the kill box and another that was a bit high in the right shoulder which had broken the big joint, splattered the bullet into several pieces and then mostly deflected up into the heavily muscled hump on its back.

Another bullet had hit it in the back leg up high, doing tremendous muscle damage and passing through its stomach, liver and corner of a lung and then exited the front shoulder. That one must have found the mark when it was spinning since it entered the left rear leg and the bear had almost always been quartering away to us and facing right.

Four of six rounds hit and in most big animals, any one of those shots would have caused enough shock to bring it down. This bad ass boar was all fight.

Frank, who was then in his mid-sixties, was nauseated from the mile long foot race executed in full swamp gear. I was exhausted, still catching my breath and soaked absolutely to the bone with sweat. With perfect timing the sun broke through and slightly parted the never ending mattress of low spitting clouds. The sun would not last an hour but was great for pictures, splashing some colors onto our photos that we had not seen since arriving in Cold Bay. Both of us shed some clothes and tried to dry out as it briefly warmed into the high 40s.

We wrestled the 800 pound mass from sprawling on its stomach to its back by folding two legs on one side of the body to a tucked-in position and then tugging the other two legs up and over. The knives came out, then the smell of bear fat, a smell which replaces every other sense vying for a synapse.

I swear each time I am in on a bear kill that I will jar up some of that miracle lard for later whiffing, for inspiration when I want to go off the reservation, to become a fugitive from the one inch world of civilization, to get me in the mood for chipping some new arrow heads from flint or spending quiet time in my cave sharpening my spear. I love the smell of bear fat because it is the smell of success and everything that came before it.

Skinning took a couple of hours. After strapping the heavy wet hide to a pack frame we took turns with it on the walk out. Our weather was changing. The sunny break was long gone and the clouds sewed back shut over us but the rain was gone and the wind which never, ever stopped blowing, was down to a steady 10 miles an hour.

Our lifeline to civilization was a hand held marine band radio that could reach across the Bay to the NOAA weather station.

Once we finished the march back to camp, I planned to call the station and see what the forecast was. As we hiked out, it had crossed my mind that sometimes a calm period meant you were in the eye of a spinning system and the nasty east winds we had been experiencing could be about to shift full west as the whirlpool of weather moved over us.

With breaks and snacks included, and stumbling around with one really heavy pack, two smaller day packs, and two rifles, it took three hours to make it back to camp.

It was time for some dry socks and underclothes and the last of the fresh fleece. The story was relived in detail over hot drinks. This time with animation, each of us taking turns playing the part of the big bear reacting as the rounds struck. Life was splendid.

Our day was dimming. With the hide spread out on the tundra we worked to remove the last of the fat and viscera layers that had clung to the hide in the first round of peeling it off the bear. Called "fleshing", the better job you do the longer it will keep prior to spoiling. Lots of salt also went on it, once the last of the fat was removed, a curing process which also extends the time you have to get it processed by a tannery. If the trip was unexpectedly extended by weather or calamity all these steps help preserve the hide. Losing a hide to rot is a hunter's high crime.

Once it became too dark to finesse the razor sharp blades without risking a finger, we threw a light tarp over the hide to keep it out of the drizzle.

Satisfied with a good day's effort, we grabbed a little squirt of dish soap in each palm and walked down the bank to the edge of the lagoon to degrease from the elbows down. I do love bear fat but I try to keep it out of my hair, my clothes and my sleeping bag.

Looking out over the lagoon and the big bay beyond I noticed that it was peaceful. The wind was little more than a whisper, the waves in the main bay had dropped to foot high chop, still pushed east to west, still from the open end of the bay into the closed end. Even with the drizzle it was actually pleasant for the first time all week.

I worked the soap into the bloody, fat caked wrinkles of each hand, grabbing some beach sand to make a scouring paste out of the soap, the sand, and 40 degree saltwater. It kind of works.

When you are all done you still feel like your mother slathered your hands with lanolin and it will be there for a while. Bear grease sort of wears off over time rather than washes off. That's why no matter how hard I try to clean up after skinning a bear, all my sleeping bags still, to this day, smell like bear fat.

It was time to get a weather report and see about getting a ride out from Dick. Our original plan was to take two bears, if we could find two good ones, but that idea began to change when we loaded the 11 foot inflatable with our gear for the first time and saw just how tiny it was. Add a one hundred pound bear hide and a skull to that and we started to look like a cartoon.

Two bears would have meant two trips in and out of the lagoon, both timed perfectly on the right tides. And if the tide was right but the wind inside the lagoon was blowing the wrong direction (opposite of the tide) we were also screwed. The outboard's three horses did not have the giddy up.

This lagoon, like many of the lagoons in the area, are known for their "world's largest collection of eel grass". The long thin strands of floating grass are impassable at any-thing but high tide.

At low tide the grass looked like you could walk on it, floating on just a foot or two of water and completely blan-keting the entire surface. At high tide the stuff floats but less of it actually is long enough to reach the surface or the running space for a propeller.   Then, it's possible to navi-gate through it but still with some amount of fuss.

Problem: If you started down the lagoon's several miles properly riding the backside of a receding high tide in order to get out, but perhaps while bucking an adverse ten mile an hour wind, and thus only making one or two miles an hour progress, you would not make it to the lagoon's out-let in that window of two hours....and then the tide would drop, the motor would choke on the carpet of eel grass, the boat would be immobilized by it (even when using just oars) and you would be stuck out there until the next high tide.

It would be like spending a damp frigid night sitting up-right on a child's inner tube, surrounded by water and not able to move. For all those reasons we thought one bear would be a home run.

When I returned up the bank to camp I used the hand-held marine band radio to reach across the water and call NOAA for weather. On another bear hunting trip during a previous year I had made good friends with a gal, Peggy, who lived in Cold Bay and ran the NOAA station. We saw her briefly when we came to town and she knew our plan and that we would be calling NOAA if one of us cut our leg off or had appendicitis.

Click, "Hunters in the field calling NOAA...Peggy, do you copy?" hiss

Click, "this is NOAA" hiss

Peggy's voice crackled with static. We could understand each other but it was like talking through a long skinny culvert in an electrical storm.

Click, "We got a nice bear! How's things with you?", hiss

Click, "Good for you! Nothing much up here. Bored mostly" hiss

Click, "Bored and warm sounds pretty good. I would empty my wallet for hot bath about now!" hiss

Click, "I'll bet. Kinda wet so far huh?" hiss

Click, "Just a little. Tell me Peg, what's the wind doing tonight and tomorrow?" hiss

Click, "let me look...it is changing for sure.... This low pressure system now centered on Dutch Harbor is moving up and out to the northeast and another one is moving up the Aleutian Chain, coming in right on its back. There will be a little break tonight; winds will be light and variable 5 to 10, remaining south by south easterly for now. The second low will begin building by 8 AM. It will bring heavy rain with winds remaining southeasterly, increasing to 35-40 knots gusting 50 by ten AM. Looks like four to five days of pure fun." hiss

Frank and I recognized a moment of silence.

Click, "Hmm. Ok. Got it Peg. So it's going to hell again... great." hiss

Click, "Enjoy fall while you can. Winter is coming." hiss

Click, "Thanks Peggy. Can you call Dick for us and see what he is up to? If he came early in the morning, say six or seven AM, we could get this done. Call him for us and I'll call you back in an hour...would that work?" hiss

Click, "Sure. Are you saying if he can come in the morning you want to come out?" hiss.

Click, "That's affirmative. We are ready to come out." hiss

Click, "OK Bob, I will make the call." hiss

Click, "Thanks much. We will talk in one hour. Over and complete." hiss.

As with any of these trips you have to prepare yourself for long periods of excruciating boredom waiting out things you cannot control. I did not like the news of a week-long storm coming with 50 knot winds. That's a lot of tent time, on your back staring into space, hour after hour, day after day. I have done it countless times. My patience meter was pegged after just two and a half days of shacking up with Dick just trying to get out to the hunting site.

We had suffered heavy weather at the beginning, then in the middle, during the hunt, it had hardly let up...and now weather was going to be kicking our ass on the way out. This is the ugly side of the Alaska Peninsula. It consistently has some of the worst weather in the world. Our adventure was quite literally an episode out of "The Deadliest Catch" but on land and without all the crab.

The twangs of stress were a buzz kill taking some shine off a fantastic hunt. We could spend another five days here, or perhaps more, before Dick-the-bird-man could fetch us. Then of course we'd have to catch him on a "good" day, between benders.

The weather and the lagoon's tides would all have to align in a cosmic union with Dick's finest moment. For such an intercourse of the divine we needed Tarot cards instead of the tide book and NOAA reports. We waited out the hour. I called our lifeline.

Click, "Hunters to NOAA, Peggy?" hiss

Click, "I read you Bob. Go ahead." hiss

Click, "What's the good word my dear?" hiss

Click, "I wish I had one. No luck with Dick. His truck is in front of his house but he does not come to the door, lights are out. I tried. " hiss

Click, "You are fucking kidding me." hiss   (I'm not sure why I was surprised)

Click, "I'll keep trying, when I get off I'll drive over there again." hiss

Click, "OK Peg. Good god...uh...thanks for that. What a deadbeat. Peg, we do have enough food for four to five days, longer if we cut back some. No real issue. We're fine. If you happen to reach Dick we will try to be on the beach at the pickup site by 7AM. Just tell him we expect him." hiss

Click, "You got it. Good luck. Over and complete." hiss

Frank and I plotted the way forward in the pressing confines of our small tent. Reading the tide book by headlamps, we noted a peak high tide of 3 AM.

Alaska Raw

That meant to even get a chance at a pickup we would have to launch at about 2:30 AM, as the very last dribbles of incoming tide were still entering the lagoon and working ever-so-slightly against us. Then the tide would go slack before shifting. We would ride the receding tide out, using the three horse motor to make better time while picking our way through the eel grass. With luck we would make it through the lagoon in just an hour or so. Then, we would wait on the beach from about 4 to 7 AM for the ride across the big bay that may or may not come. It was worth a try.

If Dick did not come, we could always just re-pitch camp at the mouth of the lagoon and wait out the week long storm. If it came to that.

All of this had to be accomplished in pitch black darkness, adding one more layer of difficulty. We needed to get camp mostly packed up so we could catch a few hours of sleep, load the boat quickly and launch. As we thought it through, it was more and more apparent neither of us had much faith in Dick coming through. Looking out over the lagoon and beyond to Cold Bay itself, in the very last glimmers of evening light, the water was nearly flat. It was eerily serene, and the calm must have seeded some innovative problem solving.

It came to mind just then, that if the ocean stayed just as flat through the next tide cycle, it could be possible, though immensely risky, to take the 11 foot inflatable from the mouth of the lagoon all the way across Cold Bay.

The motor would need to run without a blink and every variable had to fall our direction...but it was possible. We examined and briefly considered a route that would hug the edge of the big bay so we could make shore if something went wrong. But that idea presented its own problems. It was a longer distance, but even more troubling was that the wind out of the east, when it did rise, would cause breaking waves, rather than just swells, all along the coastline. We had observed such nearshore breakers on the way in. They were nasty. Being swamped 300 yards off shore would kill you just as fast as being two miles offshore. So straight across appeared to be the safer, quicker choice.

Let's see how this looks on paper; Crossing eight miles of ocean on the Alaska Peninsula in mid-October, without survival suits, in a rubber boat with eight inches of side board fully loaded, with an antique, yard-sale-quality Johnson three horse outboard...and this Journey of Miracles would be in the absolute dark for all but the very tail end of the ride.

If the wind prediction was wrong and it caught us, we'd be in serious, serious trouble. The trip would take three hours with the engine at almost full power, making about 2.5 miles an hour, which is just slower than a walk. We would have to refuel at least twice, possibly three times along the way. What a crazy thought. I shared it with Frank. Frank's response was a muted "hmm", and he did not make eye contact.

I couldn't tell if that response was meant to say "hmm (you are fucking nuts)" or "hmm (I will be nuts...if I have to spend another week in a storm in a tent with you after I run out of cigarettes)". We talked it through while packing and sorting our gear by headlamps. At first we talked like it was just totally hypothetical.

We threw the sack of problems into the center of the room so to speak, like a bag of nasty cats, and then circled it and poked at it with a stick to see if anything clawed its way out.

There were lots of potential pitfalls and really nothing in the way of off ramps once we committed our toy dingy to open water. To make an actual decision to go, you had to block out a lot of ugly eventualities. Momentum sometimes suffices for good sense. So we kept talking. A consensus began to emerge.

The plan was to give it a try if the bay looked totally flat.

But we agreed it had to be totally flat, nothing less, or we scrapped the idea. Of course there would be no time to actually wait to see if Dick came after clearing the long lagoon in order to decide.

If we waited until 7 to see if he came, we would never beat the weather front that was coming in. If we waited, we would be pushed out to a 10 AM landing in Cold Bay when the winds were predicted to be howling and the seas would be far more than our boat could take (which was like about six inches). To make this work we would have to ride the tide the two mile length of the lagoon to its exit, make a snap decision, up or down...and then keep right on moving, making the trip across Cold Bay from 4 to 7 AM, with 7 being about the time it just started to get light out.

So the decision matrix was clear. We launch in the dark, we get to the big bay and look over the conditions the best we could in the dark, and if it's totally flat, we go. If it's not, we wait for Dick, who may or may not show up. Nothing like a little gut wrenching drama to top off a good bear hunt. If we ultimately decided to go across in the 11 foot Zodiac this would be about as bold and risky of a move as I had ever taken in the outdoors.

Peggy was off shift that morning so we planned no further contact with her to try to get an update on Dick. She had either located him or not. It didn't really matter. Momentum mattered. Frank and I got up at 2:30 AM after four hours of sleep. With the cone beams of our headlamps piercing the night and guiding the way, we skidded the Zodiac to the waterline and piled it full to heaping, and then laid the folded bear hide over all of that. It was comical. It looked like a floating chocolate muffin.

The total floor space on the boat was about the same size as a very small dining room table but it was jammed packed. We had a little less food now and had shed 10 pounds of salt but added a bear hide. With a GPS and headlamps to navigate with we set out down the length of the lagoon.

At first the tide was slack to slightly against us, as predicted, but it soon changed and we could feel it aiding the outboard's progress. With just a couple eel-grass-motor-choking events we made the length of the lagoon and found the hazy dark outlines of its mouth. Maneuvering towards it, the tide boiling out now, it caught us like an uncorked bathtub drain, sucking us into the narrow channel, accelerating, and then spitting us into Cold Bay proper. Tally ho, chocolate muffin, tally ho.

I idled the boat over to the shoreline next to the mouth and out of the tidal current. It was time to think this over and make the final judgement call. We could feel a breeze coming from the Pacific side of the bay, possibly 3 to 4 MPH. The bay was not flat of course. That would be too simple. There were some very low swells coming in and very light chop on top of those swells.

It was good enough we could not dismiss the idea out of hand, but it wasn't great, and we knew it wasn't on the front edge of calm; it was on the back edge.

As I noted before, momentum often suffices for good sense. We could now see the faint lights of Cold Bay. Could we make it? We decided that we were going to find out.

With a neck full of adrenaline, some serious cotton mouth, a bottomless pit where your stomach used to be, and all the other assorted flavors of fear, you knew you were alive for sure. This was what the other side of the edge looked like. Eight miles of jet black ocean lay quietly in front of us. The faint lights of Cold Bay in the distance would guide us. Our GPS would tell us if we were making the crucial distance over time that we had to make.

From a two and a half gallon plastic fuel jug I topped off the little fuel tank that sat atop the engine and then throttled it up to about 90 percent power.

We tried to settle in for the ride and find a comforting mental rhythm if one was to be had. There was still not a hint of the coming storm, almost calm with two inches of light chop on an ever-so-gentle roller coaster of shallow broadly spaced swells.

It would either go well, and the engine would run for three hours and deliver us or it would not. The calm would either hold or it would not. It was largely out of our hands now. It was about the gamble. Putt putt putt putt putt putt putt putt. Off we went. The minutes went by excruciatingly slow. After what felt like half an hour the lights of Cold Bay seemed just as far away as when we began. If not for the GPS I would not have believed we were progressing. Frank watched the time on his wristwatch and eventually called out loudly "One hour", the running period we had agreed would require refueling the motor before it ran dry and quit. I had placed a jug of gas between my ankles to be able to access it easily.

Without pulling off the power I carefully unthreaded the soda bottle size aluminum gas cap from the top of the motor and trickled it full. The GPS confirmed we were making slightly better than 2.5 miles an hour, almost exactly as planned. It was tense. There was no small talk. There was no spatial sense of progress since it was too dark to see the water go by unless you shined a headlamp on it.

Every odd noise from the motor had my heart pounding. I could feel nervous sweat on my lip and forehead each time a small bit of chop, just slightly taller than the last, sent a few cups of water over the front and onto Frank's lap... and down to the floor. There was no space to put a bailer.

It all either worked or it didn't. Putt putt putt putt putt putt putt putt. Across the icy cold black Pacific we went, the laboring little engine did the best it could. I promised it an early retirement and spoke to it to comfort us both.

Frank just wasn't talking. Very quiet guy all of the sudden. I was stressed. I needed some company and began a conversation with myself in my head:

Was it building? Was it worse than ten minutes ago? Was it? Shit...it is worse. The chop is six inches now, I think. Frank? Oh my god, it's worse.

It's building! The chop is building!

There's another splash over the bow! We're screwed....

We are totally done! Should have never tried it! How stupid.

No... maybe it's about the same. That still looks like six inch chop there. It could be about the same.

I wonder how much water is lying in the bottom now? A couple inches? More? Less?

It's so dark I can't see Frank let alone how much water is in the bottom. Once in a while I can see the outlines of Frank's face glowing when he puts the GPS close up so he can read off our speed. How much water now Frank? Maybe a little more now eh?....could be more? You think?

I can't see anything.

Does the water make us ride lower?

Can you tell? Is that why we are taking more in?

Should we shift some gear to the rear? Would it help, would it make drag and slow us down?

We are going so damn slow now! We can't do anything that makes us slow down more!

That settles that.

Should I use 100 percent throttle? Would the motor overheat and take a shit on us? How long could we last?

We're fucked!

No...we'll be ok. I think.

Who knows?

Are we halfway yet? How long until we are halfway?

An hour later Frank looked at his watch and called out "Two hours". Without missing a beat I carefully fueled the little engine and re-capped the tank. At two thirds of the way across by then, the black eastern sky was breaking ever so slightly to another pasty, dreary morning with about as much light as a clear midnight with a full moon.

I could now make out uniformly stoic expressions on Frank's face, just what I needed in a partner right about then. He had a serene and confident look. But then I thought he could be serenely confident of the fact....that we were totally doomed.

We were still an hour out and the wind was crawling up the Bay ever so stealthily. It was more than a wisp now. It was five to eight and making chop that was often a foot tall. Six inches was a luxury and a fond memory of a more hopeful time. The stress was so intense it was making it hard to find bandwidth to think.

But looking back into the middle of the bay where we had been an hour before, the chop was bigger; it was one to one and a half feet. We had just moved through it. But the boat was now seeing more sloshes of water over the front.

Twelve inches of chop was simply too much.

Just a few cups here, half a gallon there, making every minute a breathless guessing game. Should we try to clear a space on the floor to bail the boat with coffee cups? How far down in the pile are the coffee cups? Was there room to stack the gear any higher to make any room to bail?

I could not see my feet jammed beneath all the gear. There was no more room to be found. When, exactly, should we start throwing any extra gear overboard?

If we were going to swamp we'd start shedding gear like it was on fire... wouldn't we? My mind was spinning. I began a new conversation with myself:

Are we close enough to land now that our odds are actually improving? Slightly?

Let's see....What should we pick out to throw overboard?

We better have it all selected and organized ahead of time.

That's it! I'll start organizing! Problem solving!

What about the tent?

It's old, and less expensive than guns...

The tent, it simply has to go!

What else? The cooking kit and food? That can go. Good call! We'll chuck the entire mess kit first!

Sleeping bags and pads don't weigh anything. They can stay.

Why is this boat so full! This boat is too damn small!

The bear hide? That bear weighs a ton. That's it!!

Could we tie a rope to it and throw it overboard...and then tow it?

Would it change the waterline enough to ride higher and keep the breaking water out?

We are only making 2.5 miles an hour. Would towing the bear hide slow us down much?

Uhh...It would slow us down just a little less than tossing and towing a queen size mattress and box springs.

Is that crazy?

Yes.

Am I going crazy?

Surely.

To change the geometry of our waterline, Frank struggled to fold back the bear hide to select and move some gear back toward me. The pile now was so high I could not see over it by looking straight ahead. The bow promptly tilted up a few degrees and we started to clear more of the chop and spray.

But that immediately slowed us down. Moreover, we discovered the wind then had more purchase on the bow, pushing at it, nudging it slightly sideways. This caused me for the first time to steer and correct against it, robbing us of even more forward motion. We were dragging. The little motor struggled and rattled maniacally.

The GPS showed we were down to a 2 MPH crawl. The throttle had been shoved to full open since the cargo shifting. This made exponentially more noise, scarier vibrations, and random paranoid thoughts of parts rattling off the motor and falling to the sea bottom. The engine just did not like 100 % power and it told you so.

Shifting the gear was not a solution I would've wanted to implement an hour before, but now with breaking water coming over the front we had to do something. Would it work out? Suddenly my feet were colder than normal. I looked down and saw they were in six inches of water. Now that the bow was up all the water had pooled around my boots in the stern.

What does winning look like?

We were getting closer, but it was still way, way too far to swim. Over the next twenty minutes I did get a few darting feelings that our odds were improving and talked myself down from the mind fuck of "what ifs", the endless, circular, speculations-of-doom. We could now barely make out the first forms of a few houses on the coast line, their silhouettes framed by a few residential lights scattered around the village. Then the dark grey coastline began to come into view.

For the first time in hours I am thinking this might work....

In the final half mile we actually got some cover from the approaching shore. Even though the wind was building and the storm was coming in, we were now starting into the lee of it given the protection from the side of the bay. Finally we knew we were going to make the shore. Day was slowly breaking.

We welcomed the light like a new beginning. Our nerves settling down gave Frank and me some space to almost enjoy the scene. Miles of ocean behind us, a crisp breeze in our face, and a bear onboard. After a few more minutes the little engine rattled us up to the shore. I cut the power and coasted in. The silence was beautiful.

We talked to Peggy once we got into town and she told us she never did get Dick to answer his phone or come to the door. The only good news was that we saved the $400...

like it mattered. I made a couple attempts to contact Dick to let him know we made it out OK but I never heard from him again. We thanked Peggy for all the help and left it to her to advise Dick whenever she finally crossed paths with him. The storm did come in hard that day exactly as it was forecast. By noon it was raining and blowing 40 and it raged like that for six days.

Reflecting on the trip as I unloaded the gear and bounty onto the sandy shoreline, I was sure that if we had spent any more time the day before analyzing the possible pitfalls of the return crossing, we would never have pushed off into the blackness.

Instead we got caught up in the momentum coupled with the dread of spending another week there. That everything went our way was pure luck.

The bear made an absolutely stellar rug. Hanging on Frank's wall, it will always have a story to tell. Would we do it again? The answer, stripped of bravado, is no. Never. Once was a gift. We did it. We lived several hours where everything was at stake.

Chapter 3

Winter (2006)

February can be a real hag of a month in Alaska. Ugly physically and emotionally, it's always cold, usually bitterly so. The one positive is the days are edging toward being noticeably longer, near the end of the month hitting ten hours of daylight, and adding to that about a half an hour every week. You at least start to feel like you can come out of the prison of your shelter, to witness the sun finally at something over a fifteen degree incidence to the horizon.

It's nice to experience the nearly forgotten warmth of radiation for the first time in many months, coming through a closed car window and coming to rest on your cheek. The sun's rays are at a seasonal tipping point, trying to send your eyes a different color of light, a more hopeful light, full of orange and pink shades in the evening instead of the deep blues and chromes, colors formed by what remains after most everything else bounces off the atmosphere at shallow angles.

December and January just don't have enough daylight to hunt fur, so I spend a lot of time wishing for the longer days. It was toward the end of February when I received a call from one of my hunting partners who wanted a second man for a wolf hunt. Kurt, who is a pilot as well as a hunter, had recently done some flying in the far north and located a set of ridges where wolves had worn trails back and forth in the crusty snow.

The wolves used the wind-blown ridges to stay high and out of the deeper snow while still being able to move around and scan the miles of terrain below for caribou. These ridges, known as the Alphabet Hills, are almost 40 miles long and run east-west at four degrees of latitude below the Arctic Circle. They rise twenty five hundred feet out of their surroundings, and just over five thousand feet above sea level. During the flyover Kurt had spotted several wolves moving briskly and with purpose, headed west to east, in the direction of several small herds of caribou in the lowlands. Wolverines were open for the taking in that area also, so we could hunt or trap either one.

I didn't need much of a reason to say yes. It was February. I was ready to come out of solitary confinement and get in shape for all the snowmobiling that was sure to occur later in the season, during late March and April, when I had bear hunts planned. My skin had changed over the long winter to a pasty ashen color from a lack of sun and fresh fruit. Scurvy couldn't be too far behind.

It was possible to see the sun in February, real sun. Even though it would be well below zero, the hope of natural light was reason enough to start packing.

This trip would require a long drive up the highway followed by running snowmobiles 43 miles past the nearest plowed road to a small outpost where we could base and spike from. The remote lodge, with husband and wife proprietors, was cut off from all but aircraft and snowmobile access from the first heavy snows in October until April, when heavy equipment was used to open the road again. It was a great place to get a cooked meal and a bunk. When they had it, you could also buy fuel.

Covering this forty plus miles can be a snap if conditions are good. It can be much more difficult if the trail is blown invisible in a whiteout, if the temperature is 40 below zero or, say, the wind is screaming at you from the north with gusts peaking at seventy five miles an hour.

I had made this very trip several other times, in other years on other winter hunts, and I had been caught in each of those extremes. It will spook you. It can shake your idea of competence and make you feel small and emotionally naked in a way few environments can. A breakdown along the way, or something as simple as moisture in your fuel, or just losing track of your partner in a storm can have life threatening consequences if you're not able to manage it.

Our packing took into consideration a wide variety of weather conditions and the possible mechanical issues we could encounter. You needed to have enough gear to spend a night on the trail if you had to, to dig a hole perhaps, to get a shield from the wind. If things went poorly you would need a really good sleeping bag, a tarp to wrap up in, and a glitch-proof stove to thaw water from snow. Such items were considered the bare minimum.

We were never big on carrying true "rescue" equipment, emergency flares, smoke cartridges, signal mirrors, or the like, and it was just before the time of personal ELTs or our acquiring satellite phones. We weren't big on it because at 20 below with a forty mile an hour wind no one was going to come out looking for you anyway. When bad conditions improved, we would have to save ourselves, thank you very much. Self-sufficiency was the goal in any condition. Our gear came together over several evenings.

We headed up the highway north. It's always north, it seems. It's always north because all the pussies, posers, bubbas and big talkers go south. After a five hour drive we rolled into Paxson, a wide spot in the road that acquired a name sometime before its only roadhouse was deserted. We arrived towing a trailer full of snowmobiles and gear. It was a crisp 15 below zero. If that temperature held for a couple more days we would have a great time and not spend most of it just trying to stay warm and hydrated while keeping the guns and machinery functioning.

In my experience 15 to 20 below is a threshold temperature to have a decent time of it. If you get beyond negative 20 the cold really begins to occupy the core of all activities. Everything you do seems to take longer than a chore performed by an astronaut suited up for a space walk. If it is minus 15 or warmer, the cold just informs and limits all that you do instead of entirely controlling and confounding it. At that temperature you can shed a glove for a few moments, to fiddle with a bit of nonconforming hardware, gear or clothing, and your hand actually comes back to life a few miserable minutes after you re-glove it. It makes all the difference.

The specific period when you are quickly trying to travel from point A to point B on a snowmobile in the cold will usually be the most trying since you are developing your own wind chill. Minus 15 at 30 MPH becomes something you just endure because you can't dress heavy enough to feel good about what is happening to you. Extreme cold is a thief that probes every vulnerability. The wind driving it is a ruthless assassin. The wind chill under those conditions is minus 55. In such conditions I've had water bottles and sandwiches freeze solid inside my snow suit, in inner pockets on the body side of the thermal insulation.

With your head and face swaddled like a menacing freedom fighter, topped off with a thick trapper hat and goggles, ice cream headaches are still the norm, the freeze penetrating right through all of it like a torch pointed at your forehead.

The cold no longer nibbles at your itty bits from the outside, making you temporarily uncomfortable. Rather, it inhabits your core, as though drawn there to fill a vacuum, and puts your body under siege.

At 40 below even steel gives up some of its utility and becomes brittle and weak. On a similar trip Kurt and I broke the inch and a half thick tempered steel drive axles on two brand new Ski-Doo Expedition snowmobiles, three days apart, in less than 100 miles, requiring an air shipment of new axles to replace them. But that is another story.

After loading our snowmobiles and the gear sleds we tow behind them, and layering up to Michelin Man proportions with high tech synthetics and wind stopper fleece, we were ready to make a go of it. The trip in actually went quite well. Travelling through the Amphitheater Mountains, we moved past Tangle Lakes and then past Landmark Gap and Glacier Lake.

At this time of year the country looks and feels as lifeless and brutish as Mars, every piece of it blue or white and eerily repressed by the seemingly unnatural, unyielding bitter cold. Miles of rolling alpine hills and rock covered with drifted snow lay in front of us, open to our sole exploration for many hundreds of square miles. To our left and right the hills eased into narrowing drainages lined by steep and spectacularly impassable mountains. This was our Arctic playground for the next four days.

Where the trail was rough and heavily drifted, fifteen miles an hour was pushing it. On better sections we picked up to thirty five or better.

Once we actually started to hunt, our pace would be much slower, and therefore warmer, with lots of breaks to shake our feet and hands warm, to clear icicles and frozen snot from our face mask and goggles, and scan for tracks or glass the hills for signs of life. Through gritted teeth and the 40 below wind chill temperatures, we sustained a good effort on our limb numbing run to base camp, ending the misery in less than two hours. Since the highest order of business was recapturing lost heat, Kurt and I secured our small cabin with the caretakers and poked a match to the oil stove. In the couple hours it took to warm the cabin, we ducked outside again and re-fueled and sorted the next day's gear.

Accomplishing anything in the severe cold is a paradox. You move quickly and every task takes an eternity. Activity does not correlate to accomplishment.

Getting that far brought us to the end to the day. There is nothing quite like the contrast of color in a clear Arctic sky that is yielding its last minutes of daylight. Your attention is drawn much less to any disappearing sunset orb than to the opposite sky, where the blue of approaching night is unusually rich.

The east sky looks endless and dark, its stars lending weight to the idea of absolute infinity. All the while, looking west is still a glowing, life affirming pink. Staring at the zenith line between the two horizons directly above, you feel as though you are inhabiting two very distinct worlds, like opposite pages of an opened book where one page is daytime while the other is already night.

If you have never witnessed this visual trick of nature and its subzero boreal panorama of bent light, I recommend that it makes its way to high status on your bucket list.

We spent a quiet and serene evening twisted around the small drip fed oil stove while pouring over maps of the ground we wanted to cover the next day. A new day brought a clear sky and minus 28.

That meant by 10 AM or so it should warm again to minus 15 to 20, good enough for a functioning enterprise. We larded ourselves with all the heavy calories we could choke down and prepared some carry food and liquids.

Ten hours of fuel at our slow burn rate would be about twenty gallons per machine so we strapped on two extra five gallon jerry jugs each with the rest of the gear. It was an ambitious load. Our snowmobiles were now re-packed and provisioned well enough to cut the tow sleds loose and leave them at base camp which would dramatically improve maneuverability.

Loaded as they were, the snowmobiles still handled piggishly but we could also unload and stash some of the fuel along the way to the hunting zone and use it on the trip back out. If we got on a wolf track and had to run it out for miles and hours on end, we still had the means.

With everything set it was finally time to coax the frost covered snowmobiles back to life and head east for the GPS coordinate where the wolves were last spotted from the air. If we could not find the wolves, we would look for the caribou and then hope the wolves eventually found us.

The first pitch took us ten miles down a frozen river, the Maclaren, and to the foothills of the Alphabets. Though our trip into base camp had been hard and drifted, snow on the river was deep powder. It hadn't gotten much if any wind. Stepping off the sideboard sent you down waist deep into the soft snow. The machines labored along under heavy throttle, ass down from the load of extra gear and gas cans on the tail. It's hard to know how much extra fuel you burn up hauling extra fuel.

Like a boat on water, the machines work best if you can get up to some magical speed and plane. To do that required almost full throttle and a continual stressing of the engine and clutch. We had a long way to go. Here and there, stretches of powder were so deep the machines pitched and wallowed like an overloaded dingy. There was lots of frantic engine noise and a buffet of weird hot smells coming from under the cowling. We scratched and clawed for every yard of progress. It was time to drop a five gallon jug of fuel from each of our rides and see how that worked. Like a sinking ship, perhaps you just keep throwing things overboard until you get the result you like.

Once stopped, a quick check of the GPS showed we had made about seven miles downriver, better than expected. Dropping a 30 pound jug off each tail, and topping off the main tanks from the other two jugs made a big difference.

Under half throttle we mostly stayed on top, porpoiseing our way through the bottomless white brine and swapping turns breaking trail. Where the west end of the Alphabets met the river we cut left onto them and tried to find a good way up to the top of the first arrangement of hills. It was still deep everywhere and it was a struggle to move up the foothills to gain elevation.

What Kurt remembered from the flyover was mostly packed, blown, crusty ridges. In these situations pilots/hunters often trot out an axiom. It all looks different from the air. Indeed. And never in a reassuring way.

It made sense to hunt our way over to the GPS coordinate, which was at the far eastern end of the small range, instead of simply rallying straight to it at our best clip. It was all good hunting. Why race through it? All that day we worked our way east up and down the series of scattered knobs and hills that make up the Alphabets looking for wolf tracks and glassing from high points. Moose and caribou were plentiful.

As we slowly and methodically covered each of the ridges and draws that may have held some wolf sign, we came to realize that the discontinuous ridges sucked up lots of time and energy, much of it spent grinding through the deep snow in the lows, navigating the sometimes thick alders, getting stuck and unstuck, recovering, and then finding a reasonable grade the snowmobiles could manage to climb to the next high view point. It was exhausting work and we were only able to cover about half the distance to the GPS coordinate before the narrowing daylight and plunging temperatures signaled we should be wrapping up.

The weather that was forecast to hold clear was changing and high clouds were leaking in from the west. Where we previously had good visibility, the overcast was laying a uniform gray onto all the dips and valleys, erasing shadows, definition and depth perception.

Like the fake white backdrop in a portrait photograph that erases the line between floor to walls, the features in front of us began to change from three dimensional to two. The human eyes are entirely accustomed to having their binocular and parallax capacity easily and quickly place objects in space and reveal distances.

When the eyes are denied that capacity the brain loses not only its ability to gauge distances but also loses almost all of its ability to process motion and speed. The disorientation then, is almost total. You have to convince your brain to allow the eyes to be overridden, to pull clues for motion and speed from things like the wind on your face or the sinking or rising feeling in your gut. More than a few snowmobile riders have been maimed or killed by riding off of something they could not see. We slowed to a crawl at times to try to manage the extreme condition.

Turning the machines back north we spent the next three hours backtracking up the river to our cabin, the last hour of that was spent retracing our tracks in the dark. With the sun long gone the temperature had dropped 15 degrees from the high of the day and it was again a stinging minus 25.

It felt worse. It felt worse because every article of clothing we wore, from our face masks, to our underwear, gloves, socks, boot liners and the works, were less effective than when we left, having gained moisture from each time we sweated fluid into them, which happened every time we wrestled one of the 500 pound machines out of some dung hole in the alders nested in swimmable deep snow.

In the Arctic winter all your gear is on a slow burn of deterioration and effectiveness from the first hour you leave camp.

Back at the cabin we began the process of unbundling, first beating the ice off exposed zippers, shedding layer after freeze-crusted layer, thawing, then drying. After we had attended to what looked like laundry for a family of six, all of it draped on nails over top the limited space around the oil stove, we were finally ready to pack in four or five thousand more calories, upend several beers and tell and re-tell booze propelled stories about the remarkable, action-hero-like accomplishments and calamitous missteps of the last 12 hours hard labor. The stove was at the center of the universe. Creaky joints became mobile.

Fingers and toes feel less like prostheses and more like flesh actually connected to the host. Snow blind raccoon eyes are eased and renewed. The pressure lines imprinted on cheeks and eye sockets, left by a day spent strapped in goggles, were beginning to fill back in on our weathered faces.

In the morning a light snow was filtering down through the clouds that moved in while we slept. You can't hunt what you can't see. It's a set-back. But as usual, we repeated to ourselves that if enough ground was covered one could stumble across a track, which is optimism enough to push ourselves to hunt anyway.

When the morning of a wolf hunt brings you snow and diminished visibility, the odds of success are buried with it. It could lift. We pressed ahead to get everything ready, fueled, sorted and packed. The plan was to mostly skip the lingering and glassing along the route and get all the way east this time. Down the river we went, right back to where we cut away from it the day before.

We worked the previous day's trail up onto one of the longest ridges and pushed all morning and afternoon for maximum mileage. There was still lots of combat riding to do since yesterday's trail ended well before some of the worst alder and ravine punctuated real estate.

One place was so deep, steep and cobwebbed with alders, it required some real technical weaving through the limbed jungle while trying to hold speed and momentum to make the long hill. In fact it was too steep and deep for our machines to make it in one pitch. Most problematic were the clusters of tangled limbs that sprouted through the six feet of heavy powder snow.

The only solution was to pack out a trail a piece at a time, to take turns making runs at it going just as high as momentum would allow, and turning out just before sinking. This all felt like trying to maneuver a Winnebago in a sand trap. You were wishing it was a Kia. We were stuck and digging out after every miscalculation. The physical labor in subzero temperatures was exhausting.

Further, you had to be careful not to sweat out too much or the cold would come back to devour you in your wet clothes whenever you slowed down the effort level, stopped to rest , to hunt and glass, or otherwise quit making so much internal heat. Effective body heat management had us bundling, shedding and re-bundling each time we over-heated when wrestling a snowmobile unstuck.

Variations of this played out all along our path eastward until, after six hours of intense bushwhacking, we finally made the last ridge where the wolves had been spotted and marked from the air. Sure enough, a well worn game path was notched into the snow at the top of the ridge. Wolf tracks were everywhere coming up and down in organized runs from the lookout. Wolf urine and dung littered the place and made it look as though the pack spent a lot of time just hanging out there.

It was a good place to glass, and we did that for the next hour, but visibility was sketchy and this was limiting the possibilities. A close look at the tracks could not really bring out what was new (or very new) from the "days old" variety. The light snow and constant wind hid the clues that we could have picked up otherwise, possibly identify-ing their last exit and a hunt strategy.

There was satisfaction from just making it to the spot, a culmination of plotting, scheming, flying, driving and snowmobiling that not very many people would ever un-dertake, and even fewer would do it successfully and ar-rive there. We had found wolf turds, those wonderful little scat deposits that look like Baby Ruth bars that have been dipped in glue and then rolled in caribou hair. And to us, right then, it was as confirming and rewarding as if it had been solid gold nuggets.

It was a long and tortured way back and it felt like we better get to it if we wanted to make the trip in the day-light. The light was getting better and some sunny patches were breaking through so we kept glassing a little longer. We didn't want to give up our high ground just as the light started getting good. Building wind seemed to come out of nowhere, arcing across the top of the mountain as the fronts were clearly changing back again from a low pres-sure to a high. With that high pressure came a strong and bitter wind.

I'll offer some conjecture to give the reader a better understanding of the hunt and how weather and timing plays such a big role in any outcome. Had we been able to get to this probable epicenter of the wolf pack's range in the morning, and on a day that had clear skies, we could very likely have found them, or been able to identify the freshest tracks and tracked them down.

As the clouds lifted and the setting sun was peeking under the cloud layer at a keen angle for casting shadows, we both noticed a lone set of tracks about three miles in the distance. This was a long way to spot a set of tracks with field glasses, but they were well punched in the deep snow and drew a dark line coming off a high ridge.

The straightness of it gave it away as furbearing predator rather than caribou or moose which wander. It was way too far to tell if it was a bear, a wolf or something else. We agonized over how badly we wanted to add six or eight miles, out and back, to our already slog of a trip, at this late time of day. The next few moments were spent babbling about how many brush filled ravines lay between us and the track, how little water and fuel we had left, and how hard the wind was going to blow at its peak.

This area was known for its ugly winds, a place where it could easily come up to fifty or sixty miles an hour without much notice. If it did, the wind chill would drop severely. Visibility would be obscured not by fog or low light but by blowing snow. There were demons for every occasion here.

Hunting in the winter demands extreme caution, good judgement and a unique set of skills. We needed to discuss our next moves. After we each articulated for fifteen minutes every good argument about why continuing on was totally out of the question for today, we looked at each other for a glancing, shifty eyed confirmation that neither one of us was actually voting it down because we lacked the will, but because it made no legitimate sense to go that far, as physically spent as we were, just on the hunch that it was actually a fresh wolf track.

With that decision made and behind us we were silent for a moment and glassed the rest of what was coming into view as the clouds slowly lifted. The wind was increasing steadily and as we sat sideways to it trying to glass, we noticed it drove the cold right through our snowsuits. The minute movement stopped our bodies quit producing enough heat to survive. It was a brutal reminder that we really needed to go back.

To communicate at all we had to put our heads together, yelling through our facemasks over the building wind. The conversation began to pivot.

Kurt: "...Notice how much more light there is now compared to a few moments ago? Ceiling is coming up...at least for a while."

Me: "Ya....I wonder how much time we may be able to cut off, once we do head back...if we go a more direct route?"

Kurt, taking it further with this optimistic gem:

"You know the gas gauges are not very accurate, and there is always a couple gallons more than you think."

Me: "Um hm....true. Sometimes...yep, that's right, there can be...."

These were the first signs that we might reverse our earlier decision to get back to safety. Then came recollections between us of a time when we did run way too low on fuel to both make it out, in a very shitty spot on another miserable winter hunt. In that case by stopping before both machines were totally empty and draining the tank of one into the other, and abandoning the empty snowmobile on the trail. We both rode back to safety doubled up on one. As a strategy for success, we love that solution like a dead sailor loves the sea. Leaving one snowmobile behind can also lead to both hunters freezing to death after the one remaining machine quits running from some odd mechanical failure.

By this time I had been screaming into the howling wind so long my throat was raw from yelling. In our half frozen but fully dehydrated delirium, every strategy concerning why it was physically and technically possible to extend our hunt to include just one more pitch forward was tossed around. But these things were spoken of cryptically as though they had nothing whatsoever to do with our previous conversation, and without anyone ever mentioning backtracking on the "firm decision". In fact it was full reconsideration of a debate we were refusing to recognize was just settled.

Me: "I think I saw a spot to get water a few miles back on that tight bend in the river. I thought it was steaming a little through the snow. If a guy dug down without falling in....probably some there."

Kurt: "I still have that small baggy of raisins that was stashed under the seat...you got anything left?"

Me: "One candy bar and a few Ritz."

Kurt: "I can't tell if that track is going away from us or coming towards us. You?"

Me: "I like the sound of 'coming towards us' best."

The lengthy pause in conversation that followed was interrupted only by clouds of swirling snow pushed by erratic gusts of wind.

In a sort of nervous tic that surely lacked any possibility of finding new information, our field glasses in our gloved but numbed hands kept swinging back periodically to look at the far off track.

That beautiful, straight, deep, punctuated string of impressions that continued to pull us in. We sat on our machines, trying to keep our backs to the gusts, hunched harder over the handlebars and scoping the terrain, clenching our core muscles in an effort to generate heat and stay warm without moving much.

We were at the single most critical go / no-go decision point of the venture. We were hunting in conditions so extreme that an insignificant error could kill. The Arctic, as a medium to exist in, is as hostile and brutal and foreign to the human body as anything on our planet.

The day was spent, our bodies were spent, the darkness and temperatures falling, the wind was picking up and driving the cold like a dagger through layers and layers of thermal gear. We were out of water and had all but finished the rations of dried food we had brought.

The only way to stay warm was to generate body heat through motion. Stop moving for more than three or four minutes and the balance tipped, your body heat dropped into a net loss equation...and each time that happened you had less and less ability to tip the balance back.

We were spending reserves that could not be regenerated and we knew it. We were several hours from camp and just making it back would be a deadly serious and strenuous undertaking. Absolutely every well-reasoned thought told us that it was time to retreat, to begin the return back to safety. But we were both considering the opposite and if we pulled that trigger we could count on the return being even more difficult.

Finally...from Kurt, yelling over the howling wind:
"FUCK IT."

Somehow I sensed that was coming. Even after everything to the contrary. In that situation those two words of course mean "Let's do it anyway". So that was his opinion, which meant only that the option was clearly back on the table for further debate. In those conditions we always respected a veto from the other. But in that moment we both surrendered to our predator demons.

The chase is our dope, and our bodies need just one more hit. This moment is the purest example of what it means to be a hunter, to be host to that specific string of prehistoric DNA that was embedded hundreds of thousands of years ago that confirms we are predators by instinct. The DNA is making the decision and it simply takes over. That ancient string of code had just been unshackled.

Me: "WHAT THE HELL....LET'S GET IT DONE. LET'S GO KILL A WOLF!"

And with that, the atmosphere changed in an instant from plotting a cautious retreat to preparing for a winter stalk. With the decision behind us, both of us went entirely silent as we dismounted and began shuffling about our machines stiffly, trying to keep our backs into the wind, moving slowly with our sore and tired bodies, putting things in their place, zipping up, lashing down. Loosening our seized knees, shoulders and elbow joints to ready them for another subzero cross-country trial of our limits.

I opened my snowsuit to reach into the breast pocket and check how much water was left in my last bottle. Six ounces of frozen slush. Funny, it had been liquid just two hours ago when I had been more active, riding and moving around, and before the wind picked up hard. Comforting thought.

I shoved apart the flaps on my frozen, slobber-caked face mask to wedge open a hole for my mouth, then drew what fluid I could off the ice slurpee and put it back inside my suit in the pocket close to my armpit. I pulled my last frozen Snickers bar out of my side pocket and broke it into two pieces with some difficulty, by smashing and snapping it over the handlebar. I then worked each half into opposite sides of my stretched out cheeks to thaw so I could masticate them eventually, on the fly.

Flexed, fed, hydrated, wrapped, goggled and gloved, we fired up and followed the spin drift and gusting wind off the crest, pushing down the 5,000 foot high mountain to begin crossing a series of brush-filled draws and crags that would take us to where the animal track was.

Our ride over to the track went decently, which is measured by how often we buried the machines, or stuffed them into a tangled brush trap, or had the bottom fall out of some blown over voids in a ravine bottom. At least by moving and maneuvering the snowmobiles we warmed up again. We made good time. Within an hour from the time that we had shoved off, we were standing over the track examining it. It was a lone wolverine, not a wolf, but fresh.

It was possibly just hours old, but surely no older than early morning. The disappointment that the track was not a wolf was short lived; wolverines are a real prize and hard to hunt. Immediate decisions to be settled concerned how long it would take to track it out with the diminishing daylight, the lack of any reserve fuel, etc., all over again.

There was some positive news; generally the track ran back towards camp at a quartering angle so tracking it out would bring us closer to our final destination in a tangential way. We decided we had come this far and we could take a run at it and perhaps get on it before dark. It was game on. In less than 40 minutes we had run the track over top of, and down, a 1,500 foot high peak, then through a couple of connecting shallow draws in between ridges, and finally to a point where it disappeared into a hole flush with the snow surface. Poof. It was gone.

On the way there, as we followed a long draw, the tracks had been mostly shielded from the wind. Nothing had contaminated them and it was evident they were fresh. And we knew the hole we were staring at was certainly not a den. For a den it lacked a multitude of tracks coming and going. This was just a single track in.

With those two bits of information we believed the hole was simply a place where the wolverine scratched through the hard crust and then burrowed through the powder below it. Probably to retrieve a bit of buried carrion. Frustrated that the track did not lead to a visible opportunity, we started thinking about the long ride out. But then, looking again in the hole, logic held that the wolverine was in there somewhere.

Kurt: "Get your shovel."

Me: "What?"

Kurt: "Get your shovel. Let's see how deep the snow is here under this hard crust. "

Me: "For what?" "That thing is long gone, probably squirted out some other rat hole somewhere else, or he's rallying around in a tunnel system that would make a Viet Cong proud."

Kurt was now standing directly over the hole: "Throw me your shovel. Let's just take a look."

I unstrapped the small collapsible shovel from the side of my machine and tossed it to him:

"Here you go. Have at it"

Kurt started digging. The hole went down three and a half feet before turning 90 degrees and going lateral. Admittedly, it took me a minute or two to get amped up about the pursuit. But once we started digging that changed. We traded off, each taking turns at the shovel.

Looking back, I have no idea what either of us were thinking, being out here at 20 below zero, way too far from shelter, under dwindling light, low on fuel, out of water, and physically spun out from a very hard day....digging holes in the snow looking for a lone wolverine. The answer, of course, lies buried somewhere in the prehistoric mind. About then I took a rest from the spade work, handing off again to Kurt.

That moment before Kurt began his shift we both heard a weird noise underfoot and looked at each other to check if it was imagined or mutual. As always, the wind and our heavily insulated heads made it hard to hear.

It sounds like rapid, muffled swishing and scratching! We both hear it. It's the wolverine digging! It's about eight feet ahead of where we are standing. We step over there, get down on our hands and knees, placing an ear closer to the snow.

The noise is still faint, masked by random gusts of wind, but it's directly below us. Kurt hustles back to the snowmobile and un-straps a .223 bolt action Model 70 rifle, walks back to where I'm keeping watch, and forcefully jams the gun butt deep into the snow directly over the noise.

Straining an ear into the last place we heard noise, we hear nothing for a few moments. We wait. It stays quiet so Kurt grabs the shovel and starts digging again, I pull the gun butt up and shove it into the snow a few more times right around where we heard it last scratching. Then, the scratching begins again! We hear it start digging furiously, this time a few feet left. We move left. I move to a place directly over the new noise and shove the gun butt down again.

Since the snow is crusty and layered harder on top, it takes some force to break through, but then there is little resistance in the soft fluffy powder underneath.

Just as I was working the gun up and down into the snow I felt the bottom fall out of my stomach...and the snow below my feet. I broke through the supporting crust and up to my crotch in the powder below, directly over the animal.

In that instant I knew that having a forty plus pound wolverine in an absolute fit of rage lacing into one of my ankles would be like stabbing a foot into a bathtub full of piranhas. In full blown panic mode, using every ounce of energy I had left, I jerked one foot up and got it onto the crust. I then used my hands to push up and out. For a second I was free, but that was not quite good enough....My other foot broke through as I put weight on it and I began cycling my legs in and out of the deep snow, high stepping, breaking through repeatedly.

Kurt was about fifteen feet away, probably feeling a little helpless and unable to lend a hand without presenting a second pair of shins for the taking. Of course it's a bitch to move at all, let alone fast, when you are bundled in three or four layers of clothing and then stuffed in a full body Arctic snowsuit.

In that moment, in my mind, I went from predator to prey. The tables were turned. I was in a state of raw panic as acute as I have ever experienced. Who would have ever thought?

One minute I am focused like a falcon in a dive on the object of my pursuit, and the next, I would be crying like a baby if I thought it would bring help. I was frantically trying to escape and the only thing that finally worked was to throw myself forward chest first onto the surface spreading out the weight, tug my legs up and out behind me and sort of roll forwards onto stiffer snow like a man on fire.

Through all of this I still gripped the rifle in my left hand. Kurt was manning the shovel. No sooner had I rolled out of the snow trap and got up onto my knees, I caught the blurry flash of brown out of the corner of my eye! The wolverine's head had emerged as it came clawing its way up out of the broken crust and powder. Things were happening fast! I was totally out of breath from all the energy spent trying to avoid having my legs shortened.

The wolverine's head was out and its upper back was emerging next. Facing toward us, it was thrusting spastically with its front legs, trying to get some purchase and escape the loose, inconsistent jumble of broken crust and wispy light fluff. This was one pissed off wolverine.

I had no idea if, once free, it was going to try to spin itself around and flee or attack. I'm sure I never stopped to think long enough to figure that out.

Still on my knees, with my teeth I quickly snatched the glove off of my right hand and flipped open the scope covers. (Why flip open the scope covers? Habit I suppose.) The gun came down to its target instinctively. There was little definition in the three power scope.

At 12 feet away, it was just chock full of brown fur and nothing else. As the wolverine struggled to surface I held in the middle of the image and pulled the trigger. The 55 grain round found its mark. Silence settled over what had been a chaotic scene. We took a moment to allow the tension to settle out. The prize was exceptional; the muscular male wolverine was five feet long, as thick in the body as I'd ever seen.

As thrilled as we were to have finally succeeded, there were no high fives or photo sessions. Instead, our thoughts turned once again to how dim the light had become in the last hour, how insufferably bitter and debilitating the cold was, and how we were on borrowed time. There was no escaping the fact that most of the return to camp would be made in full darkness and that would make it tougher than the trip in. It's such a dramatic shift in mindset to be whipsawed from unrestrained aggression in one instant to complete retreat the next. The sobering reality was that we needed food and shelter and that it would take a 110 percent effort to get back to safety without any issues.

In those moments I am refocused by a survival anxiety; you know that the next two or three hours really must go well. Nothing I have ever experienced makes you feel as insignificant or as naked as the Arctic in the grip of deep winter.

Interestingly, the one all-consuming emotion that sticks with me in such situations is not so much fear, or a heightened sense of respect for how quickly things can go very badly, though I have both of those. Rather, what leaves the biggest single impression on me is how incredibly alone you are.

The vastness of the landscape feels endless because it is. It feels hostile, intimidating, uninhabitable and, without a doubt, empty. You are made physically uncomfortable continuously by it and you continuously have to fight against it making you mentally uncomfortable.

We wasted no time strapping the animal to the back of my snowmobile and getting started. On the trip back we took great pains to try to follow our tracks out.

Where blowing snow had obscured the tracks, instead of just winging it over that particular stretch and hoping to connect with them again, we stopped to collaborate and then we would take some large sweeping circles out from a center point to try and pick the old tracks up again. Most of the time we were successful and slow but steady progress was made. We were stuck four or five times in the bottomless powder in places where we had lost the trail, and I'll admit there were a few times when I questioned if either of us would have the energy and reserves, or the will, one...more...time, to dig out and unstick one machine or the other.

It was very tempting to stop and try to build a fire and to rest. But then what? Without food or shelter, at 25 below zero, it's going to get really uncomfortable, maybe dangerously uncomfortable. And the longer we lingered the more of the trail would be blown to obscurity. The GPS worked great, but was useless for precisely tracking a winding course through alders, in and out of ravines and creek bottoms. So if we stopped we may be stuck until dawn, and that's a very, very long time. We kept moving, slow and cautious. The machines ran without a hitch. The gas held out. We were fortunate.

After about three hours, making the final push north on the frozen river, we saw a far off light oscillating from dim to brighter then back again as the gusts of spindrift tossed around the light reaching our eyes. We had made it. A few minutes later the cabin came into view.

We climbed the bank up off the river and rolled into camp...and out of the ink-black-frozen-loneliness. Once inside we began the ritual of beating the ice from our pant legs and boot gaiters so they could be removed, and worked our way up to the frozen zippers, the iced over facemasks and all the rest, in an effort to unwrap ourselves from the crust-encased shell that had shielded us for the day.

It's a wholly gratifying time with not much to say as you warm a little and begin to test cycle limbs, and probe muscles to see how difficult the recovery will be, and fathom a guess at how degraded you will still feel after ten hours of sleep. The difficulty of what we had just accomplished was driven home by the pain from each time you'd squat or bend to free a snap, a lace or a zip.

The next day would begin at some morning hour, sure enough, and we would do it all over again. But in those moments of physical misery your body is not subtle with its message that it's simply too much to ask. And you question if it is.

But the next day would start slowly. We would wake up and begin to move about on the small cabin's cool wooden floor, fumbling around the nails and strings above the stove for dry clothes, checking to see if the gloves dried all the way through, probing to see if the boots were still wet in the toes, looking out the window at the thermometer and knowing that it wouldn't come up from 28 below zero until the sun found it, and talking very little, but knowing that we would bring into the day everything we had, and every-thing we had left.

In my head I could hear the conversation we would have before the first words of it were ever spoken:

Kurt: "Let's go kill some wolves." "What do ya think?"
Me: "I think today is our day."

Authors note: *We didn't end up getting any wolves on the trip but we went back in the same location the following month to try again for wolf. We had great luck after a ten foot grizzly crossed the trail near Tangle Lakes and left trackable prints. It didn't take long to locate. A single .223 FMJ round squarely in the heart put it down without any drama. That was fortunate. I certainly don't recommend .223 for bear... but that was all the fire power we had. It was a close and accurately placed shot so it did the job. The photo with the bear hitched to the snowmobile puts the size in perspective. It was the largest inland brown bear ever taken on any hunt I had ever been on.*

Chapter 4

Soiled Dreams (2006)

Few things are as satisfying as taking someone hunting who really is dying to go and is new to it. Sometimes the newbies act like a child that figured out how to stay upright on a bicycle for the very first time, and you can't pry them off of it. Just as often they get all jazzed up, finally getting to the field only to find out they are really uncomfortable in tough environments. People new to hunting are often out of their element, a little spooked by the unfamiliarity of the weather, the remoteness, the risk.

I hesitate to admit that some of the satisfaction I get from taking a novice into the field comes from the stories that are later told and re-told at their expense. If you are new to the chase and you want to hang with my gang of hardcore Neanderthals, you check your ego at the door and surrender yourself to becoming the punch line. In this case I have a lot of respect for my subject. Unlike some, this man did not start out by spending a month's wages binging on Cabela's gear, or buying a new rifle, or new boots, especially for the event. He gathered what he had, borrowed what he didn't, and said "Let's do this". To use his real name would be unkind. We'll call him Moe and I'll tell his story.

Moe was somewhat of an outdoorsman, just not a big hunter. He had a lifetime dream of taking an Alaskan brown bear. When you talked to him you came away knowing that he was passionate about this chance to go. In his late thirties, he had recently moved to Alaska from the Lower 48 and was making a living teaching golf, a sport he was exceptional at.

Being athletic helped. He was over six feet tall and had a good set of arms and shoulders. As you will see, Moe proved to have a determination rare in a new hunter. When things got really nasty he soldiered on. His combination of enthusiasm and never quitting makes him a hard guy to make fun of.

The third guy on the trip was my frequent wingman Ed. Moe was Ed's friend. I had not known Moe at all before this hunt. Ed approached me and asked if it would be cool for him to come along on one of our spring bear hunts and told me how badly the fellow wanted to take a brown bear. Ed arranged for all of us to meet over a couple of beers and I really enjoyed the fellow. He was as kind a man as you could ever hope to meet, handsome, gentle, humorous, wholly unassuming and with a face that was alive with childlike energy.

Most importantly, he seemed at our meeting to be someone who would let Ed and me strip his ego to the bone during the trip and also let us be the sole arbiters of how he could earn it back. There is nothing worse than a new guy who won't let us embarrass and intimidate him when he's struggling.

It was early April when we met up for the first time. The three of us made lists of the necessary gear and pieced together a plan for an early May trip north, up the Alaska Highway, near Mt. Denali. Moe was new to snowmobiling and did not own a machine, so he borrowed one.

The snowmobiles Ed and I had were outfitted with cargo sleds that we towed behind us to carry the gear for all three of us. We had propane, gas jugs, food, beer, water, guns and the like. We were loaded a bit heavy if by chance the snow was soft. But if it was windblown or crusted from slightly lower temperatures in the early morning the overweight sleds would perform just fine. Such is the balancing act you are always trying to anticipate and get just right.

There was an old prospector's "cabin" in the vicinity of where we were hunting, 12 miles in from the road, and we would stay overnight there a of couple days. The cabin was the size of a big bathroom in a modest house. It slept two in stacked bunks at one end. It had a tiny table with a couple of steel folding chairs and five gallon buckets to sit on.

If you temporarily set the table outside, another sleeping bag could be rolled out on the floor. In the morning the guy on the floor has to get up first and roll up his bag and then the table comes back inside. This third guy sleeping on the floor is commonly referred to as "bitch" and he also lights the propane cook stove to initiate a little heat and puts the water on for coffee while the other two guys in the bunks decide when they prefer to get up.

Coming out of Anchorage we got a late start moving up the highway. It is a five hour trip and the last hour of it, after turning on the Denali Highway, is a rough gravel road that's often impassable even by four wheel drive in mid-April to early May. The Department of Transportation opens it right about then, but only after enough of the snow has melted so they can take heavy earthmoving equipment in and bust a trail through. It was not altogether a bad thing to arrive at the jumping off point later in the evening than planned. The deep spring snow is soft at midday and sometimes it can be too soft to work a snowmobile.

Temperatures range from just below zero at night to just above freezing during the day. If you get there by seven or eight in the morning you can prep the snowmobiles and towed sleds and ride them in the 12 miles of firm cool snow without much labor. Similarly, after about eight or nine in the evening the soft punchy midday snow begins to stiffen again and riding is better, but then you don't have as much light. If you hit it just after noon, especially if it has been sunny, you could be busting your ass for hours in a six foot deep ocean of Cool Whip instead of zipping over a hard crust.

We arrived about nine PM with overcast skies that made it darker than was ideal. The overcast also kept the temps from dropping as fast as a clear night would have, and it was just finally getting down to the high twenties. We got out of the truck and surveyed the situation. The snow was deep, wet and not yet taking a set. Ed and I decided that a dash into the cabin in the falling darkness, in sloppy conditions, may not be the best testing grounds for Moe's skill set. The only option open was to sleep in Ed's quad cab truck and move the next day early.

Everyone got his final snacks, and pissed, and otherwise attended to every need that could arise in the middle of the night. We had to get all that out of the way because once we took to our sleeping positions inside sleeping bags, inside the small cab, it was a big hassle to get up and out. Moe, owning the short straw on this trip, would bunk in the narrow slot on the floor between the front and rear seats. Once Moe wedged into his position and lay down, I crawled into the rear cab next and scrunched into a knees-up posture across the seat. Ed did the same on the front bench.

Alaska Raw

The temps dropped to five degrees. Body heat from three of us in the cab made it almost comfortable. I heard Ed wake up a couple of times during the night to start the truck, letting the heater run for a while to take the edge off and then he shut it down again.

Ed was smart to not keep the engine running. With a breeze coming the wrong direction there was always the chance carbon monoxide would find a crack in the cab and gas us into a permanent nap.

In the morning the inside of the truck was covered with ice crystals from our moist breath condensing on every surface. By seven AM we were stirring and trying to break loose cramped body parts. Ed started the truck one last time. We opened up the doors to the frosty box and crawled out like the hunched homeless pressed unwillingly into a new morning. All of our clothes and gear bags were in the open bed of the truck covered with a heavy layer of frost.

Bracing against the cold, the race was on to get at the bags and start layering on Arctic gear. Once dressed, the snowmobiles, sleds and everything that went in them or onto them was unloaded from the truck. We divided and reassembled the gear, strapping it on the machines. Snow crunched under our boots letting us know the snow had set up like cement overnight and was perfect for a quick gymkhana rally into the hunting zone.

Pointing the snowmobiles toward the northern mountains we bailed over the steep ditch line, into the untracked wilderness, and started breaking trail. Moe had hardly been on a snowmobile but he tucked in behind us and did nothing stupid. He wasn't towing anything so in the few spots where we did break through the frozen crust he just followed our strategic lead which was big fists full of power and doing your best to stay out of the ugly deep trenches gouged out by the guy directly in front of you.

Even with the near ideal conditions, we got stuck several times in really deep soft stretches and had to unhook the tow sleds, pack a trail out with the machines, come back, reconnect the sleds, and repeat as many times as needed to beat a trail through the troubled spots.

Moe was smart enough to stay some distance behind the main operation and only come forward when the trail was all clear ahead. So often new riders want to come right up into the hot mess to try to be "helpful" only to find themselves just another elephant in the tar pit. Twelve miles took two hours, which was a great run.

I have started that exact same trip in the morning, on other hunts, and barely made it by dark, a twelve or four-teen hour ordeal, spending hours buried in nearly impass-able conditions, or crusty snow that unpredictably gave way, dropping you into grainy loose powder devoid of any traction, or sometimes right on through into knee high slush and water.

One of the worst I can remember, the one that took all day to move those same 12 miles, involved Ed dropping his snowmobile, with an attached freight sled, through a crust that was concealing a chest deep beaver pond. But that is another story for another time.

We had the entire day in front of us and now we were at base camp, up tight against the steep walls of a long jagged mountain range and a large glacier. The clouds cleared on cue and conditions were absolutely perfect to cut a bear track coming out of the steep slopes or to power up the many valleys and crags and glass for a den. Up against the mountains it was cooler for longer and most of the areas would have a solid base to move around on.

Ed, Moe and I unpacked and unhooked the tow sleds and opened up the tiny cabin. To keep the bears from ransacking the place, hunks of plywood were screwed to the couple of glass panes that allowed light in. Uncovering those and plugging in a small propane bottle to a hose that ran to the outside was about all there was to settling in.

Within a few minutes we had accomplished those small chores, regrouped our personal gear, shed a layer of clothes, stuffed our pockets with a day's dry food, and set out.

The machines felt much different without one hundred pounds of fuel and supplies behind each of them. The mood changes when the guns go on your back and prime bear country draws you in from every direction. Our first move was into some high valleys that had always produced a bear or two. We moved along until we were positioned to see big, steep south facing walls, glassed them carefully for any den holes or tracks, and then moved briskly on to the next range.

The game is to repeat that process over and over cover-ing as much of the range as possible. Our hunting ground was immense. About two hundred square miles of poten-tial denning areas surrounded us.

Crossing from drainage to drainage down low was the only place that gave us trouble, the snow getting more and more punchy and sloppy at the lower elevations. Riding the ridges was out of the question. These mountains topped out on knife edge lines that a man could not walk, let alone thread a snowmobile along. We covered a bunch of ground, hunting all day and finding nothing but a few caribou and a couple of winter starved sheep.

After working our way in a ten mile circle that took us back to camp the sun was setting. It was time to dry out, drain a few beers, sample the whiskey selection, heat up some food, and retell the stories of each time Moe got stuck up to the handlebars in the creek bottoms, or had to take five tries to get up a steep pull. Moe was flogged and Ed and I were not much better. A day of aggressive hunting on snowmobiles makes you feel like you have participated in a prison riot and been beaten with a pillow case stuffed with soup cans. Everything hurts, which of course calls for more beer.

With Moe spread out on the floor and Ed and I commanding the steel framed army surplus bunk bed, the chatter winnowed to the last few ribald comments, personal insults and the sighs and groans of big groups of aching muscles finally letting down.

The next morning was blue bird and about 15 degrees, warm for such a clear day and with the sun not yet at a high angle. This was good and bad. The previous morning had been 10 degrees colder and that was at the truck, a lower elevation and certainly not next to a glacier like we were now. So given the 15 degree showing that early, we could plan on having a high in the mid-forties instead of the thirties. That meant the snow would go completely to hell in any low draws we had to cross. As we cooked some oatmeal and chewed dried fruit, it was decided that a circuit of glassing near to, and actually on, the glacier itself would avoid the bottomless midday snow. We would attempt to stay high.

The maps came out, a plan came together and we launched day two. Hunting methodically up to the base of the glacier took us a couple hours. Once up on the thick ice mass, the view was expansive and it was cooler, as we had expected.

Brown bears usually den high so they don't melt out before food is available. Since it was nice and cool the travelling was easy with the exception of the few times we had to follow narrow ice ridges from one big glacier section to another, which was like navigating a maze. Some of these blue ice pressure ridges had flat tops that were eight to ten feet wide, others were narrower, just wide enough to fit the machines single file with little margin for error. One rib led us to the next.

In some of the worst places these snaking elevated ice causeways fell away on either side down steep 45 and 50 degree slopes ending in the blackness of narrow chasms.

Nothing dropped away more than 200 feet. While you would surely get the shit knocked out of you tumbling down any of these slopes to the bottom of the crevasses, you probably would not die. But still, it was no place to miss a turn, to relax, or pick that stray booger. In these sections we crawled along at a walking pace steering to stay exactly in the middle of the available ice.

It was all going nicely, Ed leading, then me, followed by Moe just a few lengths behind. Ed glancing back every couple of minutes to see if I was still behind him, while I was doing the same, keeping track of Moe. The three of us snaked our way steadily through the immense and dangerous ice field, heading for the next large expanse of flat ice so we could kick back and glass some more.

Ed looked back. Check. I looked back for Moe. Check. That all worked...exactly up until the one time I looked back to see nothing but a sea of sun glazed blue ice ridges. No Moe. There were some blind corners behind me where the odd ice tower rose above us at various points, blocking the view backward.

Perhaps he is just 200 feet back, I thought, hidden by that last corner I can't see around...and he will appear any second. But he didn't. I was stopped, waiting. Ed finally looked back. Then he stopped. We waited just another minute. Maybe he was shedding or adding clothes, or peeing. The ridges were so narrow there was not enough room to turn either of the snowmobiles around. Ed and I dismounted and started jogging back to the last obscured turn.

As we rounded the ice wall and looked back another 100 feet we saw Moe's machine at the extreme edge of the skinny ice causeway and it was tilted up hard on its side. All we could see from our approaching angle was the belly of the machine, with one ski high in the air, as if it was levitating at a 45 degree angle.

Ed and I ran back calling out for Moe, momentarily terrified at the thought of how far and fast he must have went shooting down the icy side slope after apparently tipping off the snowmobile. As we hustled toward the snowmobile we were also struggling to process how it was that his machine could somehow balance itself, teetering on the extreme edge of the available ice, ready to start tumbling down with the slightest whiff of assistance. Just before we reached the snowmobile we heard a breathless whisper of a voice.

Moe: "Ya....I'm.......here"

Ed: "WHERE!?"

Moe: "................underneath"

Ed ad I both rushed to the machine arriving at the same time and grabbed the high side ski and a handlebar to stabilize it.

We finally realized that Moe was hidden behind his tilted machine, down over the steep pitched edge, sort of standing upright on his toes with his knees pressed hard into the grade, his arms fully extended in an Atlas like superhero bench press.

He was straining hard into the snowmobile, sweat pouring off his face, channeling every ounce of his fear and resolve to keep himself from rag dolling down into the crevasse, a fall that would not end well considering he would also be pummeled by a 500 pound hunk of aluminum tumbling after him.

The steep icy slope had just enough gravel and silt on it that his boots and knees were scarfing enough traction to allow him to hold on for his life. The machine was tilted towards him just past its tipping point and he had been bench pressing that weight for the last several minutes, waiting for the cavalry. It was a fine balance, but he was unable to force it upward to right it. If it had tipped any further toward him the added weight would have made his feet and knees give way, even if his arms had the strength to hold it in check. Moe was the picture of a man in distress.

He was alternately whimpering and letting out intermittent guttural noises that we could not understand. We pulled off the weight and flopped the snowmobile flat on its track and skis. Moe was gulping air, exhausted. Still glued to the incline, he lowered his arms to brace himself on the ice, then dropping his head for what looked like a prayer at the Wailing Wall. Moe was a Mormon and he had this really odd manner about him in those few moments while he was recovering.

I thought he may be receiving a telepathic revelation directly from the Mormon cosmos delivery system on how to righteously steer a snowmobile. In truth, it was a quiet, private moment for Moe that Ed and I would only understand much later in the day. He looked injured and was moving slowly but denied anything was hurt.

With a bit less zip and enthusiasm, Moe mounted his ride and gathered his bearings as Ed and I walked back to our machines. We all reformed our string.

Ed and I were a little shook up by Moe's seemingly mindless mistake of driving off the "trail" and putting himself at such serious risk, and how quickly things could have gone really bad. We tried to stay in a tighter formation and we changed order, sandwiching Moe between us like two parents boxing in a toddler.

The mountain walls containing and limiting the glacier were heavily snow covered and steep, a perfect place to find a bear den. Browns den high, usually preferring 3,000 to 5,000 feet. The sows with cubs will sometimes den even higher for safety from predators. For example, wolves can dig a sow and cubs out of their den to kill and eat them. Boars and sows both den in areas where they will not unwillingly be melted out before their hibernation schedule agrees.

The peak timing for exiting from the den for the male bears in this area was the third week in April. For sows, it's two weeks later than that. Our timing was perfect. After moving up and then down the glacier and glassing the sides of the entire bowl, we still did not spot anything. As the afternoon wore on and the sun changed angles, the temperature dropped.

Since the snow had started to set up down at lower elevations with that temperature drop, we changed strategies and moved off the glacier, down to the valley floor, crossing the firming snow, and then on to another drainage to the south.

Most of my spring bear kills have happened in the late afternoon or evening. By afternoon the bears have had a good 12 hours with the temperatures rising and sun beating on their ice burrow. This time of year the extended light allows you to hunt until about midnight on a clear night. We had hunted all day and came up empty.

About then you are still engaged in the moment but begin to pin your hopes on the next day and what it could bring, and you start contemplating what the weather will be doing then, how the temperatures will affect travel, if any strategy should change, and mentally shifting gears.

Moe was thrashed and out of steam from another long day out of his element but he had recovered well enough since the-big-scare to smile once in a while at the jokes made at his expense. This is a true sign of worthiness and the requirement that he subjugate himself to his keepers.

Alaska Raw

It was toward the end of the day, but we were still covering a lot of ground, stopping, glassing, repositioning, repeating. We came to a high bench that allowed a panoramic view of a large valley and flats beyond. We were all ready for a short break and a candy bar and some liquids. The low sun was starting to turn the crystalline landscape pink and magenta. We got comfortable again on the glasses and let them do the work, reaching out several miles in every direction, looking for the prize.

I was scanning and rescanning the same sections of flats below that I had covered about three times in the last half an hour, knowing that the sun was at the perfect angle, throwing shadows that would reveal any good set of tracks a long way out. I was straining to make out every odd impression for a pattern that we might investigate further, as I had hour after hour, when a big brown mass suddenly blasted into view from the right side of the lens!

Whatever it was, it was in snow so deep its stomach was plowing a trench. It could be moose, caribou or bear, given the color and size. After watching just a few seconds I could make out from its gait and deliberate path that it was a big bear. The rush is always just as satisfying...no matter how many times you have hunted, spotted and stalked, the endorphin spike of a big bear coming into view ratchets the heart rate up and focuses every sense to a fine edge.

The bear was moving fast for some reason, right to left almost two miles away, heading out from the mountains onto the flat. Beyond the flat lay a dense tree line and once the bear made it to the trees it would probably be lost. From our perch in the high bench we had an outstanding view but we were a long way away. I blurted out the news to Moe and Ed.

Me: "I HAVE ONE!!!"

Moe: "One what?"

Me: "A bear, A BEAR! Way out! It's moving fast! It looks like it could be a good one! Are you ready?!!"

In seconds Ed found the bear in his glasses, lit up his machine, and was ready to launch off the mountain. My machine was also running by then.

Moe struggled, still panning his glasses over the landmarks and reference points I was frantically calling out to him so he could line himself up on the animal. Finally, giving up on Moe actually getting a long view of his prey, I barked "let's go!" with enough urgency for him to sense it was not a suggestion but a demand.

I tried to get him moving without demoralizing him by taking away the only chance he had to actually see a bear, something he had been pouring his heart into for the last two days, and dreaming about for years more.

Me: "IT'S HAULING ASS!   IT'S CHASING SOMETHING.....YOU WILL SEE IT WHEN WE GET THERE!"

Moe: "Where? I don't see it!"

Me: "I WOULD DRAW YOU A PICTURE BUT I'M ALL OUT OF CRAYONS... LET'S GO!! WE SEE IT !......... IT'S A BEAR!.....SLING YOUR GUN, PUT YOUR SHIT AWAY, PUT YOUR GLOVES ON, START THAT FUCKER UP AND LET'S FUCKING GO!!" "NOW!... LET'S GO...NOW!"   I was screaming at him by that time. Only then did Moe finally act, scrambling to secure his gloves, hat, binoculars and helmet, and prepare to follow Ed and me off the high bench.

I mentally logged a couple of distant landmarks from the bear's last confirmed position, pointed the machine accordingly, dropped my goggles down and pegged the throttle. Raw horsepower screamed from under the cowling and exited out the bottom of the track, catapulting me off the bench and down the side of the mountain.

Glancing around for a second I found that Ed was immediately to my left. Moe, surprisingly, was not too far behind him. We were scorching across the tundra at 65 to 70 miles an hour, gathering up and spitting out the waterfalling cascade of foothills that formed the base of the high bench.

After sending some arm signals to Ed that he instantly understood, I broke left twenty degrees from the course to cut a path that would place me half a mile out front of the bear's path. The bear was moving like it was chasing a moose or a caribou, the only possible reason it would be burning so much precious energy resources in deep snow. Still, the bear had no idea we had lit off the cruise missiles and were closing in.

Ed motioned for Moe to stay behind him and they stayed on a true course headed directly toward the bear, still at warp speed. At the very bottom of the hill we bashed through a couple of heavy patches of eight foot high alder like it was cat's tail, throttles hammered to the bar, the powerful machines blowing through the heavy brush like a pickup truck full of drunk rednecks blows through a corn field.

As we hit the flat and broke out of the brush, our two paths split wider and in moments I could see the bear still crossing far out front, still running after something, and without a clue that we were coming. We covered the last mile at a blistering pace catching air over the bumps. At the end of the run I turned more south so I ended up about 1,500 yards out in front of the bear's path on a high dome. I wanted to keep an eye on it while Ed and Moe got themselves into position. Ed and "shooter" Moe arrived a couple hundred yards behind it.

I shut down my machine and parked, waiting to see the action unfold. As I watched through my field glasses, Moe jumped off his machine and readied his gun.

The bear had made no changes in direction as they came in from behind it. It was headed somewhat towards me and was hell bent on chasing whatever it had caught the scent or sight of. Looking over top and beyond the bear I could see Moe and Ed clearly and Moe was handling his gun but I could not tell what he was doing with it. I kept waiting to hear the shot and hoping he would drop it before it got any closer to me or the tree line.

The shot never came. I was parked, my snowmobile still shut down, and the bear was still coming my direction. The snow was deep and punchy and not worth a damn for making emergency maneuvers on a snowmobile. Even though I was still a long ways away, it seemed a really good idea to start the motor and move out of the bear's path.

As I continued to motor off, quartering away from it, and out of the line of any potential fire, I looked back and saw the bear was turning 180 degrees, lunging through the snow, heading directly back to Ed and Moe. Was it possible the south wind was carrying my engine noise directly back to the bear? It was carrying Ed's and Moe's directly away.

The bear still did not see my partners, but since it had reversed course for whatever reason, it had now closed the distance to Moe and Ed to about 150 yards. This entire stalk was not playing out like it was supposed to. I waited and watched through my glasses, listening for a shot to ring out from Moe.

Nothing.

As I watched the bear hit a stretch of some better snow, either harder or thinner, and picked up speed. Things were now happening very fast. From what I could see it looked like Moe was still fiddling with his gun scabbard.

Seconds were ticking by, the bear was getting better traction the further he retreated towards Moe and Ed...who were now standing waist deep in wet snow. Moe was about to get his ass wrecked by a 500 hundred pound brown bear. As the bear closed to 100 yards and was on target to run Moe over, I could not understand why he could not get a shot off. It just never came.

I watched in the field glasses. Any second...I thought, the shot will come, or Ed will drop it for him.

I could see Ed was still sitting on his machine and guessed that he was getting as panicked about the situation as I was. He had not unslung his rifle because he was sure Moe was going to get the job done any second. Ed knew he had to do something or Moe would be road kill and I was much too far away to do anything. Ed lurched into action, jerked the pull starter on his machine, gassed it, and ran himself in between Moe and the closing bear. It was a risky move. The bear instantly turned off his path, cutting to their left but never breaking stride, nostrils ejecting funnels of steam and snow flying from his haunches with each muscular thrust.

KABOOM !

Moe had finally freed his scope covers, or his safety, or otherwise put his dick away and at long last... sent a bullet out of the end of his rifle. Bravo my man... Here's to your health! The bear went down like the unfortunate victim of a lightning strike. It took not one more step after the round exploded in its chest.

The only remaining movement was a visible wisp of hot steam curling upward off its wet brown mass. A .300 Win mag at 60 yards has a truck load of power and every ounce of it went into the bear's chest cavity and not one sliver of that energy came out.

Ed was close enough to the shot, and so directly in the line of fire, that he must have felt the shock wave on his face. Only when it's over do you notice the metallic taste of stress in your mouth, the sweat rolling off your face and down your neck, and the quick, short breaths that come from too much adrenaline pressed into every corner of your mind and body. But that all flips in an instant, perhaps like finally having your parachute open so you could begin to really savor the rest of the ride.

Wrapped in a perfect evening sun, shimmering over an ocean of flawless white, it had all come together. Moe was THE MAN. When I reached him he hugged me. He was weeping. The strong feelings of fulfilling a lifelong dream just came pouring out. The three of us gathered together. Standing up to our waists in snow, we leaned in to congratulate him and celebrated his wonder.

Moe's emotion became our emotion. It was an unusual few minutes that took me by surprise. Actually, the impressions those moments made on me seem to come back to mind whenever a new hunter asks to go with me. Yes, it's a hassle to bring them into that world but the rewards are uniquely rich.

The brown bear was superb, its hide a chocolate color with bright gold highlights and without a single rub. It squared just over eight feet, on the large side for an inland grizzly. After rolling it up onto a flat spot where we could take some pictures, it was clear Moe had indeed taken an excellent animal. Confirmation of all of this was reassuring since things happened much faster than we would have liked, and initially there was little time to be sure of much more than: It was big enough to be a real trophy and it was not a female with cubs.

It had been on the move, big time. Minutes later it would have made the tree line and blown any chance Moe had. It would have been nice to spend hours looking at it through the glasses first, and critiquing its every characteristic, but that was not the play available to us. In those circumstances you feel greatly relieved that it was an exceptional bear.

Our light was still good and the sun would hang lazily above the west horizon for another two hours framing everything around us in hues of soft pink and orange. The bright but filtered light was absolutely perfect for pictures. After the pictures the knives came out. Within an hour we had coaxed the thick fur off the carcass.

The kill was just a couple of miles from the cabin so we had two options for finishing the night. We could run back and grab our tow sleds and head out for the pickup... or spend another night in the field at the trapper's cabin. After some discussion we ran back and picked up the gear, shuttered our hut, and set out for the twelve mile trip to the highway.

With the sun just setting below the western mountains, the cool evening air again put a firm set to the snow making running on it relatively fast and smooth. In an hour and a half we pulled onto the snow drifted highway, located the truck, and started pulling off layers of clothes and loading the pickup and trailer.

As Ed and I scurried around packing and securing the machines, Moe was unusually quiet. He must have been totally pooped. It was a long, long day of aggressive and technical back-country riding. Moe, we remembered, had a really tough time on the glacier, bench pressing his borrowed snowmobile over his head with nothing but a toe hold on the ice-shelf-of-death.

Ed and I had changed out of our Arctic gear and into street clothes but Moe was still mostly suited up.

He was darting around, digging in the pickup cab and then the bed looking for something and behaving oddly. As Ed and I loaded the last of the gear Moe began stripping off his clothes standing in the gravel road, but behind the back of the snowmobile trailer and mostly shielded from our view. I thought maybe he did not want us to see his magic Mormon underwear, or maybe he was just shy about his small penis. Who could know?

Moe was back there for what seemed like a very long time so Ed and I went back to see what the hell he could possibly be up to.

When we came around the back of the trailer the first thing we noticed were wads of newspapers, paper towels and a few balled up fast food sacks all over the ground surrounding him. Moe was standing there in the gravel, surrounded by the confetti, in nothing but his shirt and socks with shit smeared from his knees to his belly button.

He was bathed in brown and wiping down....with anything he could find. His head hung low and his eyes were looking everywhere but towards us. He had the expression on his face that can only be described as roughly matching how he looked when first caught by his mother masturbating.

Finally, Moe breaks the silence: "I had an accident."

Ed and I stared in disbelief before folding in half with uncontrolled spasms of laughter. Moe had found and used every spare bit of anything he could find to de-poop his torso and the ground around him was littered with these shit stained wads.

Important to the story here is that Moe had pioneered a new type of spring riding gear since he did not own good snow pants to wear on the trip. He wore chest waders. Actually, chest waders are a   resourceful and inventive solution for spring bear hunting on a snowmobile. You can layer as much as you want underneath and they are waterproof, a huge plus in sloppy wet snow. After seeing Moe wear them I even thought they would be good to try sometime. But in this case, instead of keeping the snow out, the rubber body sock kept the poop in.

Moe's bowels had blown on him early in the day when he had the big scare on the glacier, straining to hold his borrowed machine from tumbling into the crevasse.

Back at the glacier he had the sheepish look of a shamed man when we saved him, not because he fell off his machine, or because he was getting revelation from his Celestial Dictator, but because he had just fudge packed his pants with an especially soupy load....and did not know what he should do about it. He chose to soldier on, like a man's man, and keep right on riding and hunting...like nothing ever happened. Hour after hour Moe rode on, pounding his rear on the snowmobile seat, turning his chest waders into a human colostomy bag and his ass into a dumpster fire.

That is why Moe is our hero to this day.

Back at the snowmobile trailer, Ed and I could not muster enough compassion to quit laughing, but during the convulsing we did help round up some more wipe worthy materials so it can't be said we didn't do our part. We dug out what little water we had and tossed it to him and, while circling from a safe distance, encouraged him to work some fistfuls of snow into the more stubborn poo streaks before getting into fresh clothes. It all helped. But the minute he got into the truck, new clothes and all, the cab was shot through with the smell of sewer.

The ride back to town with turd boy was four hours that we thought would never end. For weeks afterward people getting in Ed's truck would be instinctively checking the bottom of their shoes for dog shit and then cracking their window.

It was all worth it. Moe got his bear. Ed and I got enough adult diaper jokes to last a lifetime...

Moe at the supermarket getting supplies to go spring bear hunting:

....."Sir, do you have any Depends in a size X Large that come in a winter camouflage?"

....."You do!" "You have them in all white!!!" "I can't believe my luck!"

....."Those will be PERFECT!!"

Chapter 5

Killing Machines (2008)

"Many of us are hunting mice while lions devour the land."

Leonard Ravenhill

This story begins at a pub where again I find myself in the company of Wingman Ed, a solidly reliable brute of a hunter who is always up for anything. With us, "up for anything" is a disposition we cultivate and guard from any attempts by the other to temper. The more outrageous the plan, the better.

Some hunting partners are reliably a "fit". A good partner has to be a peer in strength, skill, endurance and determination. In the perfect union, without even recognizing it, you take turns at being the catalyst for making a move the other would grimace at the thought of ever attempting solo.

Ed is a few years younger than I. He previously played college football at a high level and is one of those guys who, in his prime, could bench press a small car. Even still, well into his late forties and early fifties, he remains a raging bull in the outdoors. He's a thinker and a strategist. His manner is direct, often to the point of being blunt. He is a gambler of some significant success.

Ed can play the mental short game, or the long one, depending on what's called for in the moment, and can toggle effortlessly between the two mindsets. When instincts are driving our team, especially when things get dicey, it's necessary for me to have confidence in his instincts like I have confidence in my own. Of course, we both have outsized appetites for risk. It's all so perfect.

As can be all too common with my pals and I, the scheming to launch a major adventure gels after about the fourth beer. That is when we get down to the base elements regarding which Cro-Magnon itch really needs scratching. We decided that evening that it was the need to mix guns and snowmobiles and to dominate the landscape in an Eskimo Braveheart sort of way. My conversation with Ed turned to wolves, the indefatigable killing machines that they are.

Between swills I relayed a couple of tales in years past of putting the hurt on those shifty eyed, elusive assassins. As the night grew longer the challenge took shape: how can we turn the tables, or at least change the odds, that for a few days in the middle of nowhere a couple of the planet's more aggressive two-legged beasts would outwit and out maneuver the gloriously fanged four-legged ones.

Why would we do it? Who knows? But near as I can tell, deep down, hunting wolves must have a component of reasserting command at the top of the food chain. It's about pure aggression, imposing your will on something that never gets imposed upon, but rather is the predator, coordinated into a pack of death so efficient nothing ever escapes it, let alone challenges it. It's about reversing the natural order of the jungle while knowing how incredibly difficult that can be.

More people have summited Mt. Everest than have tracked down and harvested a wolf, or several. I believe it's just an exercise in setting free your DNA to do what it has always done, what it's pre-programmed to do.

At its core the hunt is an absolute frenzy of high speed, pull-out-all-the-stops, eyes bugging out of your head, adrenalin spiked, sweat soaked contest with a very fast, smart, dynamic and unrelentingly durable opponent. And for those people who absolutely despise wolf hunters or people engaged in state sanctioned predator control programs, there is an upside, something for everybody, because for every dead wolf several hundred moose, caribou and their calves get to live another day. Clearly, my pals and I are closeted conservationist. This is a coming-out party.

I know that if the State of Alaska did not think that controlling the numbers of wolves was critically important, and had the science to back it up, there wouldn't be sanctioned predator control programs or the generous daily bag limits still being used today.

I have personally seen wolf populations in certain areas expand exponentially over a few years, then all the caribou and moose and sheep begin to disappear, then the wolves start eating each other, and the ones that don't eat each other starve to death after they have vacuumed the landscape clean of everything up to, and including, porcupines and ground squirrels.   So which scenario is less kind, thinning the pack, or cyclical genocidal mass starvation?

A plan came together that night which involved driving 800 miles from one end of Alaska to the other. No shortage of ambition there. We had to get up to the specially designated areas north of the Yukon River where snowmobiles could legally be used as we were utilizing them. There, we would visit the wolf in its most vulnerable range.

"Vulnerable", as it concerns a wolf's habitat and range as understood by a hunter, simply means no trees and no place to hide. No packs scattering into subparts and heading for the first stands of trees only to vanish. They would still have the safety of the mountain peaks, but only if they reach them before you killed them. It's the difference between combat in your opponent's jungle versus the better odds of hundreds of miles of overexposed snow panorama. There, the opposition is stripped of everything but its wit and speed. There can be no argument, even under those circumstances, that the wolf remains one of the most difficult animals in the world to locate, hunt down and kill.

The plan would involve high performance snowmobiles complemented nicely with semi-automatic weapons. It all sounded absolutely irresistible. This was not my first wolf hunt on snowmobiles above the Arctic Circle, but it would be Ed's. So even though the team was new it had some history to build from.

Officially we could have been either "trapping" or "hunting", using sections of the Alaska regulations that suited our purpose given the laws as they were many years ago and given our designated location. Both hunting and trapping under Alaska regulations at the time allowed the taking of wolves with a rifle using a snowmobile in specific far north Game Units, with the condition that you cannot shoot from a moving snowmobile, which is almost impossible to do anyway.

Alaska Raw

After driving north across the Yukon River and continuing through to the Brooks Range, our plan called for sleeping beside the road in the snowmobile trailer we would tow behind a pickup. Stocked with some cots, a propane heater, cook stove, small generator and plenty of instant food, we would have a crude but mobile platform that could self-sustain for a week.

Our high horsepower snowmobiles would chew through vicious amounts of fuel, as would the tow/haul chariot, which was Ed's Dodge mega cab and 20' enclosed snowmobile trailer, affectionately nicknamed the QE2 for its likeness of the cruise ship's imposing bulk and appetite. About 400 gallons of fuel should turn the trick. Some could be purchased along the way, at least until we ran out of roadside services above the Arctic Circle. For the rest, every nook left unfilled by cold weather and hunting gear would be packed with fuel in plastic jugs.

In late March the weather in the Brooks Range can be 40 below or 25 above zero. There is no predicting it so you need to have storm proofed your pickup, your camp spread, your snowmobiles and your personal gear as though you were headed to a tailgate party in Antarctica. It's never going to be easy.

The endeavor usually allows brief moments of enjoyment inside the bitterly cold, highly challenging experience that makes up a week in the outdoors in the Arctic winter. And for those who think late March is spring...it may be where you come from, but not here. Even April is still an unmovable sea of ice and snow with subzero temperatures being highly probable.

Throw in a little wind and some whiteout conditions and you have all the ingredients of a combination survival / fur hunting trip...a gig where just returning with a few of your body parts not frostbitten to black spells success.

More than a couple times I had wished I was more of a barstool hunter, the type of person who drinks too much, blathers on too much, talks big and then goes home, never really walking the talk when it comes to hunting. But neither my partner Ed, nor I, trend in that direction. We're just not satisfied telling and re-telling stories about "The One" that you're always going to go back and kill next season, if you can find him.

For better or worse, we just aren't built that way. With us, anything worth doing is worth overdoing. The plan started getting more legs.

To feed any wide eyed, crazy man plan in the Arctic you have to have the tools. A couple of absolute key items would be reliable snowmobiles and weaponry. "Reliable" as it relates to the snowmobiles is really a secret code word we substitute for "indestructible". The test for this attribute, to be candid, is more like this: if a wolf hunt reduces the near new machines to a smoking pile of rubble, sporting wire and tape and bungee cords where fasteners once existed, with skis so damaged that each have their own unique idea about what forward should be, both of which are at odds with any given orientation of the handlebars, when the odd noises emanating from god-knows-where begin to be accompanied by odd smells or little fires...will these machines still limp us the 50 or so miles back to where we can thaw out, re-group, and contemplate the repairs over a plastic cup of Crown Royal. These are big and important questions.

About the weaponry. I have to get up a head of steam to explain anything technical about guns since, surprisingly, they aren't really something that makes my nuts tingle. A sturdy gun that fires when called on, and hopefully more than once at 30 below zero or colder... is a good one. A good gun is also one that you can actually hit something with in the mental confusion and mechanical chaos of a good dog fight. The gun has to be as familiar in your hand as your favorite hammer.

To me, a gun is just a tool, not a lot more interesting than a Skilsaw. It's a tool to be maintained, worked hard and stowed in the corner until next time you have a job for it.

If it rides well slung on your back without banging bruises into your spine when charging over the snowdrifts at sixty miles an hour, if it readies quickly even when fumbling with frozen fingers, if it scores its mark sending showers of bone bits, hide and gore all over the snow scape, we're mostly done jabbering about it. If I could kill all my game with a spear I would. I would enjoy it more. But I'm just not that nimble, or brave, or skilled. My arms may also be too short. So I use the other tool, a gun.

Since this screed is nearly all about hunting, I feel a thin but nagging duty not to disappoint the gun heads that are grinding through my pile of chapters impersonating a book. I really do owe you. I am aware that guns are just short of a masturbatory aid for many outdoorsmen. Accordingly, we'll all circle back later to those destruction spewing extensions of manhood and everyone will have their moment of orgiastic satisfaction.

So back to the hunt....let's review Sturdy Tool number one, the snowmobile. A lot has changed in a short time with the design and capability of the modern snowmobile. By the late 1990's they were becoming profoundly capable, faster and lighter. Major changes in snowmobiles over 25 years have yielded an incredible result. The steering geometry now works for you instead of solidly for the gremlins. Insanely powerful engines are inspired by NASA booster rocket technology.

Longer and vastly more aggressive tracks harness all that horsepower and carve it into the landscape, blowing scenery out the rear at warp speed, catapulting the Master and Commander forward at blistering acceleration rates. Nothing really compares.

Power to weight says it all. Let's look at some metrics. A top of the line, $200,000 plus supercar, like a Ferrari F430, a Lamborghini Diablo, or even a new LS9 Z06 Corvette all have power to weight (PW) ratios in the 6 pounds to the horsepower range, give or take. By anyone's measure these cars are wicked fast. By comparison, the large displacement snowmobiles I speak of have a PW ratio in the low 3s, roughly twice as maliciously potent as any supercar car you can buy and drive away in, no matter how exotic the price.

Take a new generation Turbo 911 Porsche and replace the engine with one twice as large producing 1000 horsepower and you will finally be approaching some parity with a high performance snowmobile. Can you feel the magic yet? There is nothing hypothetical here. If you drop one of these fire breathing sleds straight onto some asphalt beside the Ferrari, or the LS9 Corvette, for some zero to sixty truth-squad runs, the supercars will be left for forgotten... at least for the first 150 or 200 yards.

Moreover, they steer precisely, carve deep snow nimbly and climb whenever called upon like a goat with a jet pack. In powder so deep and fluid it would stop a man from physically doing anything but belly crawling, these sleds suck in massive amounts of snow-covered tundra and then puke it out the back at a clip that turns your face white and rolls your lips back double. They can blow through dense brush like it was fireweed, mow down eight foot high alders at speed, or rocket down dry river beds (handy, but not for long) and keep throbbing for more.

For wolf hunting such a tool can be just the thing. Wolves aren't afraid of much but when they get a little taste of your action, when you swing a leg over one of these 160 horsepower snow sleds and begin acting like a 500 pound wolverine on methamphetamine, you will have their full attention.

Did I mention you also have to be half a mechanic to partake in this sort of pastime? The machine also represents your survival platform. If you don't have the knowledge to keep your sled running, this probably isn't your kind of trip. They are durable in a sense, but very high strung like any technology taken to the edge. If one of you t-bones a hidden ice shelf or rips a ski leg off in a dung hole someplace, you must be capable of either repairing it or else your partner's sled needs to be able to drag both of you out from wherever and however insane the inbound route was. It is your life raft in a vast ocean of snow.

Ed and I took three of these machines, one as a spare, just in case one took a dump and could not be artificially resurrected with our stock of wire, tape and bungee cords. We never needed the third machine but as you will see later, it wasn't for lack of trying.

Our drive up to the hunt area went well enough; no major mechanical or biological issues. Giddy anticipation overlaid most of the idle time and tempered the boredom of the Infinitely Long Grind.

Whoever wasn't driving got to sink a few beers, get his glow on, become the lead storyteller and animated entertainer, and then sober up for a couple of hours, just in time to take the wheel and alternate duties, guiding the 10,000 pounds of truck, trailer and gear down the long, long thread of a dead end gravel road leading to the vast and desolate Arctic plains.

We crossed the Yukon River just about in the middle of its 1,200 mile span and the trees began to look tortured and weak. Too little light, horribly tough winters, high wind, and a lifetime nested in permafrost makes for some bulimic, tattered looking boreal forest. The sick, scraggly spruce resembled draught killed corn stalks more than timber. About all you can say in their favor is they could make a fire and possibly save you from freezing to death.

As mile after mile rattled by, we finally made it over and through the breathtaking and rugged Atigun Pass. By then even the scrub pine disappeared and gave way to low, denuded rolling hills reaching northward for 150 miles of emptiness, terminating at the frozen Beaufort Sea. You really have to want to do this, and you remind yourself of that repeatedly, because it's a 22 hour drive in good weather.

It is unusual to find a big grizzly in March at subzero temperatures. We tracked this one out near Tangle Lakes and it was taken quickly and cleanly with a single .223 round.

These wolves came from the same Drift River area where I was predator calling and the bears attacked. Bears and wolves share the same dwindling salmon in November.

We are loading up my Super Cub after a Unimak caribou hunt.

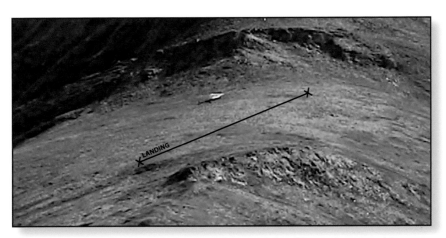

To hunt Sheepzilla we touched down at the lower left, rolling to the upper right.

The Unimak clouds breaking in the evening for a rare treat of dwindling sunlight.

My father, Bob Sr., and I savor the moment with a nice Unimak bull caribou.

A group of walrus we encountered on the Alaska Peninsula.

Bears den in outrageous places. This picture is at 7,000 feet, climbing up to a known denning area.

The high saddle landing that made Sheepzilla possible.

This is our comfortable shelter on the Maclaren River for wolf hunts.

Getting high and staying there for grizzly in the spring. Ed and I are scouting dens at 6,500 feet, looking east toward Valdez Creek.

This is the aggressive bear that almost ended it all for me.

The Alaska Peninsula has produce some big bears for me. This example is 11 feet 4 inches squared.

Introducing "Sheepzilla"! It is among the largest rams ever taken in the Brooks Range.

I can't get enough of the geometry of Sheepzilla.

If you are a sheep hunter this is your candy.

This is a great example of a 120 pound wolf we took on the Arctic plains.

Another Arctic plains wolf well over 100 pounds.

Wolverines are quite a prize.

Ed Gohr zooming in on a bear den with a spotting scope.

I enjoyed this waterfall found on Unimak when scouting for Caribou.

Our bear hunting cabin named "freezer house" we used for Moe's bear. The whiskey bottle is still full so it must be lunchtime.

This is a nice example of a spring grizzly we found at 7,200 feet.

Ed is trying to position the bear for skinning.

Loaded for bear.

Wolves are "Killing Machines". We interrupted wolves savaging this muskox and managed to track them down.

Nelson Lagoon was our stopover point for the Ruger hunt.

This was a lifetime dream for Moe. He earned every minute of glory!

Mike Fifer and I are taking a break after a long day.

This is Mike Fifer (left) and Randell (right) and we are showing off the prize.

Mike Fifer had a beautiful mount made of his trophy Peninsula Brown Bear.

Mike Fifer got what he came for.

This is my father checking out a dead walrus.

This big fatty has expired...and is ready for its neck surgery. It's a great find!

I have had good luck in the north eastern Brooks Range for sheep.

This battle scarred ram with both horns broken off (broomed) came from the same area as Sheepzilla but a couple years prior.

Alaska Raw

An ideal trip is one where you don't have both your head-lights and front window broken out from ice road truckers going the opposite way, don't have to install chains on your tires going over the icy Atigun Pass, and don't suffer so many flat tires that you still have some spares on hand for the long trip back.

This trip would go pretty well on all of those counts. But I recalled one that didn't and all those past lessons added to the database that informed the current trip. Headed up the same road for wolves a couple years before, a different partner and I were driving his new Ford F250 crew cab with less than 5,000 miles on it. It had Firestone tires. Apparently Firestone could not be bothered with the cold weather testing part of their quality program before selling Ford about 800,000 tires for these new trucks.

Firestone's blind spot involved 30 and 40 below zero temperatures while thumping over gravel and rocks for hours on end towing heavy loads. Imagine that. We know this because when we made that trip it was that cold and we had three tires self-destruct along the route and they did so in a very strange way.

On that trip we had only two spares but bummed a third in Coldfoot, a tiny truck stop above the Arctic Circle. When we got to Prudhoe Bay, the end of the road, we went on the prowl for some new skins all around. Finding them at a hole-in-the-wall oilfield tire shop was a very lucky break. This "tire shop" looked like a crusty WWII vintage Quonset hut with a gravel floor. Ratty and dank, creaking against the Arctic wind, the assemblage of salvaged tin and plywood over a well rusted steel skeleton was straight out of a Road Warrior movie after the bad guys pillaged and torched the enclave.

When we dismounted the tires the problem became ob-vious... big handfuls of powdered rubber inside each car-cass. The tires, which looked quite good on the outside, had inside layers that had disintegrated to dust the consis-tency of fine coffee grounds as a result of the subzero beat-ing. This made them leakers. We were both shaking our heads in disbelief and discussing the real possibility that Fred Flintstone rolled on better goods than Ford provided as original equipment on this factory new F-250. Our tire mechanic was a man of few words, a greasy little fellow with his black hair falling over his eye on one side and tucked behind his ear on the other.

His face displayed a smoky grey pallor complemented with eye glasses so smudged and filthy he appeared to have just used them to spread mayonnaise on a Spam sandwich. Tire Man was impressed by the damage. A little Copenhagen spittle leaking out of both corners of his all-knowing smile, he rendered his technical opinion: "Firestones no good up here".

So noted.

In addition to the tire issues on this earlier trip, it was 4 for 4 in the broken glass department. We lost both headlights, the front window, and a skinny skylight glass which spanned across the front of the truck bed's fiberglass topper.

All were smashed by rocks on the way up. Some of that had to do with a serious lack of snow that year, turning the hundreds of miles of gravel to a real stone chucking gauntlet as industrial trucks roared by in the opposite direction. Some of it had to do with the high speed driving pace we set, progress be damned the consequences.

It's what I call the "Shred Now – Pay Later" plan. There were, after all, wolves getting away every moment we tittered. Perhaps it was hard to ratchet back our speed once the heavy hunting tales broke out. I can't really remember all the details of why we pushed so hard. But that was of course a different hunt and I like to think I learn something each time. We did get three wolves that trip, so if I had not learned to slow down, I did discover that wolf hunting was nothing short of euphoric.

Ed and I would escape the really cold weather on this drive to Prudhoe Bay. In fact it barely reached zero the entire trip so we didn't get to put our tires to the Ice Road Trucker test. By the time we reached the hunting zone the temps were climbing due to a big low pressure front that was actually following us up the highway. After twenty plus hours at the wheel we were finally looking for a place to get off the road, scratch and yawn, peel ourselves off the truck seats and draw a deep lung full of the Arctic air. The first order would be to unload the snowmobiles.

From that emptied space in the covered trailer we would muster our living quarters. Our final docking spot ended up right next to a frozen river, just off the road, a great ice causeway providing access to endless hills and multiple drainages stretching far to the east. Once the sleds were driven out and the small generator, fuel cans, propane bottles, tow sleds and other gear was removed, the cots and folding cook table were set up.

The 20 foot long, eight foot wide trailer had a not-large-enough propane heater which we fired so that the food, water and other stores all packed and stacked in Rubbermaid totes would begin to thaw. It was quite a process to keep perishables cool and fresh while keeping snacks, water and other goods warmer. To make something colder or to keep it temporarily frozen (yet still accessible inside) you shuffled its container out toward the corners of the trailer, away from the small propane heat source.

Every morning and evening was like a game of jumbo checkers, moving one plastic tote over and past another in the tight quarters, shoving another across and back, stacking two up nearer the heater since they froze slightly overnight, then kicking the water jug a couple times, testing to see if it still sloshed nicely or had begun to rattle some with forming ice, and thus needed to be repositioned.

It was by then snowing pretty good outside and the temperature continued to come up, reaching the low twenties, a real nice break from what I had experienced every other trip up that far north. Before, it had always been well below zero and twice 30 to 40 below, turning simple things into an exercise in simply staying alive. After several hours of work, camp was shaping up and getting nicely organized. The best evidence of this was the plastic cups of Crown Royal that we treated ourselves to as we sorted and sifted our way down through the layers of supplies and gear.

As a result, the organization effort was for sure getting happier. The tin box trailer began to produce and capture some propane heat and when it did, frost on the walls began to melt and run down in streaks, freezing again in glossy puddles when it met the floor. It was a real layer cake of thermal existence, about 20 degrees at the un-insulated steel floor, 45 or 50 at the level of the cots, and about 80 at head height when you stood up.

We settled in for an evening around the two burner folding Coleman cook stove, the closest thing we had to a campfire. It's funny how we are all programmed to stare endlessly at the flicker of fire.

You understand just how little man has evolved when, given the chance, you spend hours acting like a moth attracted to a street light. Somehow the fire always becomes the center of things and everyone goes into a slow trance by watching it. When there is a pot of hot water going you can get double hypnotized since you have those steam swirls to lock on to. With all that entertainment who needs television?

Circling back to those guns, because I promised I would: that night, as we sat on our cots and readied our kit for the next day's excursion, out came the guns. Safety is of paramount importance to Ed and me so we have some hard rules when it comes to firearms. Rule Number One is: "WHEN THE BOOZE COMES OUT THE GUNS GET PUT AWAY". Our problem is that once the booze comes out neither of us can remember the fine details of Rule Number One.

What too commonly happens is that one of us witnesses the other spilling his third drink down the front of his shirt while trying to shove ammunition into his gun. Then, the red flags go up and one of us finally says something to the asshole offender. Something like this:

"Hey bitch, get the fucking barrel out of my face and point that thing at the wall if you're going to play with it."

Admittedly, that's not the highest call to responsibility but it is slightly better than this:

"Hey bitch, that's my .223 ammo you're trying to shove in your 7MM-08, here's your magazine, use that!" "I'll hold your drink".

Ed was sporting a high end AR15 in .223. He liked to be able to shoot fast and often and had fists full of clips at the ready. Ed's rifle was scoped with a one power Aimpoint and was quite a nice piece of expensive weaponry. I was using a Remington Model 7 in 7mm-08, a very light youth model, with a slim 18 inch barrel and a fiberglass stock. You would have a hard time getting $300 for my gun, scope and all. It was a real Plymouth Fury of a beater weapon.

The stock was a raw, unfinished fiberglass affair with a scope from I-can't-remember-which pawn shop. The thing was 5.6 pounds loaded and adorned with a sling. It shot exceptionally well and had never let me down even in very cold weather. But I admit, I envied Ed's gun, the black AR.

It looked cool with steely mechanical knobs and levers and handles poking out in every direction like it belonged in a movie with avenging mercenaries destined to settle a score.

My Remington also had its advantages and all the versatility of a Swiss Army knife. For example, if you broke your leg someplace you could use it as a crutch to hobble back to camp and it would look absolutely no worse when you got done.

If your pickup was stuck, for example, and you needed to use the barrel to pump a handyman jack, you could do that. This was abuse that Ed's AR would not rebound from. I recall paddling a Zodiac with it. There are other possibilities, I think, but they are not coming to mind right now.

Alaska Raw

Just in case the 7mm-08 had an issue I brought along a 6mm Remington in the exact same model rifle, one I borrowed from my father. The small calibers, fully jacketed, keep the fur damage to a minimum.

The next morning was spitting snow with low clouds just above the plains to the North, and settling in the foothills and obscuring the mountains to the South. We scurried around getting ready in a push that was buzzing with anticipation of how the day might unfold. Fuel and gear were stashed and lashed on our snowmobiles.

Some sandwiches and snacks that we put together the night before were zipped into inside jacket pockets where they wouldn't freeze hard. We had rope, shovels, spare parts, tools, GPS, maps, brush saws, bungee cords, knives, water bottles, cameras, binoculars, ammo and other essentials occupying every spare nook on our snowmobiles. Second sets of gloves, extra socks, extra face masks, goggles, ear plugs, and other spares began to round out the kit.

Actually getting into the launch mode is a special and highly enjoyable hour. It represents everything coming to a point. Mostly, it's where the speculative jaw jacking stops and all efforts become pointed at the goal. A trip like this takes determination and sheer force of will to even get to take a swing.

As incredibly remote as this venture was, as tough and changeable as the weather could be, with unfamiliar terrain and unpredictable visibility, you are at the mercy of an exotic mix of variables. Circumstances can turn on a dime and the hunt can quickly become about surviving rather than hunting. As we eased the sleds out onto the frozen river to really get a look around, we found the visibility quite poor.

Yellow lens goggles helped but it was still demanding to tell the sky from the surfaces that pushed up grey and smeared any hope of a recognizable edge. Once we got beyond the river, our path out across the plain varied with rolling terrain, drifts, shallow draws and the occasional machine bending sheer drop off (usually a river bank). Imagine driving over the mixed terrain of a hilly golf course blindfolded and you get some idea of what it's like to make forward progress in a true whiteout. You are transformed into an albino zygote, blindly swimming around in the murky amniotic fluid of a space without borders. Yet, if you wandered just a couple yards too far away from your twin, you totally lost track of him and everything else that connected you to mother earth.

Coming in and out of view were scarce patches of scattered grass clumps poking up on low ridges which had been blown clean of snow. These were welcome reference points that you could look ahead to and temporarily connect your brain to land.

Vertigo and less severe disorientation was a ubiquitous stressor which detracted from the mission. Hunting is really about seeing. We moved slowly but methodically that day.

We were at the northern face of the Brooks Range mountains (which run east west) where they break down to the rolling hills before giving way to the vast tundra plains that reach 100 plus miles to Alaska's northern coastline.

This transition zone between mountains and plain is braided with rivers and streams of various sizes running south to north. Our path had us transitioning all these frozen and semi-frozen waterways as we eased along the base of the mountains on an east-west track.

In a whiteout, on this course, there were a multitude of places to blindly fall off a cut bank, plunge into a ravine or otherwise end up in a wad. Eyes that are conditioned by nature to find and orient on the horizon are repeatedly tricked and confused. We were usually moving along at no more than 15 miles an hour, straining to make out features ahead or looking for the next scrap of wind-beaten sedge poking up, giving meaning to what looked and felt like floating around in a sensory deprivation tank.

Whenever we came to a small river we made a solid reference point with a GPS and from it turned south. This led us gently upslope into the selected drainage and more into the steeper foothills where any wolf sign would likely be more consolidated as the terrain climbed and narrowed. If we did not find wolf sign we would backtrack downriver, returning to the somewhat flatter ground where it was safer to proceed in poor visibility, and move along the foothills to our next favorable scouting opportunity.

That first day was part shakeout day and part hunting, making sure we had all the right gear and the machines would be running well, and the hunting... getting a feel for where the predator feedstock (caribou, muskox and sheep) were located and how those prey animals were browsing and moving around.

We covered only about 40 miles, picking carefully through the whiteness, looking mostly for tracks crossing our path since glassing was so limited. We paused often and shut down to silently take it all in, like a couple of hungry eagles sitting out a dense fog with a light dusting of snow collecting on their hulking backs, we were similarly ready to launch if only we could sense a productive direction. When the snow let up periodically we could see perhaps three miles and glassing was some benefit. As the day shortened the grey terrain began to dissolve into the sky, eventually erasing even the slightest remnants of a horizon.

We stopped and pulled a couple of partially frozen sandwiches from inside our snowsuits and took a quick chow break. The ride back was going to be less exciting than covering the new ground had been. It always is. The good news was everything was clicking and with some good visibility we could be lighting up some wolves. The day wound to a close as we eased back to camp paralleling our morning trail but covering slightly different ground on the return run.

Back at camp that night we topped off the fuel, checked and rechecked our equipment and heated up the tin box to thaw and dry out everything that needed drying including our firearms. Though we both have soft cases and places to lash our rifles to the sleds, stowing them like that makes it impossible to react quickly. Most of the time we sling them on our backs when we are anywhere in the zone.

Thus slung, the guns get a constant misting of snow and require quite a bit of attention during and after the day's run. The guns get deiced and shot up with WD40 once back in camp. This happens as soon as the propane heater has taken the edge off our ice box hovel and before we start rooting around the collection of Rubbermaid tote boxes and putting together a meal to thaw on the small cook stove.

In any event, the Arctic post-hunt is an enjoyable time, lots of heat pumping in, steam rising off everything, body parts relaxing, the smell of food, the taste of whiskey, the endless flow of wild speculation and what-ifs regarding the pursuit, which then spins off into one-upping, name calling and juvenile manhood challenges. This is followed by the fart jokes, dick jokes, asshole co-worker jokes, rude slander of anyone holding opinions different than ours, and often some deeply intellectual musings about the allure and biological wonder concerning fit, lithe, petite women. And on and on it goes.

If either of us happened to have wrecked earlier in the day or just fell off his sled, it's worth at least a half hour of ribbing, followed by recommendations that the underperforming slum dwelling rider should really be drinking his whiskey from a sippy cup and appropriately belongs on a children's snowmobile instead of his man-rocket. Before bed, final insults are usually nourished by making fun of which one of us is crippled the most from the hard days riding, who is walking bent over at some odd angle, or who is so spent they are reduced to slurring and mumbling and no longer making any sense. All of this is testimony to our lifelong aphorism: "Anything worth doing is worth overdoing".

The morning of the second day looked promising for hunting. We made coffee and packed on a bunch of calories while trying to wake up. A bracing cold breeze to the face always snaps you to attention no matter how sluggish your weather beaten corpse becomes overnight.

Broken clouds over stratified and misty lower layers meant some glassing could be accomplished, at least intermittently, and we could make favorable time hauling ass from drainage to drainage, poking in for a look and then moving on. Wolves are highly territorial and generally stake out a definitive range to operate within.

Each of the large drainages running north-south was reported by High Authorities to contain at least one wolf pack and therefore we would try to inject ourselves into as many of these drainages as we could reasonably reach and reconnoiter. Either caribou or muskoxen or both could be found scattered in these drainages and that's what would keep the wolves interested in hanging around. They also kill plenty of sheep late in the winter season after the sheep become thin and weak.

Early in the morning we were glassing and saw a few magpies and a nervous raven or two a couple miles out, coming and going from a northwesterly spot all the way across the drainage we were exploring. It wasn't obvious, not like a swarm of winged bone pickers all frenzied up over a delicious road kill moose.

Rather, just a couple birds leisurely heading away from a general spot in the distance and a couple more inbound. This would have been easy to ignore but birds mean some scavenging is going on and that means something got whacked. We decided to run the couple miles over there and see what the attraction was, if it could be pinpointed at all.

Picking our way over there took only a few minutes and a few more birds lifted off in front of us as we approached making the final locate easy. A muskox was spread out dead in a shallow depression that hid its body from our prior glassing location.

The fresh carcass, lying on its side, had a basketball size hole in its forward ribcage, some lung parts missing, and some of its flank had been pried open but everything else was looking new, as though it could have been killed within the last day sometime. It was not steaming, but neither was it at all frozen, ruling out anything over 48 hours prior.

The hair is so long, and its insulating qualities so high, that it was hard for us to judge exactly how many hours old the kill was. It had been stormy and mild for the last couple days, high teens to mid-twenties during the day, so with the mass of hair it could stay thawed for a while. A big male, the ox had a nice set of horns which we should have immediately hacked off its skull but we made a plan instead to keep hunting and backtrack later for the booty.

Looking around the kill very quickly we saw a parade of wolverine and wolf tracks decorated with piss holes and a few hair stuffed turds but it was hard to tell just how fresh the tracks were given the spitting snow the night before and light blowing snow then at the crime scene. The tracks could have been just hours old or 24 to 48 hours. While scanning the horizon for any tracks or activity, off to the north some small movement caught our eye. A wolverine was just breaking over a low hump in the distance, moving slowly away over a series of hills.

An endorphin rush washed over us stripping away every thought not having to do solely with the prey. We jumped for our machines and fired them off. We would have to move fast in order to position ourselves on the far side of the hill to intercept the wolverine as it dropped over the backside. To me, climbing the first hill directly ahead looked too steep. We needed to go around it. The tundra was blown bare of snow in many places where high wind funnels through the Brooks drainages. This entire section of territory was one of those bare zones with skimpy pockets of snow laying only in the dips of the four foot high tussocks.

The terrain the wolverine was headed up and over was a steep sided jumble of three or four almond shaped hills laid end to end and stretched about three quarters of a mile, paralleling the river bed and pushing up about five hundred feet tall out of the center of the two mile wide, miles long drainage we were square in the mouth of.

The drainage was itself a mixture of braided, rocky riverbed interwoven with heavy tundra tussocks. To get where we wanted to go from our spot beside the dead muskox, we had to first navigate through one of these brutal tussock fields, about a quarter mile of abject cruelty, and then either climb over the first entirely bare and very steep rock and gravel hill, clearing the five hundred feet in elevation... or go around it.

To go around it meant staying in the rough tundra and the rocky riverbed. Ed, thoroughly ladled with adrenaline that squeezed his pupils to a pinhead, chose the direct route, slamming the throttle down. He was determined to close the distance at light speed even though it meant crashing over the tops of the four foot high bare tussocks, each one ricocheting the machine upward and at some odd angle only to return to earth and hit another frozen lump that tossed it some new direction. It was like running a speedboat in four foot high ocean chop...but the chop was frozen solid.

In theory, if you hold the throttle open long enough and accelerate hard enough, you can begin to skip over the tops of these bone jarring, equipment crushing moguls which were also salted with sizeable rocks. As Ed disappeared in a frenzied display of athleticism, smoke, sparks, flailing handlebars and unusual mechanical noises, he was about to prove up that theory or expose its flaws. I saw lots of elbows and knees rapidly swapping places as the terrain tried to tear him from his ride.

From my vantage point his head yo-yoed above and then below his shoulders, like a prize fighter taking the beating of his life. His knees and legs unreliably followed his torso, depending on how high the mechanical bull sent his ass into the air. It didn't matter. Instinct took over.

I punched it and hung on.

I followed Ed for a good while, with my fist stuffed in the throttle until it became an uncontrolled handlebar slapping, knee banging carnival ride from which a return without something really ugly happening was not a good bet. My forearms were melting to junk, my legs were burning and my ability to muscle the sled straight was slipping a little more after each hard deflection pin balled me in weird and unexpected directions. My suspension was bottoming hard and repeatedly, and my skis were bashing side to side onto the stops with such force I was just waiting for the inevitable.

The machine had to break somewhere, nothing manmade could take such a pounding. And yet...there was Ed, always just a little bit out in front of me, proof that wherever that point of mechanical meltdown was, I was not there yet. Wingman became the team canary. If his machine held up, so would mine, but my body was going to give out before the snowmobile broke. I had to change strategies.

Seeing an opening to cut left onto flatter terrain that was generally more river wash and less tussock, I pointed and shot that direction. My new path allowed for even greater speed and the surroundings were soon a blur. Glancing right I noticed I had caught and slightly passed Wingman. I was outflanking Ed and hopefully would get well in front of the travelling wolverine. It was still unclear to me what was going to happen when Ed finished hurdling the tussock field, providing such could even be accomplished without a mechanical failure. This tussock run terminated at the base of the first hill, a short but super steep 50 degree rock and gravel slope. The slope was without trace of snow on its face. In fact, there was no snow within 1,000 yards of that hill. Not a thimble full.

The terrain was smoothing out on my alternate path. I was blazing down the wash at over sixty miles an hour on ice and gravel covered with patchy thin snow that the wind had missed, and either jinking around the big rocks as they came into view or deflecting off of them.

It was at least better going than where I had been moments before. My grey matter had just quit banging around in my head from the earlier beating when I looked right again and saw Ed had cleared the jumble piles and immediately shot three quarters of the way up the bare rock hill before he ran out of momentum and stuck it hard.

The snowmobile was spun out, buried tail down in gravel where it had rototilled itself in under full throttle, the entire nose of the sled reaching for the clouds like a missile waiting on its launch pad, the skis swinging free in nothing but air. From a distance the sled looked like an oversized lawn dart poked ass first into the rocky hill.

Surrounded by a cloud of smoke and steam, Ed wrestled to get it unstuck while at the same time holding it delicately balanced to keep it from flipping over backwards and tumbling down the steep grade, leaving a trail of tears and broken parts. This was pure insanity, especially considering how incredibly remote we were.

That second I caught a glimpse of the wolverine far above and to my right. He was on a high ridge, at the crest of the hill and a couple hundred yards beyond where Ed had augered in. It looked like I had decent positioning for a shot if the wolverine stayed travelling along the ridge. I had to decide in an instant whether to break off and help Ed, or push on to get into position for a shot.

I tried to process it all in an instant. First, my wing-man was stuck. He needed help. The sled was perched in a truly fucked up spot, clinging on an insanely steep grade on a bare slag pile and was at real risk of tumbling if he tried to un-stick it alone. If it tumbled over those several hundred yards it would gain momentum as it cart wheeled. This could end the hunt. Duct tape and wire, though we had lots of it, is no substitute for a welder. If Ed was patient he'd just hang on and wait for me to come back.

Another consideration was that if I went immediately to help him get unstuck, and we accomplished it quickly, he would be hunting with me, increasing our chances. We would also be safer if both sleds remained in good working order. All that calculating came to a fine point in micro-seconds:

Ed...can wait.

You really should not leave your wingman, and we rare-ly leave each other because of the serious safety issues that can arise. If you got knocked unconscious a couple miles away in a ravine in the fog and snow, no one may find you until it was too late. It's just not a good idea. The more remote, and the colder it is, the more important it is to hunt as an inseparable unit.

I kept up the speed until I was well in front of the wol-verine. It was above me but still slowly coming my direction laterally high on the ridge, still unbothered. It was time to try to make the shot. Instantly the throttle came off, the brakes were jammed on and a tightly choreographed pat-tern of urgent tasks took place. With the sled slowing hard, the left hand grips the brake and steers one handed while the right hand reaches up to flip off the goggles. As the sled skids to a final stop the left hand comes off the brake and reaches over to un-glove the trigger hand. Then both hands un-sling the rifle off the shoulder while you're simul-taneously slipping off the sled into a squat to get a rifle rest on the snowmobile seat.

Scope covers flipped open, safety flicked off... acquire... shoot, all in 6 to 8 seconds. For the untrained this simple sequence can burn up 20 or 30 seconds, if that time even allows one to get all of it correctly accomplished. That's way too long. If you can't do this under ten seconds you will never get a shot off let alone kill anything. By then the wolverine had finally noticed me. It accelerated. The shot

I had was running, right to left, at about 175 yards. It was way too small a target. James Bond would have been hard pressed to connect it all. I shot twice, missed, and watched the wolverine, looking unimpressed, shuffle off over the rock face and disappear.

It was over for the moment, time to breathe again, clear the steam rising off the sweat pouring out of my face. I opened some clothing to purge some of the sweat running down my chest and back.

I also put my kit back together, reversing the order: safety back on, scope covers closed, right glove on, goggles on, sling the gun.

It was time to see where Wingman ended up and if he still needed a hand getting yanked around and pointed downhill or, if it hadn't gone well, some help picking up the stray bits of aluminum and plastic. Going back around the hill I found Ed still stuck but progressing well all by himself. On closer inspection the slope looked unnerving if not full blown scary. I was now rooting strongly for a solo save from Ed and not wanting to join him on the steep rock pile. Hiking steep rock in bunny boots is a drag. The boots have zero side-hill ankle support. It's as if you had stuffed your feet in a couple of watermelons and tried to lace them up tight.

The key to my being able to avoid the long climb up, and still save face, was to linger at the bottom for just long enough for Ed to question my will, but not long enough for me to clearly look like a lazy pussy. Ed was making progress which I encouraged and cheered on while offering continuous and highly valuable advice.

"Looking good bro! You got this. Just pull the front a little more left..."

He finally worked it loose by pirouetting it around 180 degrees while still balanced on its tail, shoved the nose over and came rocketing down slope in a halo of dust, sparks and purple exhaust smoke. We high fived the engagement of man, machine and fur bearer and collected our wits. We could have continued tracking the wolverine but we both had enough of that action for the day.

We circled back to the muskox carcass to take another look and snap a couple pictures before heading back toward camp. About an hour later we made it back. Inspecting the sleds closely seemed like a really good idea given the torture they endured. To do this we first spent half an hour chipping and banging ice off the frame and running surfaces until most of the components were visible.

The ski bottoms were pretty well hammered and ground to a thinning profile from all the dry running. There were a few smaller dents in my running boards and a bigger one in the tub. The muffler exit was bent partially shut. Other damage no doubt existed but was not immediately visible. Rubber tracks, especially our high lug "paddle" tracks are prone to overheating without deep snow to cool them, especially at high speed. The same overheating is a problem for the Hyfax runners the track glides on. These hard plastic rails are designed to use snow as their sole means of lubrication. The consequences of breaking something visited a heaviness on us right then.

Sure, we had an extra machine if we broke one. But we still had to be able to get back to the truck to retrieve it. It was way too far to walk.

The insult imposed on these snowmobiles, in the tussocks and in the rocks, was nothing short of reckless. The thrill of the hunt caused a temporary suspension of sanity. The conversation that night included firm plans for selling the tainted iron to the highest bidder once we were back in the city. An appropriate Craigslist ad swirled in my head: "LOW LOW MILES, HAS ALMOST NEVER SEEN SNOW!"

A new day opened with about the same high overcast with some lighter holes, with all of it overlaying some lower mixed smut of inversion fog and stratified intransigent grey gloom. With a fresh supply of food, fuel and motive we struck out to the south once again. Our plan called for a swing by the muskox kill for a quick check and then to keep moving east.

Between camp and the kill was only about eight miles. Just to keep things interesting there happened to be a deadly serious river crossing at about the halfway point. The river must have been fed by some warm springs somewhere in the foothills as water was running heavily under and over the ice. Some ice was broken and moving, some was stationary and well set against the banks.

The open-running sections had floating slush scooting downriver at a good clip which curled under the stationary ice as it met. The fully obscured surface hid any possible shadow of the river bottom and it made it impossible to gauge how deep it was, anywhere, and where it may be the safest to cross.

Now for the good part. This was not a seventy five foot splash and dash. Bank to bank, this water was one hundred yards of malice. It didn't look safe anywhere. If you were to fall off or suck in a carburetor load of water, things could go from bad to deadly in a flash. Wingman could not sling you a lifeline, or buzz out to you and help save the day. You could easily die there.

In such case the best crossing, if you are going to do it at all, is where the bank's ingress and egress is as smooth as possible, no big dropping transitions going in, and no abrupt ice shelf to ram into on the path out. We thought it over for a long time. It just looked grim, like something to be avoided entirely. But being prisoners of our own testosterone, how bad it looked rarely stopped us.

Picking a "good" spot, we took a full breath, stabbed the throttles, and moved back on the seat to lift the skis. We both rocketed into the slush packed river and tried to surf the first mixed open water patches with as much speed and composure as we could manage. Once in it and under full power, we were like two boats going cross current. We had to keep adjusting the angle upstream or be swept off target and hitting the far bank in a place that was not as "aimed". This all was sketchy to the extreme, but it worked. We cleared it all without getting completely soaked, thankfully, but from the thighs down our snow pants got a drenching and froze into statue like rigidity in minutes. This was nothing too serious given the moderate temperatures, then in the low twenties.

Moving along past the river we turned south to pick up our trail back to the muskox. A few miles later we found it and approached it slowly. An eagle, several ravens and a couple magpies lifted off and split. We pulled up to a much different kill site than we had left less than 24 hours earlier.

Expecting nothing much to be different, save perhaps a few more pounds of flesh lost to the birds, we were shocked to find the entire side of the animal opened up and mostly devoured. Wolves had been back. It was likely that they heard us coming, probably from many miles away, and bolted. Our first order was to glass the immediate area. Finding nothing moving we took a much closer look at the heavy array of tracks all around the carcass. The prints peppered the dirty, bloody snow like a thousand hooves in a feed lot, overlaying each other in a confused jumble. Birds, fox, wolverine and wolf were all pulling off that meat stack.

Walking outwards in a radius from the kill the volume of tracks thinned out. However, the farther out, the more definitive the prints became. Soon we were carefully walking in hundred foot circles around ground zero and picking out and studying distinct sets of tracks coming and going. Some were much newer than others. Overnight there had been a slight wind and a dusting of snow which made the reading newest ones easier.

We picked up a set of three wolf tracks at the far side of one of our walking loops. The tracks headed directly east and out to the river, then north continuing up it. These were clearly the freshest. It looked as though they could have been made hours or even just minutes earlier.

Jumping on our machines we powered up and got mentally organized for action. Before tearing off upriver we drove a couple of slow 100 yard circles around the kill to prove up the hunch. There was indeed only one exceptionally fresh set of tracks leading outbound. There was no doubting a pack of three adult wolves could be killed at the end of that trail if we could keep sight of it and navigate ourselves to the end of it.

It is then that the beast within makes an entrance.

But instead of little voices in your head, it begins with a cortisol and dopamine cocktail that rushes through your limbs and boils like a river inside your chest. It prepares you for a fight, just as it has for as long as man has walked this earth.

There are surely all sorts of feats in this world that demand an outpouring of struggle and resolve when set upon, and which evoke all manner of emotion when finally accomplished and owned, but there is something a little different going on here.

It's animal on animal.

The rush comes at you in an unexpected way. It comes to you much harder than it should, and in a way you never knew existed, so all you can figure is that it's from parts of your brain that must have laid down the wiring for risk and reward scenarios hundreds of thousands of years ago. From a time when tracking down an animal and thrusting a spear into its chest, or jumping into a pit and cutting its throat was a really big deal, a time when it was connected to your very survival.

Hunting and killing was such a life affirming event that whatever was programmed into the wiring then, still comes gushing up to the surface in the present. At least with some of us. It is at that moment that you separate your conscious from everything except breathing and hunting. Your pulse quickens, your breathing becomes deeper, your eyesight sharpens. The reactions are automatic. The focus is so singular that everything else falls away. How grand is that?

We spooled up the throttle and shot upriver.

The tracks ran straight and could be seen pretty well in the half inch of fresh snow and frost that coated the river ice which was mostly hard and as flat as a billiard table. After covering about a mile at 35 or 40 miles an hour we co-ordinated in a tried and true method to allow the symbiotic team of two to pour on a little more speed. One of us kept his eyes almost exclusively on the wolf tracks while the lead driver watched the trail ahead, following the curves in the river, avoiding the occasional bare gravel bar, boulders, or ice pressure ridge. The guy with his eyes on the wolf tracks watches the other driver peripherally for guidance, for any sudden braking or dodging. We ramped up to about 50, as fast as we could go and still maintain control with the visibility we had.

The thinly imprinted wolf tracks continued in a straight line over three miles.

Ed was tracking the wolves while I was focused on the terrain immediately in our path. Two sets of eyes focused on different objectives but coordinated and acting as a single hunter. Heading straight upriver at a scorching pace, I saw an abrupt transition up ahead where the ice threw a shadow and looked like it formed a ledge. The ledge looked to be diagonal angle across the full span of the river. It appeared we would have to jump some sort of transition onto a lower elevation of ice.

I dumped the throttle, grabbed some brake and glanced over to my left to make sure Ed had seen my move. He had, but at that very same instant he was also scanning the horizon ahead and had picked up one of the wolves. He saw me slow and braked for the obstruction ahead at almost the same time.

We had no choice. We both recognized a big problem with the ice shelf, and that it led to swift running open water, and we were each in a panic to size up a way forward. As we both pulled down from speed and skidded sideways on the ice to a stop, one wolf, a black one, stopped about 250 yards out and was silhouetting on the horizon, just off and above the river, on its steeply inclining left bank.

It was worth a shot, if it stayed put in full broadside profile, so I quickly went through the (goggles, trigger glove, unslinging the rifle, safety, scope caps) routine and took a quick rest over the handlebars.

I was far too winded, sweating like a madman, and generally too amped up to make the long shot. It was a long
reach for the short barreled 7mm-08. I missed. The wolf
bolted. We had a river crossing in front of us and seconds
to decide how to tackle it.   To recap, here is how it looked
on the ground: Our brief stopping point had been just 15
yards short of where I saw what looked like the elevation
change in the ice, cutting from bank to bank at an angle.
The shadow that had looked like an elevation change was
all of that and more. It was open water, running hard.

Looking slightly left and a couple hundred yards ahead,
we could see the black wolf running straight away at full
tilt. Looking harder left we caught a glimpse of the other
two which were light grey and blended in with the bare river bar better making them harder to spot. These two were
also running flat out, just off the river and about a hundred
fifty yards ahead of us.

All the wolves had cut left off the river, back behind us
about five hundred yards, where the ice was still solid bank
to bank...but prior to our spotting them for the first time.

It was deceiving. We saw them just ahead of us on the
bank, and just assumed they ran the river ice to get there,
when in fact the river ice ended, right in front of us. They
outsmarted us. In a split second Ed and I assessed the
options. The river was in a somewhat narrowed gorge now
and running deep.

It was a roiling, churning, span about 60 to 70 feet wide
hissing with power and whitecaps that disappeared as they
were forced under the five foot high ice ledge we were peering down from. There was really no good way forward. A
high speed backtrack of five hundred yards to get off the
river ice and onto the left bank to follow the wolves path
would take precious seconds we did not want to forfeit.

As we hesitated there for a second, sitting on our idling
machines, the wolves were still running flat out. Ed, in a
state of arrested reality, spun his sled around on the ice
until it was pointed at the lip of the ice shelf and across
the span of open water. I was not entirely sure what he
had planned. In one glorious blur he lit the fuse, bolted
forward, and launched off the five foot ice shelf and into the
river at full power. All I saw after the impact was a huge
cloud of steam that obliterated everything but a twenty foot
long rooster tail of misted water ejecting rearward like a
jet's afterburner.

I guessed that meant no more talking and lots more
action. I didn't wait to see if he made the other side. Rath-

er, I found my balls, right there in my left pocket where I had been keeping them on warm standby. All the spare fractions of a second I should have spent analyzing how crazy Ed's move was, were instead spent calculating how much more of a run I should get at it than he did. Ed had launched into the river from just about nil.

I could not tell how far he sank before the horsepower clawed its way up and out, unsnorkeling him, and roosting man and machine upward to where he had a fighting chance to make a go of it. For sure, it did not look like a move I wanted to mimic. I spun around 180 degrees on the ice, blipped the throttle, ran back down river 30 yards, quickly spun 180 again, and smashed the throttle to the stop. I need just a little speed.

Right before I left the ice lip I saw that Ed had made it across, crashing onto the bank and over the serious looking one foot diameter boulders lining the bank on the other side. I aimed for Ed. It was a bigger drop than it first looked like. As I went off the lip the next thing I remembered was hitting the water and a big burst of steam coming out from around the cowling enveloping everything. Then a big shot of ice cold water over the hood, into my face and over my head.

I had been at wide open throttle but still did not gather quite enough speed on the short run up before hitting the water. I was sure I would mostly plane out on the surface. I tried not to think about the air intake swallowing in a big gulp, or rolling the machine over, falling off and getting sucked under ice. The motor either ran for those couple of seconds, and I stayed straddled on top of it, or I was a fucking dead man. When I left the ledge it felt like too far to the surface below for a smooth entry. (Should have practiced that more.)

My weight was just a little farther forward than was ideal. This caused the skis to hit first when I was really looking for a nose high X-Games sort of vibe, so that the track and horsepower could immediately work its magic. On impact the hood shoveled a huge shot of water over the windscreen, douching me and instantly coating my goggles which flash froze in the frigid air.

Luckily the momentum was enough. The water impact jolted the nose up while the track finally came down under full power. It was all nice and sloppy.

Riding the machine across the rolling water without seeing anything through my goggles was a truly nauseating feeling. In any other situation where my goggles iced or frosted over I'd steer one handed for a moment while reaching up to tear them off. This was no time to steer one handed. The bank on the other side was coming. It was going to be one ragged mother. I could make out only its dull outline coming through my iced Mr. Magoo glasses but there was no way I was backing off the throttle to moderate the bank landing.

Just before I hit I braced off my arms and stiffened for the body shot. The joy of making landfall actually blocked out all the loud, expensive sounding noises coming from the undercarriage. Once safe on hard ground I ripped off my goggles, spotted Ed a hundred yards ahead, and once again laid the hammer down.

All three wolves were now just 250 hundred yards ahead. We needed to get closer to them to have time to get stopped and still be well placed for a shot. Had there been any snow at all we could have quickly closed that distance. If we would have had deep snow the wolves would be dead already.

What we had, once again, was wind scoured bare rocks and tussocks, this time lying in a narrow band of terrain about one hundred yards wide and several miles long. This band bordered the left hand side of the river we had just vaulted.

To the left of that section was a mountainside. We were between the river and the mountain on this hellishly rough ribbon of ground. Since snowmobiles are for snow, and there wasn't any, we were firmly in the zone of Research and Development which is a fancy term for "You-go-first… I'll-hold-your-beer".

If you took the tires off your car and ran it on its bare rims down a potholed gravel road, you would, in some small way, begin to understand the abuse we were heaping on these sleds. Of course you would also have to drain the coolant out of the radiator, since the sleds are not only cushioned and lubricated by snow, they are also cooled by snow.

The electronic overheat alarms had been going on and off for a good while now and you could fry an egg on any part of the heat exchangers. It was hard to escape the smell of burning paint and melting plastic. Suffice to say the time allotted us to close the gap on the wolves was now measured in seconds.

The strategy, where there is no deep snow to modulate the pace of the prey, is to get close enough before braking hard to a stop and trying to configure yourself for a shot.

If you pull that close, or even up alongside of a running wolf, by the time you brake hard to a stop, unsling, pop scope caps and un-glove one hand, the wolf is 100 yards out and running. You have his rear end for a target which is the size of a pie plate. That's still a tough shot. All of this was either going to happen in seconds or the sleds were going to melt down. Fortunately the scent of wolf blood was blinding us to the limitations of our hardware. Our cringe reflex was long gone. We scorched across the rocks and beat what was left of our sleds over the tussocks.

It was difficult to focus up ahead on the prey even though they were now only 150 yards out, as every ounce of our coordination was being used to stay upright, at speed, in the rough, as slamming the bumps and rocks jerked the handlebars out of one hand or the other, and the back end of the sled kept trying to swap with the front. Sweat pouring out of every crevice of your body, down your face and into your eyes, snot falling out of your nose, your heart racing, and muscles screaming to end it all.

Beat up but gaining ground, we closed to 125 yards.

That instant two of the three wolves cut left and in several seconds they were at the base of the mountain on our left and starting a 30 degree climb up the rocks. The big black one was dead ahead and it was staying in the open and flying over the tussocks as fast as its dog legs could carry it.

We closed to 100 yards.

I made a split second decision to stay with Ed on the closest black wolf so one of us would be assured a shot. Physical exhaustion was fast becoming the absolute choke point. You could only keep the steering controlled and throttle mashed if you could hang on to the bars under the relentless thrashing.

The sleds had long since overheated and were running on good will. As we closed the final distance I swung left to get between the mountain and the wolf. Ed kept a direct line until he was in a good location to stop and still have time to make a shot, or several.

By the time Ed was stopped, positioned, and unslung the wolf was back out to 75 yards and running at a scorching pace. Ed took aim and started unloading his AR. Bullets were whizzing and tundra wads flying as the wolf started an even more erratic dodging routine, finally cutting further left for the safety of the mountain. I had just gotten stopped and started to unsling when I thought better and decided to try and re-position for a follow up shot, and to get between the wolf and the mountain.

Ed emptied his AR as the wolf kept running and lurching from one tussock to another and getting smaller. Nothing connected. Ed hurried to put himself back together, remounted and joined me in another high speed push to get positioned again.

Moving to the left and closer to the mountain was great strategy for the wolf. The ground was rougher, the tussocks even stiffer and more pronounced as the slope rose up at the base of the hill.

I tried for a few moments but could not catch up with the wolf and still have anything resembling a snowmobile to carry me home. Fully spent, I pulled off and took a quick look to my far left to see if the other two were even in play anymore, spotting them 600 yards up the mountain and climbing like they were on fire.

Ed blew past and continued after the black one for another 500 hundred yards until it rounded a corner at the end of the mountain and disappeared up a small drainage. This hunt was over for now, and it was time to collect ourselves, shed some clothes, wipe down, calm down, re-tell the story play by play a few times, celebrate the intersection of man and wild dog, reclaim our brains, and....have a look at the damage.

The equipment was, shall we say, well used. One dent I had in my undercarriage was deep enough to mash the frame up into the alloy chain case and deform it. This highly engineered, thin aluminum casting holds oil for the drive unit and if it cracks open and runs dry you are snowshoeing home.

It had oil weeping from the deformation which had broken the oil seal. It was that close to puking its guts out on the tundra. My handlebars did not line up with the direction of either ski. Everything else was looking dented and gouged, especially my skis, which would have to be replaced. My exhaust was also bent shut, which happened right at the last, thankfully, since I it would have cut the power a bunch while increasing the engine temperature. I was able to pry it back open in the field with a pair of plyers and a flat screwdriver.

The weather was moving in again, light snow began to fall and our daylight was shrinking to a bluish grey wedge on the horizon. We allowed the sleds to cool completely down and then set out to find a way back that had some snow cover. After returning to camp that evening we were able to get a weather forecast from a Department of Transportation staffer than operated a remote maintenance outpost in the area.

He confirmed the weather was not going to lift. In fact it was going to get worse, especially the visibility. We both had work commitments and the forecast looked like a five day storm was coming in off the Beaufort Sea. Hunting in fog is just so damn unproductive we decided to call it over. We did not have time to wait out a several day storm.

The next day we folded up our cots and the rest of our gypsy spread and headed down the highway for home. The ride back felt longer than a life in chains. Less chatter, more pain. A rented mule after a hard week's work would have felt better than we did.

At least another 20 plus hours driving home gave us plenty of time to understand how to do it better the next time. To us, the hunt is the thrill, with or without a kill. On that score, this trip was one of the most exciting I have ever been on, even without the prize. We found wolves and gave it everything we had.

Of all the thoughts about this hunt that I recall years later, one stands out. I am still taken aback by how unusually consumed by aggression a man can become when predator hunting, and how that aggressiveness can transform us back into the animal that we evolved from. Something in us takes over to make us so singularly focused as to be forceful and incautious to the point of recklessness. And when it's over, and you come down from the exhilaration, and your rational mind is handed back to you, it gives you pause and you ask yourself: Where in the hell did all that come from?

Chapter 6

The Odds Were Never Worse (2003)

The West side beach of Cook Inlet, across the water from Homer Alaska, is richly subdivided along its length by salmon bearing streams. For bear, wolf, small predators and scavenging birds, the streams provide a dependable, high volume food source from late summer up through early winter. As late as November when the snow pack is building and running waters are flashing over with ice, bear and wolf steadily work all the remaining pockets of spawning salmon for low effort meals. As the glaciers tighten up, water levels drop in the streambeds sufficiently to trap salmon in small, concentrated pools.

Evidence of high activity around these natural stockpiles is revealed along the shoreline in the first snows, and sometimes by the bear and wolf tracks breaking ice to do the last, most determined fishing. For the bears it's a final pig-fest prior to hibernation. For the wolves, it's apparently just too hard to resist, and the opportunity comes without potential peril that accompanies bringing down larger game, a practice best left to a time when such game is belly deep in snow and can't return the violence. For sure, for any predators utilizing these unique feeding holes, it is the final feast before five dark and cold months of very slim pickings.

Hunting this area in November is always an interesting proposition. Alaska's coastal weather conditions can be challenging. From driving rain, to 80 mph winds, to several feet of snow, anything is possible. At the mercy of the Pacific Ocean and the Bering Sea jousting side by side with one another, trying to build the perfect winter storm, a hunter is caught in the middle trying to scratch out a sliver of accommodation while preparing for maximum ugliness. The odds of a peaceful, comfortable time are not great. On a positive note, by November the leaves are long gone and visibility through the alder and willow is greatly improved.

I had made a trip into this area in a previous season with a friend of mine and we were lucky enough to smack two wolves after staking out one of these iced up salmon holes. By the first of November the draw of a repeat hunt had me twitching and packing for an airplane ride. Admittedly, wolf hunting was the big draw, though bears were open for the taking as well.

On the previous hunt the wolves came into the fish hole, apparently part of their regular routine, and no calls, decoys or the like were necessary. Though I wondered what a predator call would do in a game rich area like this, it was almost an afterthought on my part to borrow a call from a friend and throw it in with the gear as we left his house.

I had never actually used one on any previous hunt, but thought it could at least break the boredom of long hours on the stump. I brought along the written instructions too, so I could screech and howl like the pro the manufacturer's data guaranteed I would quickly become. Having no available partner on this trip, and planning for a short, four day hunt, there wasn't much gear to pack.

A .300 Win-Mag Sako for starters, lots of warm clothes, including a head to foot snowsuit, and plenty of freeze dried food was the bulk of it. I threw in some luxury items, chemical hand warmers for inside the foot of the sleeping bag, lots of AA batteries for the headlamp, and some reading material.

Two factors consistently shape winter hunts in Alaska, weather and daylight. It would be too dark to hunt by 5 and stumbling dark by 5:30. Given that light did not break until 8:30 each morning there would be a lot of time to get to know myself in the tent, about fifteen hours at a stretch.

Reading would help kill the downtime. The other all-time great, tent-bound time burner....eating, can only be drug out so long. Walkman and headsets were out of the question. While lying in a tent, in the dark, in concentrated bear habitat, your hearing can come in handy. Bears, much like neighborhood missionaries, have a habit of dropping by when least expected. They are also quite nocturnal, moving and feeding most often at night.

Without enough daylight to see a threat coming, listening to a favorite CD could render oneself as defenseless as a doughnut. Bears favor doughnuts, I thought to myself, a good reason to be reading a lot with my ears wide open.

Just three weeks prior, on October 6, 2003, and a short hop down the coast from where I was hunting, the two adventurers, Tim Treadwell and Amie Huguenard, were attacked and consumed by a bear. Associated Press, CNN and BBC carried the news worldwide. AP reported that an air taxi pilot who arrived to pick up the couple near Kaflia Bay contacted the National Park Service and Alaska State Troopers to report a brown bear was apparently sitting on top of human remains in the camp.

A ranger brought in by helicopter shot and killed a large brown bear when the animal charged at them through the dense brush. Troopers and rangers later killed a smaller brown bear that they reported was stalking them. The story was later shared with the rest of the world in the documentary Grizzly Man.

It was against this backdrop of potentially tough weather, limited daylight and recent tragic consequences I planned a solo hunt. It did focus my attention. The airplane ride in, just over an hour long, was peaceful enough. It was a Thursday night and 34 degrees with fog and drizzle. I would usually have flown my own airplane into a hunt like this but, as it happened, my bird was at the shop being worked on and I had to beg a ride from one of my friends.

My pal had set me down at a makeshift river bar airstrip about an hour before dark providing just enough time to set up camp, which I pitched in the scattered thin brush of the dry river wash, beside a salmon stream, but one quarter mile down river from an active fishing hole.

This was a minimum separation distance that served to reduce my scent track in the hunting zone and limit the walk to and from the stand area that would necessarily be accomplished in the dark or near dark. Bears, like many other big game animals are most active in the half hour or hour near dark and beyond. If you are walking into the zone after it is getting light, or departing while you can still see much, you are missing the best hunting.

With camp set up and only about twenty minutes of light available, and not expecting to see any game after the aircraft noise we just made, I walked out of the thin brush and onto the river bar just far enough to get a clear view across and up river and survey the area. To the East, behind my position, was several hundred yards of flat gravel river wash. It was slightly elevated from the active stream beds and beyond that it was several more miles of flat mostly dense brushy plain and swamp terminating at the Pacific coastline.

To the west, in front of me, was more gravel wash varying from about four to six hundred yards across and braided with small streams, then the landscape jutted abruptly upward into near vertical hills rising into snowcapped mountains that topped out at three thousand feet. It was a perfect setup. Your imagination could not provide you a better landscape if you tried to dream one up.

A main stream wound through the boulders and gravel wash that could probably be crossed, in a pinch, with just hip boots. Four miles further up, the stream gave way to its parent glacier.

Between my location and the glacier, caught in pockets and eddies at various points along the stream's west shore, the salmon concentrated into several of nature's finest predator bait stations. The view was unobstructed for several hundred yards in front and behind my position and I could see a mile each direction up and down stream following along the length of the mountainside.

Incredibly, just a few minutes after sitting down on the edge of the streambed, a solitary, large dark brown hulk appeared five hundred yards away. The bear quietly eased out of cover along the stream and waded into a pool of fish. Stalking to within 300 yards for a better look, I watched until dark and then slipped back to camp behind me. Had I arrived to hunt in any manner other than aircraft, this would be a story about a thirty-minute brown bear hunt. (Flying and shooting same day air-born is against the law in Alaska.)

The bear was in the high eight to low nine foot range and I could have closed the distance and taken a solid shot that allowed plenty of opportunity for back up shots. This place looked immediately promising, for bear if not for wolf, but in either case, the shooting would be reserved for another day.

On the second day, hunting from dark to dark, nothing moved but the birds. Eagles hung in the trees as plentiful as ornaments, perhaps thirty-five or forty of them in all, diving, eating, and eyeballing the ravens, which in turn were eyeballing the magpies and camp robbers, all recognizing the established pecking order. The eagles surprisingly never appeared to fish for themselves, rather, they let the bears do the heavy lifting, satisfied with the second hand salmon.

The eagles swooped in for a molested carcass and carried it high onto a perch. The other scavengers took turns at the leftovers sometimes waiting directly under the eagle's high perch for droppings.

I was tempted to try the distressed rabbit predator call that day but I felt that a screaming noisy intrusion may disrupt the natural order of things. It would be a shame to run everything off; it was a slow, slow day and bird watching was my entertainment. Did rabbits even exist in this part of the country? Who knows? Back at camp I settled in for my second fifteen hour stretch of blackness and getting a few things ready for day three.

Saturday broke with decent weather, still foggy, with a light dusting of snow and zero wind. Things were eerily quiet and it punctuated my "aloneness". This day called for a move down river almost two miles to another known honey hole. This was the location that had produced the two wolves a year before. Though I saw only two new sets of wolf prints, and a few bear tracks, the fish were in reasonably thick and it looked like it should produce some action.

After burning nearly the whole day watching birds again, I moved back up river to the fish hole near camp, hoping for a return of the big bear during the last bit of light.

Sure enough, just twenty minutes before dark a head poked out of the thick brush cover just behind the feeding area. Inspecting the grounds for several moments and slowly moving into feeding position, this bear appeared much more cautious than during my earlier observation. When two small, first year cubs followed the sow out of the brush it was clear why. This was a different bear.

It was now alternately raining and trying to spit snow globs. More snow than rain. As I sat there in my hide, the combination piled up in a coating of white slush on my folded arms and thighs. I was blending in better all the time.

I briefly watched the bears feed as darkness and overcast once again dimmed the show to silhouettes. When I could not see any longer I slunk backward over the wash to the tent. The cold sandwiches and nuts were becoming a bit boring but cooking so close to the zone would spread stink increasing my scent footprint. With another fifteen long hours to kill I pulled on my headlamp, tucked into the bag and alternately nibbled away at both the food box and some well-thumbed magazines.

Alaska Raw

My ears were on super alert, straining to stay in front of any unwelcome noise from the great dark outdoors. Other than the streams gurgling in the distance, and the odd magpie fluttering in for some of my leftovers, it was dead calm.

Better weather opened the fourth day, a Sunday, and made it easier to shake loose the stiffness of a long night on a chilly, thin rubber sleeping mat. Just cloudy, no rain or wind. As with the evening before, you could hear a pin drop in the vastness that just somehow seemed like it should be generating more activity.

Since the original plan was to depart on Sunday in time to get back to work in Anchorage, it would be a short day, lasting only until the pilot managed to arrive, perhaps late afternoon.

Moving out into position on the wash, once again in the early dawn, I began to wonder if these animals ever ate breakfast, or even if they fed every day, or alternate days, or only under cover of night. The slow, steady, often monotonous waiting game resumed.

Daybreak came and went and by ten o'clock I was numb with boredom and fiddling with an empty candy wrapper inside of one coat pocket and the predator call inside the other. Nothing showing. If ever there was a good time to harass the critters with noxious dying rabbit noises, perhaps it was now. The positioning was good. I was well out in the open on a slightly elevated dry river braid, with a couple hundred yards behind me to the brush line and open all the way in front to five hundred yards, to the fish hole, and beyond that to the foot of the steep mountain.

With this buffer and unlimited view north and south the length of the streambed, just about anything presenting itself would be visible and, as an extra bonus for the solo hunter, nothing could put the sneak on me. Tucking myself slightly into a solitary, skimpy, leafless willow that barely caught purchase in the silty clay, I began to blow through the call.

For the next couple hours I tooted away ambitiously, advertising myself as both helpless and immediately available for consumption. Just as the instruction on the packaging had promised, mind bending screams of pure rabbit terror poured forth.

No question, everything for a couple miles knew some really bad shit was coming down on a rabbit. The eagles glared, keeping a distance, as did the ravens. The magpies came to a close branch and inspected. One magpie eyeballed me from its perch just three feet away. All things visible and living (and no doubt some not visible) were looking in my direction. After a time a beautiful martin quartered by, angling within twenty feet. Although after not seeing whatever he expected, it did not loiter for even a moment but kept shuffling along.

As for bear or wolf...nothing. The fish hole was Dead-Winter-Quiet. Once the magpies deserted me altogether the boredom returned. I put the call away. Just past noon the sun edged through the clouds for the first time in days. A celebratory snack was in order. It would, at least, give my aching jowl muscles an alternate workout, from puffing to chewing. Mix a little warming sunshine with food, immobilize, and you have the precise ingredients for a nap.

As the temperature rose from the mid-30s to the mid-40s, I dozed off, curled up in a depression in the rocks, hat pulled down tight, gloved hands in my pockets. It was a decent nap though it lasted only half an hour before the chill woke me. My body wanted to sleep, even after fifteen hours of tent time for the last three days. But the cold slowly seeps through all your layers and begins to make your ass and thighs and back feel like they were sides of beef left for dead in cold storage. The cold begins to ache its way through your muscles until it can't be ignored.

With me, my hands and feet are usually fine, the last to go, actually, but the big slabs of muscle laying like a hobo in the rocks bleed out all their heat and begin to throb. I had to get up. The nap was way too short.

Stepping out beside the single scraggly bush that had been a partial cover all morning, I stretched. I tapped some of the cold out of my feet. I lazily recast my field glasses back to the brushy border of the fish hole.

I saw....Nothing.

Standing in the wide open for the better part of fifteen minutes I pondered a quick trip back to the tent for a hot drink. Just then I noticed a very faint, rhythmic sort of rumble. It seemed to be coming from directly behind, sounding a bit like horses or cattle in the far distance. But for me, where I was, it was a misplaced, unfamiliar sound. Turning around to see what it might be generating the noise, it was instantly obvious. There were four large brown masses spread 30 yards abreast, about 150 yards away, all coming at full sprint directly at me!

I could now hear the strained chuffing noises of expelled breath, each marked by streaks of white vapor, and all in odd sync with multiple bounding sets of hoof strikes. There was so much to comprehend in that instant. It may be that the brain refuses to process that which it's certain is an impossibility, or that hours and days of distilled solitude slow normal reactions.

Whatever the reason, my impression in the first fractions of a second of this encounter was: these were four moose spooked out of the brush, charging hard, and they had not yet seen me. But my first impression was terribly wrong. They were not moose at all.

They were running in an orderly spacing with about five yards between each of them in half a V formation.

I remember that I was struck by the image of the forceful ejection of steam from the nostrils of four sets of snouts. The rhythm of the bursts of white mist was out of sync with the chuffing noise that was slightly delayed reaching me. The wisps of vapor shot out, drifted up and clung to a streamlined path over the animals backs and then vanished in the cool still air.

I continued to believe the forms were moose.

That was it. It had to be. What else comes in fours? It reminded me of an old western movie. I thought...wow, would these moose be surprised once they finally saw me, in my camo, hard to spot, but eventually they would. Eventually they would see I'm human, and to be avoided at all cost. And then they would break it off in another direction, and hard!

Should I wave my arms? Should I yell out? Man, they are still coming! They must not see me. I must blend in well! What scared them? Is there a brown bear chasing them?

Fuck me...here they come!

In the next second, the raw explosiveness of the charge, the undeviating directness of path, and the incredible rate at which ground was being gobbled up between them and me ...all finally registered a message in a very serious way. These are not moose!

These are bear. I am their prey. Disaster is unavoidable.

All parts of mind and body were defining the urgent tasks of survival. I wanted to live. There was barely time to get a shot off before they would be on me. Reaching for my rifle which had a round chambered and was leaned against the bush immediately at my side, in a single fluid motion, I swung it up, flipped off the safety, and centered the barrel on the closest bear. There was no time to flip open the scope covers. I looked past the barrel and centered it on the bear's chest and fired.

In the time between my reaching for my rifle and getting off the first shot, the bears had shrunk the one hundred fifty yards to fifty. Recounting now, from the first instant I had heard the faint drumbeat behind and turned around, to getting off the first round, was between three and four seconds.

The round missed.

I jacked another and aligned the bear's chest again with the barrel and fired, this time at thirty yards. The bullet smashed into the bear's sternum, its front legs buckled momentarily, it stumbled noticeably but quickly gathered its balance and, barely missing a stroke, re-accelerated to cover the last thirty yards. The other three bears dissemble a little after the two shots, startled for sure but not breaking stride. Instead their heads bobbled back and forth a little, looking at one another and searching for any sign of trouble, a little less organized, a little less sure, and a little less uniform in their raging formation. Apparently undeterred, all were still coming at full steam.

I rapidly chambered the third round just as I did the second, on the down-stroke of recovering the barrel from the heavy recoil. Again, looking alongside the scope, I aimed down the blued pipe like I was tracking a clay pigeon and let fly another nasty dose of .300 Win Mag.

This one hit square in the big bear's chest, this time at ten yards, and the crushing impact dropped its head to the dirt. As its head and then shoulders hit the ground it let a violent deep throated bellowing roar, the momentum rolling its huge body tail over head and nearly into my lap. I re-chambered and instantly swung left ten degrees to acquire the next closest brown mass.

Everything I had accomplished since reaching down for my rifle and shouldering it had been all instinct. Acting without thinking, shooting without taking the time to aim through the scope. There was no time.

My time was up.

There were three more brown bears charging in full attack mode and I was a dead man with a pulse. It would be possible to hit one of the remaining bears at ten yards, at full speed, but the other two would be on me before the echo of the last round settled out of my ears.

At least it would be sudden, and final.

When the fatally wounded bear hit the gravel it did so with a lot of speed, energy, noise and theatrics. The three other bears noticed. Seeing their companion go down hard finally flipped a switch in their heads that the noise of the gunshots failed to. At about 25 feet they broke off the charge and slammed on their thrust reversers in a way that is seared into my memory forever. Each of them instantly banking their bodies over left at extreme angles in near unison, and jamming their big front paws deep into the sandy gravel, gouging out ruts in the process and attempting with every bit of their athleticism to go from a straight ahead run at 30 miles an hour to a 90 degree turn.

One of them lost traction on its front legs as the high speed pivot proved too extreme, and it actually skidded toward me on its two back legs and rib cage, in a mad scramble to right itself. Needless to say I was stunned, in sort of a sensory shock from way too much stimulus, way too fast.

I remember two things vividly. The first was that the air was dead calm and at the moment of maximum chaos, when the three remaining bears executed their full throttle turn, I could feel the column of wind that was generated by them rushing at me. The second memory is of sand and gravel flying off the front paws of at least one of the bears and hitting my jacket, making a little splattering noises and then falling onto my boots. These two sensual confirmations of the actual proximity added to my sense of shock.

I not only heard and saw them but felt them. The entire episode lasted about six seconds, just as fast as you can pick up a rifle and fire three rounds, skeet style, it was over. For the better part of an hour, I spent the time pacing, gathering myself, breathing, and feeling fortunate to be alive.

From where I stood, as they charged, all four had looked identical in form, size and color. I selected the first bear to shoot only because it was at the point of the half V formation. I had a clear shot at any of them. The first bear I killed turned out to be a thick shouldered, heavy bodied, 8 foot 6 inch sow. The three others in the formation were very nearly her clones but were slightly smaller, and each having the same medium brown to blond color. These three were the sow's three year old "cubs". In their third year, they are actually referred to as juveniles rather than cubs and are legal to harvest as they are considered mature if not adult.

It is not unusual to run into very aggressive juvenile bears that are sometimes still travelling together for a short period before they become fully independent. They are quite a dangerous mixture of youthful exuberance and incautiousness. They are like a crazy teenager all jacked up with something to prove and testing every boundary.

The fact that the sow was leading the group and slightly ahead of the others in the charge probably saved my life because I instinctively picked her out based only on the fact that she was in front. Had one of the juveniles been slightly in front, or even alongside of the sow, I may well have picked that one. I don't think it would have ended well, or that I would be alive to be telling this story at all, had I shot one of the juveniles first.

I skinned the sow cautiously wondering if there was any chance anything else would put the sneak on me. It was a long paranoid afternoon with a lot of time to think about what had actually happened.

My informed theory of what all took place is this: the bears were a mile or more away and heard me calling for quite some time that morning. They probably just kept slowly working their way my direction as they picked up my intermittent screeching. Then, about the time they all reached the brush line of the river that I was sitting in the middle of, I had stopped calling and dozed off in my hide.

The bears, hearing nothing then, probably wandered up and down the river staying just inside the brush, as they prefer some cover, and peering out onto the vast braided river bar to see what it was that had been in such distress. Then, at some point I woke up, stood up, and very visibly started to stretch my arms and legs. That was the sort of visual clue of prey that the bears were looking for.

Know also that I was fully aware I could have called in a bear. I was expecting wolves, and that would have been more likely considering it was a rabbit call, but I had a strong hunch bears could react to it. Understanding all that, I placed myself in a location that had a vast amount of open space in every direction.

It was calculated for safety and of course to be able to have a good long look at any incoming game and making the shot. What happened was, I made the mistake of thinking the call had not been effective after blowing on it all morning to no result. Spending four days there and seeing almost nothing added to my complacency. Nothing was happening, and nothing was going to happen, or so I thought. So I took a nap. That was the single biggest error that made this event my worst hunting nightmare.

I documented the kill and especially the size of the juveniles' paw prints with photographs. What actually took place was memorialized quite well by being inscribed in the sand. I was able to relive it that entire afternoon and the next day, unfortunately.

The bears were stalking me from the brush line and you could see every move and paw print, when they accelerated, when the sow was hit by the first round but recovered herself, when she then went down for good, and when the juveniles slammed on the brakes and decided to avoid me. It was chilling. Sickening, actually.

After returning to Palmer I discussed it with the Department of Fish and Wildlife just to inform them what had happened and to get some insight, if any was to be had.

I was surprised at the bears' aggressiveness toward a distressed rabbit. Not that they would respond, but the aggressiveness of the response. What was that all about? A biologist explained that this was the second report they had received of a sow and aggressive juveniles coming in to a hunter's predator call. In the other case it was also an aggressive charge but not nearly so close and the juveniles retreated when the hunter fired warning shots.

The biologist theory on the aggressiveness toward a distressed rabbit is that they were not charging in and burning all that valuable energy to eat a rabbit. Rather, the bears believe that you are also a predator of some kind and you are already on the distressed animal and they want to run you off of it and run you out of their territory altogether. They want less competition in their range.

The impact that this close of a potential mauling had on me was a lasting one, and is counter to the image of the indestructible bad ass that I like to think I am, full of optimism and scrubbed of fear. Apparently I am all-too-human. That day, after it was over, and I managed to get the bear skinned, I still could not calm myself into believing the danger was behind me. Knowing what I know about bears' habits, and that is (and was) considerable, there was almost zero chance the juveniles would return to harass me any further. I should have been able to relax within several hours. Being alone no doubt added to the irrational fear.

But I was no stranger to hunting alone. I did plenty of it. But right there, right then, I wanted out. I wanted to be away from the scene and to be in a place where my security did not depend on my ability to hear, or see, or shoot, or kill, in an instant. I wanted the taste of panic out of my mouth. But my pilot would not show that day because of weather.

The long night the tent was borderline excruciating. I lay awake of course, and with my rifle chambered and my thumb never very far from the safety.

The absolute blackness beyond the tent and the dead silence created a vacuum in my head, a vacuum that strained continuously to pull in sounds, sounds of the tiniest disturbance that could be processed in the forced pause between my exhaling and inhaling, sounds that did not exist.

Was the fear irrational?

Sure. Mostly.

But after all, I was camped in light brush just yards off the stream bed, and my tent was bookended by two significant bear feeding buffet stations, one 200 yards west, the other about 1,000 yards north. I was very much in the thick of it. The only reason I was not seeing bears every day was that bears slow way down by November, and they often feed only sporadically, and that schedule between meals keeps stretching out as they slowly but predictably keep slipping further into their winter stupor. Some brown bears are still out and roaming around in the middle or end of November but are only getting up to eat what's left of the fish every couple of days or maybe twice a week.

About three in the morning, with five more hours to get to daylight, I picked up a faint noise of something on the way inbound. I could hear the dry fall leaves rustling from an animal moving. It took a while to convince myself the sounds were real and not a product of my paranoid brain that had taken my senses hostage. As I lay there on my back staring into the blackness as I had hour after hour, the noises were getting closer. Each time the leaves rustled it was amplified just a little more than the last, and the wad of mucus in my throat was gelling into a solid knot of immovable goo.

It just...kept...coming.

When I thought it best to get proactive rather than reactive with the intruder, I sat up in my sleeping bag, slid out of it, and then got to my hands and knees, which was all the height available in my two man tent. After getting my headlamp ready to flip on and locating the zipper on the tent, I was ready to confront the threat, whatever the hell it was.

In one well-rehearsed motion while still on my knees, I unzipped the tent fly, flipped on my headlamp, and immediately raised and shouldered my gun.

At about 15 yards a very alert martin quickly decided his surroundings were way too bright to be healthy and dodged right, scurrying away towards the river. Having been certain I would have to shoot my way out of another bad scene, my pulse was again hitting about 200 and I became aware of the beads of sweat on my face only because they were now cooling in the chill air. It was time to breathe again. The deep concern that the three juvenile bears were never very far away was real enough. They were likely within a one mile radius. But the fear that they would return for more of me was irrational. Trauma can take you places you don't come back from right away.

The long night turned into another grey morning. My overdue pilot was going to arrive whenever the weather and his personal schedule married up. I had a lot of time to think about how organized I was for death. The answer was "not very". When I got back home I made some calls to look into life insurance. It seemed like the responsible thing to do. But ultimately I had a hard time with the concept of betting on my own death and paying monthly for the privilege.

For many months I had distressing dreams, the plot lines all beginning and ending with visions of the bears in their unforgettable charge. The eight contrails of steam from their lowered snouts, the urgency of the bears' paw strikes, and the rapidly disappearing terrain between life and death. That one clip played over and over.

In the dreams, strangely enough, I don't have a gun, so I don't shoot, but the dreams never ended in me getting ripped to bloody pieces either. They just end, mid charge, and I wake up wondering how long it will be before I don't have them anymore.

Overall, the feeling of the dreams was mostly a helplessness, a total inability to effect or even influence any good outcome, like I was an incidental spectator of my own unfolding death, that it was inevitable, a feeling that my very significance on this earth could be much smaller, and much more temporary than I had ever imagined.

When I got home I knew I needed to start a writing project, though it may not have been the best time to write a will. I think it should be done with a cold eye for detail rather than an emotional heart.

I used what I had.

Chapter 7

One Miracle Per Customer (2010)

The spring of 2010 was late coming to the Alaska Peninsula. In early May you always see snow at low elevation and some scattered here and there on the deck, lying in the pocked tundra landscape. Hardly any of the grasses or tubers are greening up in early May and the freshly emerging bears have to pay attention to find much for a salad. The 2010 season was unusual in that it snowed and stormed daily well into the third week of May. Consequently, the bears were late emerging from their dens, never the best for trying to find a big one.

Brown bears are no different than humans in some regards. They are not exactly thrilled about going out in 20 degree weather, with the wind blowing 30 miles an hour and snow being delivered sideways. They are trying to conserve energy and the food value in greens, usually their first available food, rates low on the cost / benefit scale.

They hang back, taking a pass on the low calorie rabbit food in a blizzard.

That year I was able to do a little guiding under the employment of an established bear guide who had thirteen or fourteen hunts booked for the 20 day season. Among the client list that year was the president of Ruger Arms and one of his chief lieutenants who oversaw their marketing worldwide. The two Ruger executives booked the trip not only to hunt but to make a cable television movie which entertains while it promotes their brand. Unfortunately, as scheduled, I would never get to meet them or their camera crew since they had booked in the first week of a two week-long season while my slot was to arrive and guide hunters in the second week. We would pass each other somewhere in transit.

Arriving in Cold Bay a couple days early for my week long commitment would ensure some slop in my schedule in the event bad weather slowed my insertion to bear camp from the main commercial airport. The tiny one room airport itself looked a little constipated. Many of the secondary bush plane flights into the actual hunting sites had been delayed or cancelled, a result of bad weather.

A gaggle of 20 to 25 wannabe hunters were milling around the small lobby in a stewing mixture of excitement and surliness, some looking like they had been there quite a while, all waiting for their respective guides to fly in from their camps and load them up for an outbound flight and kick start their great adventure.

When a fellow pays anywhere from $15,000 to $20,000 for a guided hunt he expects service. Of course, unless you have done this before in this outrageously difficult, remote part of the world, you would not know what to expect while trying to get into camp or what it will be like once there. Some anticipate it will be just like it was in Bubba's Excellent Elk Camp with shuttles on the hour, satellite TV, and a game room to pass the time while the animals inside the fence are being groomed for next-day stalking. Clients with such expectations are usually in for a tough time.

So there I was...at this Cabela-infused ego orgy in a very small room where everyone wanted to be somewhere else with someone else and the wind was blowing a gale and the three well fogged windows in the place were further glazed over with sleet and frozen ice being served up at odd angles that changed from moment to moment. The thinly skinned, tin sided building sounded like it was under assault from all sides which depressed hope.

As evening wore on a few determined guides were able to get their small bush planes in for a pickup and some of the pressure came off the vessel as hunters trickled out to the waiting airplanes with their shiny new gear, guns and all manner of camo adorned gadgetry they believed they could not be without. It must have felt to them a little like a kid getting stuck for days on a stranded bus halfway to the big "away" game.

The little dribblers who had responsible parents were fetched reliably early in the calamity, leaving all the rest to wonder why all things had been so insufferably unreliable since the divorce, or if mom was smoking pot again, and when it would ever end.

The place did empty out a bit over many hours as the weather cleared up some. The daylight held reasonably well until past 10 PM. The remaining orphans slowly gave up and either booked one of the twenty or so $80 rooms at the scarcely habitable Barefoot Inn, or rolled out a sleeping bag on the lobby floor and waited a little longer. Naturally all the available rooms for rent soon vanish and then the time came when the proprietor, PenAir, wanted to lock up the airport for the night. Then you really are humped.

Being exceptionally resourceful, I looked around for a shelter of a type that has served me well several other times in just such a situation. I found an empty airplane parked in a "revetment". The plane had experienced some engine trouble and had been left there awaiting supply of repair parts. A revetment is a purposely excavated hole below grade, one of several big depressions dug along the side of the runway to park in when the weather is severe.

If it blows 80 or 100 miles an hour, and that happens fairly frequently, your airplane is tied down within this hole that is big enough for a couple of airplanes. I still don't know who the plane belonged to but "Thanks man...I appreciated it" even though sleeping while sitting upright fully dressed in outdoor gear leaves me feeling like I crashed in my office cubicle wrapped in a raincoat after pulling an all-nighter at the company Christmas Party.

And if I slept much at all I could not say. The downside of sleeping in a parked airplane in a storm is motion sickness from all the rocking. The revetment takes the edge off the wind but by no means is it calm inside that hole when the wind is howling. I settled in as best I could while sitting upright, slumped into the side window. For a while I watched my exhalations make frosty billows that soon had condensed and freshly coated white, all the smudged and dirty plastic windows.

As overcast daylight edged into the cockpit of my commandeered suite, I wasted absolutely as much time as I could before rolling out of the captain's chair and back to the Mossy Oak cultural exchange. Coffee was on and the place was abuzz with the shiftless, the wandering and the disappointed. Another commercial jet came and went, delivering more hunters that would need to be distributed to the field. The mix of faces had changed somewhat with new arrivals replacing some that had actually gotten out. The crowd looked to be thinning overall. The group had slimmed to about fifteen. At some point that day I noticed three guys hanging together in one corner of the room who had Ruger hats on. Cool hats. Great color.

It made me wonder how the guys from the Ruger team were doing in the field, what sort of bears they may have taken, and what kind of a hunt they had experienced given the extreme lateness of the snowmelt. I also wondered briefly if maybe the shit weather had completely bombed their hunt. That was another possibility. Once I got into Base Camp I would hear the entire story for sure. Something to look forward to.

The wait continued.

Towards noon I happened to notice one of these three fellows taking some expensive looking camera equipment out of a bag and fiddling with it. The lights in my head, sometimes slow to glow, flickered on. Could it be? No way! But if it was, they must have had major problems somewhere in the supply chain...and they must be unhappy. I recklessly made direct eye contact a few times before approaching them to ask a few questions. Maybe they were the tail end of the Ruger team who were stranded in the second of two loads? My mind invented a few scenarios just because it likes tidy answers.

The answer was not intuitive to me because these guys with the matching hats were present in the airport several days past the time they should have been hunting bears and making movies. After just a little bit of back and forth I find out these guys were, in fact, the hunters from Ruger Inc.

I never did fully understand all their logistical issues but it sounded like they were just a little late getting into Alaska, and then a day late getting out of Anchorage, all to the souring effect of burning through the first part of their total days available to hunt. They also had commitments back at the gun mill, pressing the back end of their schedule. They hadn't been able to reach the guide on his satellite phone, and he was many hours late, and to say they were not happy would be the Reader's Digest version of their stress laced invective.

In fairness, we found out days later the master guide was stuck with other hunters in the same heavy weather, unable to move at all, and with a ruck sack full of exhausted satellite phone batteries....as a result of trying to manage the ebb and flow of multiple assistant guides and hunters arriving and departing, or wanting to, or trying to, while being stranded himself. It was a classic cluster hump...in the outback, in a snowstorm. There was nothing anyone could have done much different. It just was.

Once they found out I was working for the guide they had hired there were some knotted up faces. They had a few questions for me, the first among them was:

"WHAT THE HELL???" .... Maybe not in those exact words, but close, with all the subtlety and warmth.

I did my best to explain how anything can happen in Alaska, once you get away from available infrastructure and beyond that into the field, how there was no way to order a bacon-ranch pizza, for example, or lay your hands on some curly fries, or even hail a cab. Once they discovered I was part of the guide operation it was difficult for them to not flash just a little ax to be ground.

Almost cordial, but tense, showing some fang here and there...would be a way to describe it. But ultimately they were gentlemen all.

I explained my limited involvement overall, as any capable politician would, and that my charge involved the second-half-of-season clients. The lobby was still teaming with a moderate sized scrum of stragglers still waiting on an airplane ride to the field in the charge of their respective keepers.

In general, the Ruger fellows understood after talking to me that it was the terrible wind, rain and then fog that likely kept our pilot grounded. The conversation then pivoted to what the best way forward may look like. But they were at the end of their patience and running out of time. Platitudes about how this was "just the way it was in Cold Bay and to relax and enjoy the experience" would not get us out hunting.

Notably, Ruger CEO Mike Fifer had the same determination about this venture that likely took him to the very top of his game in the worldwide firearms business. He was driven to succeed at whatever he set himself upon and this problem was just a roadblock to be calendared, managed and overcome. Mike was a serious man, handsome, fit, compact, and not given to arm waving at the first sign of a problem. He was a guy who I suspect rarely, if ever, took his eye off the ball his entire life.

His inquisitive and academic mind peppered me with questions and I could tell from interacting with him that his brain never stopped. He was calculating the several probable outcomes of my answers at the same time he was chambering his next line of inquiry. Mike wanted to get this hunt back on its legs. I liked Mike's directness, the mark of a military man. I saw him as a fellow who made very few mistakes of judgement, and this hunt would not go down as one of them.

Randell Pence was Ruger's Executive Director of Marketing. Another serious businessman, one who knew all about focusing to reach a goal, Randell had this even and easy manner about him, even under pressure, which was further sweetened by his deliberate and measured commentary delivered with a rhythmic southern accent.

Randell, in his early sixties, had a few years on both Mike and myself but he was bigger than both of us and looked like he may have been a college or professional football player in his prime.

His banter was always jovial and kind hearted and he was a nice offset to both Mike and me. We both seemed to have a tendency to be a little too serious when there are problems to be solved. Randell reminded us often, usually with a wide smile and some whimsical quip of southern wisdom, that all of this was supposed to be fun, all the time.

Danny Dodge was the third man of the Ruger team. Danny was a contract videographer who had worked for Ruger on other successful projects and was one of their favorite hands. I can see why. Danny, like I'm sure anyone in his field, has to understand how to make a film out of a thousand unorganized snippets of time. It is that talent and vision that comes through in the artistry of a finished product. What I saw, as the days unfolded, went far beyond that.

Danny was a guy who could dismantle the space shuttle with nothing but a Swiss army knife and a plastic spoon, then troubleshoot the problem, and reassemble it in the dark, stopping only to blow warmth back into his fingers after they quit working entirely. He performed just such miracles for the Ruger team, by keeping the cameras functional, and he did it in 95% humidity in blowing rain and snow.

Danny was our Pit Bull and you would have to beat the man unconscious to get the bone out of his mouth or the camera out of his hand. What a superstar he was.

So I could not have had a better gang to go bear hunting with, if only we could find the means.

I had a few contacts from past hunts in the area and discussed with everyone how we may be able to at least get started toward the field with the hopes of finding the Master someplace between one of the numerous spike camps, the

Base Camp, or the tiny village of Nelson Lagoon where we staged out to the Base Camp. Everything involved hiring an aircraft. Importantly, we were not the only guys thinking the same thing. If an air taxi operator with a pulse and a capable airplane were to wander through the Cold Bay Airport lobby it would have caused all the stir of a sandwich tossed into a circle of hobos.

Nearly everyone with an airplane had it put to work already and the rest were stuck in weather. Nevertheless, we all agreed it was worth a try. I would work the coin operated payphone and try to find any pilot coming back from other hunt-staging locations, such as Sand Point, or trying to run south to Cold Bay, for fuel, from any of several villages to the north. We needed to snag someone working for one guide operation or another, someone who had a narrow window of availability and wanted to make a couple thousand dollars for half a day's work.

To fail would mean a large prepaid hunt for two with a planned film, worth many tens of thousands of dollars, would end in ill will and harsh words, or worse. I worked the pay phone with all the desperation of a man with a garage full of Amway to sell. In no time I had reached a number of wives, children, girlfriends and the occasional grandpa of someone with an airplane and the credentials to be hired to fly it. Word gets around in the Alaskan outback by CB radio, by cell in the few places they function, and from neighbor to neighbor.

After the calls went out it was a matter of crossing my fingers and waiting by the pay phone. I had some confidence in my sales pitch that we just needed to get to Nelson Lagoon, we did not have a ton of gear, we would pay well, the weather was looking, uh, better here actually than what was last officially reported.

At least some of it was true.

The airstrip at base camp was an abandoned oil exploration remnant common in these parts of Alaska. It was volcanic ash and some organic soil, reasonably long, but with a tendency towards softness in the spring. A specialized aircraft was required, one with just a little bigger tires than standard, to be able to manage the condition.

It was a fine line whether a mid-size, six place bush aircraft could operate out of it with heavy loads. If it was soft from a recent rain or snow it would not work out so well. If it had firmed up from a day or two of wind blowing across it, no problem. Soliciting a trip from Cold Bay Airport to the Nelson Lagoon Airport with any potential air taxi operator was easier than convincing the taxi to continue on and get us all the way into the base camp, the unimproved airstrip farther to the east.   If the pilot we hired had an appetite for a little risk, and needed the money, he would take us all the way. If not, we would need plan B. Another plane, a smaller, perhaps two or four place...more rugged aircraft.

As the day ground on I fielded a few calls from different entities that had received my request. The responses ran the range of offers to come within a few days, to several days, to assurances from the wives or relatives of the pilots that if they could ever reach the pilots themselves, to ask, they would surely be interested and available...eventually.

It often went like this:

Someone's wife: "Yah, we'd love to help, just not sure when, but my husband, he can take you, he does that for people, he's flying fuel into Port Heiden now, so maybe he gets done with that later this week, and then....when he comes back. Do we have a deal? We need a deposit.

Me: "Sure thing. Thanks."

Or this...

Me: "Hello, uh...is your dad home?"

Kid: "No."

Me: "Is your dad Earl? Is he the pilot?"

Kid: "Yes."

Me: "Do you know how to reach him?"

Kid: "He's not come back from up the lagoon."

Me: "Does he usually stay gone long?"

Kid: "Sometimes."

Me: "Do you think he will this time?"

Kid: "Will what?"

Me: "Stay gone long. This time"? ...... "Like when do you expect him...your dad?"

Kid: "It depends if he got the boat running again...."

Me: "Ok. Sure thing. Thanks. I will leave you my number. Can you have him call me?"

Kid: "If he comes back."

At least some interest was stirring. About the time I was going to get back on the payphone's heavily soiled cream colored handset for what seemed like round seventeen of checking back with everyone's wives and children, we heard an airplane land out front and spin up the engine as it taxied closer. Several airplanes had come and gone over the last two days but always for someone else.

With our noses pressed to the sleet-obscured window, an aircraft hove into view, this one a six place Cessna 206, just what we needed, but our hopes were not on high alert since the wide but dismal range of responses from the phone campaign had been much too demoralizing to hold any hope at all that this bird was for us.

But apparently one of those calls had hit pay. When the pilot walked in through the small grey metal door and blurted out my name I felt a wave of relief. The pilot first wanted to talk about the only thing that matters in situations like this. Money.

Once he knew I could pay we cut a fair deal, if there is such a thing when you already have your panties pulled down around your ankles, and we wasted no time sorting gear and packing the airplane. The weather was better, the fog had lifted and the wind was off from 40 to about 25, still raining some, but a parade-worthy day for the Alaska Peninsula.

It took two loads for four of us and gear, plus the pilot, and as soon as we were airborne I began pitching him to extend the trip past Nelson Lagoon and on into Base Camp. I must have lost my touch. He was only up for the trip into the improved airport. We would soon be back to begging for a lift, closer to goal but with a big logistics hurdle remaining. We needed another air taxi. On the positive side, we had salted all the nearby communities with the news that stranded but solvent white men were looking to hire an airplane.

After landing in Nelson Lagoon we unloaded gear and took up refuge behind a runway equipment maintenance building to get out of the wind. The building was locked but a little afternoon sun was peeking through cracks in the overcast and hitting the west side. Word arrived from a pilot who was passing through that another aircraft, this time a Cessna 185, was going to drop in and help us get to Base Camp. If it would be hours or days was up for interpretation. Mike, Randell, Dan and I waited three or four hours squatting behind the maintenance building until the sun started to let us down and the wind, diffused as it was, was grinding its cold through our many layers of thermal gear.

It was time for a walk. It was also past time for dinner. We had a few fistfuls of trail food to our name and that was not going to get us through the evening without some discomfort.

Nelson Lagoon is a very small Aleut settlement on the Bering Sea shore, located on the northwestern coast of the Alaska Peninsula. It has a population of 52 people in about

22 households. A narrow sand spit that separates the lagoon from the Bering Sea makes this a place with unlimited ocean frontage right outside its inhabitants' front and back yards.

Think of the Outer Banks in the Carolinas, but fifty degrees cooler and with a really nasty meteorological attitude. The elements blow right over this impossibly hardscrabble fishing outpost situated in the middle of rich salmon runs. Recently, before we arrived, a suicide had disrupted the village's peace and tranquility and left its inhabitants full of bewilderment and sorrow. It is a difficult place to stake out a life.

It is a short walk into the village from the airport. I thought there must be someone nested in their home who would be getting ready for dinner themselves at this hour, and even their leftovers would be a gastronomic home run. My plan was to literally go door to door and ask for a meal. We would offer to pay of course, but inviting strangers in "off the street" was asking a lot of people who don't live on impossibly small slivers of shifting sand in the middle of the Bering Sea for no reason.

It was worth a try. What was interesting is that after several doors no one was answering. It was hard to believe that no one was home. After all, where could they go? I never will know if people were just inconvenienced enough to not want to get up and see who was knocking, or if they were clustered up at a relative's house, or gathered somewhere mending nets, out of sight, in their version of a sewing bee. One quiet house led to the next.

"Knock knock".

This time was different, I heard footsteps and then the door knob squeaked and the door swung open. A neat and motherly Aleut woman, compact in stature, quite pretty, perhaps early fifties, stood in front of us. Her flawlessly smooth olive skin did not correlate with her age, a probable result of never getting much sun. She had an apron on over a thick sweater and black slacks. I really liked the look of that apron; it was the perfect accessory to her outfit. It made me feel like I had cold called on exactly the right house out of the twenty or so square plywood abodes strewn down the narrow spit. She was alone in the home.

"Hey there! I'm Bob, nice to meet you! I hope we are not...interrupting?" (Much)

Tempered to establish an appropriate social boundary, a quiet and measured "Hello" was offered to me in return but without the completed greeting of a smile.

"We were just out walking and were wondering if there was anyone in the village that maybe we could pay for a meal, or some sandwiches?"

Blank stare.

"We walked from the airport. It seems we may be stranded here for a while."

The woman nods and reaches behind her middle waist to untie the apron and pulls it off, setting it aside on the back of a chair beside the door. I'm guessing she does not want to look quite as informal as she now does with guests at her door.

I can see she is processing the out-of-nowhere request of the four gringos, in full battle camo and rubber knee high boots, standing on her porch, gringos who have come only to pillage game from her backyard.

Still no hint of a smile. So I continue my sales pitch, but it felt weird because I was buying, not selling. It did not help that my delivery was too anxious. I could smell the food on her cupboards.

I had worked and lived among Alaska Native people in several villages in the past, for infrastructure projects related to my regular work, but forgot for the moment that I needed to chill out, slow down, and not necessarily look for, or expect to rely on, all of the visual facial affirmations from her that would further inform me, either positively or negatively, as we visited.

"We're hungry so we just thought....if anyone, you know, does that sort of thing, like a bed and breakfast or...you know...just anything really." "We, uh... We are not particular." Without eye contact she bends her lips slightly to an accepting if not welcoming gesture and says... simply:

"I will."

Clearly we have sprung all this on her and she is still processing. We all stand there for a few more awkward seconds before I lend some continuity to the stalled, one sided conversation by offering for all of us to remove our boots. She nods approvingly at the suggestion, turns away, and retreats further into the room toward the kitchen.

Since I think all of that means "come on in" we wrestle our footgear off and move from the doorway into the small one room living-kitchen-dining combo space and squeeze into the several chairs around the small white legged wooden table. The house is neat as a pin and smells strongly of food security. Bread I think, and something sweeter like cookies. She has not yet introduced herself but asks in her clipped and sturdy Aleut accent:

".....Spaghetti OK?"

"Yes! Yes! That would be great! Uh, what was your name, again, ma'am, I'm not sure I caught it if you told me?"

"Auntie."

Finally a few words of small talk between us starts to melt the social abyss. Auntie's face warms to the home full of strangers. Her voice, as little as we hear of it, possesses an anodyne tempo that I enjoy very much. She begins boiling water for the noodles and putting some minced caribou in a fry pan.

Her apron never left the back of the chair, apparently of no utility any longer given the changed circumstance. The meal is served with love and fresh white bread.

As the room and food warms us we are peeling layers off and I'm just a little embarrassed by the fact that Auntie's house does not smell as good now with the four sweating men inside it. The tiny room seemed to amplify this and the echoes of odor were becoming hard to miss, like too many of us in one small vessel were changing the pH in the fishbowl. We chatted for a short time after the meal and then thanked Auntie for her courageous hospitality. I never could get comfortable with the thought of just hanging out there until a plane came for us, or asking for a place to sleep if it came to that.

I don't think Auntie could either. Though the custom and social practice of Alaska's aboriginal people in general is very low key, indirect and non-confrontational to a fault, Auntie sent enough signals for me to be aware that she was agreeable to helping out but also that she did not run a hostel. Gracious as she ultimately became through the meal, I could see that we should be on our way. I pulled out some cash to square up and she seemed pleased to have experienced our acquaintance.

The next chore was finding a place to stay since the possibility of an airplane ride was looking less probable. Again I went door to door. After some inquiry a story emerged about why people were not exactly jumping at the chance to rent us a spare room and feed us. The word was that the bear guides didn't often hire and use the locals to help out in the guide operations and the community was less than pleased about it.

It was not easy finding a couple rooms but ultimately we did and we were lucky to have them because we then spent the next four days waiting out the weather, our hopes rising then falling day after day, with every teasing improvement in the dreadfully unsettled sky.

Late in the afternoon on the fifth day we got word an airplane would be coming for us, a pilot that I had called days earlier. So when we finally heard the sound of an airplane descending over the village I quickly squared up our bill, stepped outside and flagged down a young boy who happened to be passing by on a four wheeler. Perfect timing, I thought to myself. It was almost divine intervention given our hellish luck so far.

I asked the boy if he knew anyone who could give us a lift back to the airstrip. He said he knew a gal with a pickup that was actually headed out that way momentarily. There was, after all, only one main gravel road, and it ran to or from the airstrip, so exactly half the traffic going by us at any one time was going precisely our desired direction!

Sure enough, within a few minutes a severely used black Toyota pickup chased by a column of dust rattled into view. The boy waved her down. A deal was struck. Back to the remote airstrip we went, all in a pile in the bed of the dusty Toyota, the wind chill of the Bering Sea clawing at our exposed hands and faces and impressing on us that progress was being made.

A 185 Cessna had arrived. Word had gotten out. After several days the available airplane inventory had finally limbered up a little. A fair deal was negotiated and I was, finally, feeling genuinely hopeful. We would soon be headed to the Base Camp despite having to overcome a couple of major hurdles.

Gear was again loaded strategically by the pilot to ensure proper weight balances and two of the Ruger Team piled in for the fifteen minute ride. I held back just enough gear for me and the camera man to take shelter up against the building if we had to, just in case. We then stayed put and waited for the empty plane to return. As the horizon dimmed in the east and an hour passed, I was hoping the 185 had not stuck a wheel in a soft spot in the remote airstrip, or something worse. After another 20 minutes and evening fully settling in, I was sure we were fucked. All I could think of was how to find some better temporary shelter out of the wind if the wait was going to be several hours or longer.

At the north end of the airport's gravel parking apron there was a crippled 172 Cessna. At least I think it was crippled. It's always possible it was just resting its rust because you can see some real junk that still takes flight in remote parts of Alaska.

Alaska Raw

The entire plane had a month's thick layer of dried salt mist overlaid with silt and dirt. It had that abandoned-after-it-ran-out-of-oil look as it rested on one full tire on the right main, a flat on the center front, and something in between on the left main. Was it going to be our suite for the night? We didn't dare take the walk back into town for fear of missing the pilot. The airplane's door was unlocked. I'm feeling better all the time. It smelled of funk, like a badly mildewed car interior. In the front seat, what looked like the coveted contents of a homeless person's push cart had been stacked up from floor boards all the way to the seat backs.

There would be some work involved to clear a space if it came to that. But the ragged loose ends just kept mating up. In the far distance, faintly audible over the ever present thrum of the Bering Sea wind, we hear an airplane.

The noise gets closer though we can't pick up any motion on the darkening horizon on account of the low altitude the pilot is arriving with. As the Cessna's navigation lights come into view a mile away we are relieved to know we'll have a cold tent to sleep in with a cot, both of which will be much more comfortable than the alternatives. We loaded some gear and then joined the pilot in the luxury of the heated cockpit.

My eyes were burning and my face was raw from the wind and constantly wiping snot from my nose and upper lip. I hadn't really noticed either until the warmth from the airplane enveloped me. The heat was relaxing and allowed me to destress enough to begin thinking more about what I would do with these clients, once we got to camp if we couldn't make contact with our master guide. My hope was I would just be the traffic coordinator and facilitator and soon I would get Ruger back on schedule and on task with the original preplanned guiding crew.

Our trip into the base camp was quick and easy. But the short break in the darkening evening sky that allowed us to sneak in there was taking a turn for the worse. Snow was just beginning to drive in at a sharp angle carried by an unbroken line of squall from the east. As we arrived overhead there were no extra airplanes tied up at the airstrip so it was clear the guide was still out in the field... someplace.

After settling everyone's gear into one of five available tents, I coordinated some cooking with a couple of other hunters and another assistant guide.

Ducking between tents with my headlamp on I could see we had about two inches of dense wet snow accumulated in just an hour and a half. Some snow was melting, some was sticking. It depended, it seemed, on the temperature of the gusts that delivered it. On the windward side of the tents the walls pushed in with the snow and wind load, on the leeward, they bubbled out in the vacuum and clapped noisily and cleanly.

Inside, each of the squatty aluminum and fabric structures tilted and swayed in each gust, rocking the small gas lanterns that hung from their apex and causing a light play of moving shadows that were choreographed by the forces at work. The wind was rising with the oncoming storm and was now blowing 40 to 45. The Bering Sea and Pacific Ocean were again slugging it out over a narrow piece of land that divided their continually unbalanced pressure systems.

The temperature was hanging right at 30. Inside the tents, the steamy condensation from our overwrought voices pushed first out of our mouths in clustered puffs of conversation that hung in miniature mid-air clouds for a moment. The little clouds then pushed and pulled rapidly, jerking oddly through space in lock step with the air mass inside the tent caused by the gusts outside. It was a visible, dancing remnant of the last few words that came from your mouth. None of this relaxes. Your senses tend to remain in a state of overstimulation.

Morning brought a little better weather with the wind off by half and the snow only coming in sputters but salted with rain. I started the day by sweeping layers of ice and snow sheets off the tents that had taken a sag under the load. Everyone was up at the crack of 9 and coffee was on. Still no master guide, which was understandable given the weather. Looking north by north east the mountains were still layered in a mayonnaise mist.

Unless your spike camp was at 300 feet or less in elevation, essentially on the flat, you would be unlikely to escape it by airplane in those conditions. We finished breakfast and waited.

A decision had to be made soon regarding the Ruger hunt. There were two options as I saw it. To wait for a third aircraft that typically took hunters to spike camps at the traditional hotspots, or to strike out from basecamp and try to find a bear. The plusses to waiting were several. Primary among these, was that Ruger would reunite with the master guide to produce the film.

Alaska Raw

The spike camps had about a 90 percent chance of producing a bear, verses wandering off to the distant hills from base camp, trying to stumble on one. That was a much longer shot. In a spike camp the close proximity to a potential stalk or kill site was a big consideration for the hauling of camera gear.

All of us wanted the "Production" to be about the taking of a bear rather than a marathon endurance test, lugging all our high tech shit, to even get to where we could see one...maybe. The downside of waiting was we may never get to hunt.

All of those things swirled around in my head in an endless caffeine propelled loop. In general, I am not much on dithering but prefer to lurch even if it ends up being wrong. It's a personal trait that serves me well exactly 50 percent of the time. Without the master to allocate specific clients I was supposed to be tending, I concluded the Ruger's stature if nothing else dictated that I get them out hunting. All of the proper licenses, tags and contracts for Fifer and Pence were in camp, signed and complete.

We were solidly in bear country just by virtue of being in basecamp. By example, nearly every season (at least during the spring hunt) someone in or near camp will spot a bear off in the distance or crossing a big open plain on one of their never ending searches to feed. Bears were killed from the main camp and, once in a while, they were some good ones. However, when you have a sizeable contingent of people, and smells, and odd clatter, and aircraft coming and going, and hunters sighting in their guns, and all the rest... any nearby bears tend to slowly but steadily migrate away from that focal point like ripples from a stone cast in the water. Bears don't welcome the company.

It did not make sense to share my head-full of deliberative process with the Ruger crew. What they wanted to hear, and what I wanted to tell them, was that we were now, finally, in "The Zone" and it was time to finally go find a big bear. I gathered the three of them into one tent for a pep talk. As they finished coffee and some eggs with toast I went over what a splendid opportunity we had in front of us and how we would strike out from camp, move across the flats and up onto to the rising hillside two miles distant.

The camera man, full of energy and seemingly ready for anything in any conditions, was gearing up before I had even finished. He had seen some poor conditions in his days in the business. He was impressive in that regard. The two Ruger executives were also no lightweights. They had come this far, waited this long, and overcame a few bad logistical breaks already. They were anxious and eager. All they needed me to do was point. They readied their gear.

In the spring on the Alaska Peninsula you find bears most often feeding on dead whales or walrus washed up on the beach or up on the hillsides looking for green tubers and sprouts. Accordingly, you can also find them travelling between the two possible opportunities, from the hills to the beach...and back again.

From the high vantage point of the distant hills we could not see all the way to the beach but we could see much of the plains that a bear would traverse when going either direction, and we had full command of the several areas on the hills that were greening up. For us, high was the choice.

It's also self-evident that a hunter can move rapidly down to intercept but not the reverse. Many, many times it ends up being a foot race to head off a travelling brown bear and to get enough out in front of him to get a quartering shot on the way by. By 10:30 AM we were ready and headed out. Travelling first across a mile and a half of difficult and terribly uneven tundra, we worked our way to the foothills where we connected with a shallow gravel bedded stream that allowed us to snake up through the thick alders without much heavy bush whacking.

After a couple hours of slogging it uphill we were on a bench at about 900 feet of elevation which was also the bottom of the cloud layer. The layer moved up and down the mountain with each new onslaught, and then subsequent retreat, of blowing snow cycles. When it lifted periodically, green sprouts were visible in several of the gullies that ran from just in front of us upward to the mountain tops. 800 to 1,000 feet of elevation separated us from the very top of the ridgeline.

Where there was green there could eventually be bears. Looking back westerly (the direction we came) we were in a position to see the flats for at least ten miles though our hunt radius was probably limited to about three, possibly four. The layout of the bench allowed for us to split into two groups, with one glassing the flats below and the other facing straight up the hill with good visuals left and right across the rising terrain for 1,000 yards each way. This was the best location we would likely ever have given our transportation handicap.

We would play this patently mediocre hand of cards to the best of my ability and to the best of my clients' patience.

I gathered up the crew and, with an animated enthusiasm that was just short of genuine, I went over all the benefits of the site and the possibilities of various plays that could take place from the several available fields of view. High up on the ridge in a head to head huddle I found myself still having to yell to be understood over the wind. We paired up and took up the two positions.

As I noted earlier, all three of these gents were more hardcore than expected. I saw their bags of gear. As instructed, they packed little more than the necessities. Being anywhere near the Bering Sea in a blizzard makes it impossibly hard to stay warm, dry and viable in the field. These hunting conditions would be very near the end of anyone's misery index. The wind claws the heat from your body and you are continually challenged mentally to resist taking the slightest shelter from it.

If you take shelter by turning your face to the lee, or ducking in behind a thicket of brush, you are not hunting. And if you are not hunting, and hunting every moment, why the fuck did you come here? If that's who you are, you should have just stayed with your chicken wing sucking, beer bellied pals gathered around some sports TV program where the only balls that matter are the ones being kicked, bounced or bunted.

On the ridge, hours felt like days. Every 30 to 45 minutes another pulse of wind driven snow and ice would roll across the ridge from right to left. The wind rose and fell in chaotic pressure waves that you could hear coming for 20 or 30 seconds before they caught up to you. Trying to keep field glasses clear was a nagging chore, as was trying to sneak peaks windward when it cycled between gusty squalls. What started as a small problem, keeping the big camera gear functioning, became an ongoing and critical problem.

In fact the main camera was fogging internally and showing intermittent fault codes on its management screen. Batteries were becoming cold and were rotated inside jackets to have a warmer one always one armpit away. Continual tests were being done by filming small parts of the storm and each of us in our makeshift blinds. About half the time, if not more often, the camera fault screen was showing internal moisture levels beyond allowable. Sometimes it made film, sometimes it wouldn't.

Our camera guy Danny was such a pro. Throughout the blizzard he never let up trying to keep his several pieces of critical equipment as operational as humanly possible.

As the day wore on the camera faulted a higher percentage of the time during test runs and it became clear we would have to try to disassemble and dry it thoroughly over heat back at base camp.

The camera simply had to function or there would be no kill shot recorded. With no kill shot there is no movie. It's not marketable. Had a bear presented itself that afternoon it would have been a crap shoot if we could have gotten it all.

We had "in the can" snippets of the hike up, scenery from Cold Bay forward, base camp shots, and lots of footage capturing the snowstorm that surrounded and harassed us. A lot could be produced from these pieces.

The entire 30 minute movie could be stitched together and then in a pinch you would add a couple seconds of dead brown bear lying in a wad complete with smiling hunters in the background...whenever we could get the big camera to come to life. Or we could use the GoPro if we had to, which never quit working. The end product would look not only funky but desperate. No matter, without the money shot, it was not fit for living rooms across America. Danny had to get the big camera working more reliably. He fiddled with it under a piece of plastic on the side of the hill while the snow, and the wind, and the rain, and the day...ground on.

We watched and waited for a bear.

In the early evening, during a brief period where the long distance visibility improved, we did spot a very big bear several miles out on the flat below. Probably three miles out and moving from inland to the ocean, nearly directly left to right, but at times quartering slightly away from us as he ambled along briskly. The bear's pace was deliberate, quite different than when they are feeding along a path of some emerging grubs. The massive animal was on the path of something specific, probably stinky carrion or a stinky sow. Both were on the menu this time of year. Maybe he was motivated for dinner and a date.

On inspection, it was absolutely a huge slob and almost assuredly a boar given its immense and dark chocolate profile. A quick calculation told me our gang would be 30 to 40 minutes bailing off the hill if we pushed it to a near run. But the camera gear, tripods and the like would slow us down a little, perhaps to 50 minutes. Then to cross two more miles of tundra, another 45 minutes on a good day.

We would have to take an angling direction off the bench about 30 or 40 degrees in front of the travelling bear in order to intercept and get into shooting position. Then of course you had to get the camera gear in place and functioning. We were as nimble as the two hundred pound girl at cheerleader try outs. I couldn't see us making it. Rather, it looked like we could get down to the bear just as he walked by us at about half a mile away, and he was walking faster. I made the call. We would pass.

What I made sure to not leave undiscussed was the fact that just a couple of us hauling ass, with no cameraman or gear, could have gotten on that bear and killed it. The bear was in the high ten foot range or even bigger. From a distance, it looked like a ten-passenger Ford van painted black.

Spirits settled back down into the emotional space that lies between low physical activity and hypervigilant sensory attention without an outlet. It's an odd mental state, unique I believe, to hunting. In that space, a person's tolerance for inactivity gets smaller and smaller as the hours tick off and probabilities slip. My goal was to grind it out on the glasses until 10 PM and walk everyone back, slogging into camp just after dark.

Bears are often nocturnal, especially ones that have been proximal to some man-made activity, as any around our base camp would have been by then. Even without man-made interferences that push them to be nocturnal, bears are often quite active at dusk and a couple of hours beyond. One theory to explain this goes back to the weather.

The bears wait in their lair, sometimes all day, for some decent weather, maybe some sun, maybe less wind, always for purposes of spending less calories than they bring in. By the beginning of evening after hanging around all day with no weather breaks that looked compelling, the bear decides it's now or never and starts to forage. So then, we would do well to try to hunt until we could not see to shoot, which we did.

Score: Bears 1, Ruger Arms 0. We collected ourselves and headed down the hill and back to camp behind the bright, bouncing cone beams of our headlamps.

It is never the best idea, but often an operational reality, to push through brush that is over your head in the dark in brown bear country. By the look of their darting wide eyes and stress tangled faces, my clients knew this instinctively. With their newly minted Ruger .375 rifle barrels thrusting forward, as though clearing house to house for rebel Al Qaida, they talked among each other loudly and often, but communicating not much of anything, making as much noise as possible to avoid any ugly surprises.

No one in the crew had a cow bell but I could have made a few hundred bucks in side change if I had brought a couple with me to sell. It's a real danger obviously, that I tried to minimize at the time with humor. Since I was usually leading, my bigger worry was taking a .375 round in the back. It happens all too often. Hyper alert men stumbling though the brush in the dark with guns pointed toward your back and fingers on or near the trigger. What could go wrong?

We made camp and were damn glad one of the other assistant guides had a pail of hot water on. After slipping out of rain gear and then layering on some dry fleece, then a down vest, then a full blown parka, I was ready to join some of that hot water with a handful of dry food pellets for a hot meal.

This proves to be the best hour of the long and physically taxing day. It represents the end of a 13 hour thermal assault wherein your body is turning everything inside of it to heat. And when your body finally gets the loud and clear signals of dry clothes and hot food and drink, it knows it can shut off that machinery. The cold stress is over, the food stress is over. It's all about the total flow of calories moving from one direction to the other like current moving back into a depleted battery. I had reversed the polarity of a long day and I was glowing.

Danny the cameraman knew he had to work some magic to get his equipment dried out. The only tent with any heat was the one used for cooking and the heat was usually just a side effect of having a propane burner or two going during meal preparation.

As a treat, once or twice a day, and only for an hour or two, someone would leave one of the stove burners going and the tent would get to 50 degrees. This usually occurred when three or more people lingered after receiving their morning ration of coffee and hot water, the latter of which was turned into breakfast by rehydrating oatmeal or something similar.

We did not have a supply of propane to heat spaces. Fuel was for cooking. Since 90 percent of the food was freeze dried, if we ran out of fuel we would soon be eating the equivalent of handfuls of beef and chicken flavored sawdust and rinsing it down with a gulp of water.

While no one was happy about the camera problems, there was keen interest in watching it be disassembled, dried out over a propane burner, wiped with paper towels, reassembled, tested to failure, disassembled, reheated, wiped and on and on for hours. It was the subject of much chatter and speculation while also being an extended, and most importantly, guilt free source of heat to luxuriate in.

The propane made moisture as a byproduct of combustion...as everyone who has ever used it in a tent knows. The trick was to warm up the camera parts in the moisture laden heat and then pull them away into drier (but cooler) air in another tent to evaporate all the moisture. It was a hit and miss proposition.

Eventually the apparatus went together and was powered up without flashing a fault code. It was then deemed ready for the next day's work and carefully double bagged for the trip up the hill.

About 6:30 in the morning a muscular gust of wind swatted my tent sideways hard enough to mash the aluminum tent frame into my cot and jar me awake. The gust reversed, just as I opened my eyes, and the vacuum sucked the sidewall back out forcefully with the cracking sound of a snapped towel. Welcome to the day.

A peek outside through a short slice of opened zipper confirmed we had a little storm going on, though nothing exceptional, just light snow blown at right angles to everything vertical, just below freezing, and just enough of the thick, wet, white goo sticking to impress a few mental low notes and put me in the mood.

This is when I root around for just the right over-garments before exposing myself to the outside, having woken up fully dressed in the same clothes that I had worn for many days. My socks change, my jacket and hat selections change, but all else, right down to the skin, is more of a hassle to remove and replace than it's worth unless it's wet.

It's a good signal to send your clients to be the first one out of the cocoon, but with the Ruger crew, it was not likely. I wondered if they ever slept, or if they would one morning bring me warm bread and a frappe to reinforce the point they were all business. They were all of that, for sure, but more importantly they were just pleasant, fun and ambitious human beings. I can think of few gentlemen I have ever enjoyed more in the field. I wanted to make something happen for this crew. They had a lot of time and money invested and a short film they really wanted to produce.

I can't remember the exact content of the morning pep talk but there is no doubt it centered on the presumption that the blizzard we were in the belly of would pass by eventually, and no matter when that happened, we all needed to be back up high, in position, and tucked out of sight as soon as we could get there. The cameraman gave a thumbs up that all his gear, though tenuous, was reassembled, functioning and ready to cart back up to elevation.

During the walk up this time it began snowing, dampening sprits. One plus was it was slightly colder making the snow bounce off your clothing and gear rather than clinging to you like you were a ship slowly icing up in freezing spray. Visibility was about a mile, possibly a mile and a quarter, which did not allow us to actually see our familiar hunt location higher on the hill.

Believing that we were walking up only to be surrounded by overcast was depressing, and glassing the hill on the way up was a waste of time, but our spirits were lifted each time Randell remarked at how the previous day's visibility had ebbed and flowed making for several intermittent hunting opportunities.

After reaching the familiar bench and staking out positions that once again allowed four of us to scan separate parcels of mountain and flats, the waiting began. I could say that the "hunting" began, but in reality an instinctive hunter is hunting from the moment he departs camp with a gun over his shoulder, with eyes continually strained for the odd movement, or the discontinuous pattern broken by the glint of a horn, or a patch that in the distance reflects light ever-so-slightly differently, because perhaps it is brown fur and not decomposing foliage.

We waited.

Hour after hour we waited. The snowstorm proved itself to be a vigorous and snarling living beast with unpredictable moods and greatly varying levels of energy. Once again, the Bering Sea and the Pacific Ocean were locked in a fit of nastiness with both oceans trying to lay claim to the narrow sliver of wind beaten tundra and volcano sand that we were interlopers on.

Noon came and went. Lunch consisted of big handfuls of nuts, cheese squares, dried meat and the ever reliable CLIF Bar. Peanut butter chocolate, I want to say. It was hard to stay warm, just as it had been the day before, mostly because you can't get out of the path of it. You must spend every moment either glassing, or trying to, or shuffling around within your six foot square hide, like a caged animal, trying to build body heat and fight the demons of mental tedium.

Of course this is exactly when you ask yourself if you're still having fun, and the answer comes back....No, Not yet...

and any fun seems so distant a notion, so impossible really, that you know you have spent all day shitting yourself that any part of this is actually enjoyable. I like to hunt. I enjoy a physical challenge if it ends in success or failure. However, when it becomes just an exercise of waiting, while preserving body heat, while beating back boredom, then joining the North Korean Army has got to be more rewarding. And I'm thinking right about then, that I could do with much less of that in my life.

If only I could be walking it would feel, and be, more like hunting. But the game here is waiting. As so often it is. And so the hours drag on.

Each time the blowing snow eases or pauses altogether we are all on the glasses, commenting just to comment, on anything having to do with the break in the sky, or the steadily dimming of light that reverses itself each time the clouds lift, giving more length to the possible time we can stay in the game and perhaps make all of it count for something.

It was about 9 PM, with only about an hour remaining of shooter's light in our evening, when Danny drew my attention to what looked like the front quarter of a dark bear, head down, feeding, barely showing itself. It was well up the ascending slope directly in front of us and moving near a shallow gut that was full of taller foliage. The cameraman and I had taken the position facing uphill and the two Ruger executives were staked out facing downhill, viewing those slopes and the vast flats beyond.

I spent just a few moments on the glasses before walking the fifteen paces over the ridge to summon our two hunters over to my side for a look.

By then the bear had stepped out of the low foliage it was grubbing through and was slowly walking and sniffing along a lateral path about 600 yards above us. A lot of excitement built fast and all of us were soon whispering intel as we searched for visual clues that would reveal if it was a boar or, with the more time and inspection, would we end up seeing small cubs trailing their mother. We studied the bear.

It's such an advantage, being able to first see prey but not be seen. We had four sets of eyes all trying to pull details in the last bit of daylight. With whispered affirmations back and forth, we knew it was dark toned, boxy headed and had a nice broad ass that made its head and shoulders look smallish.

As it moved its head up to travel periodically, and then back to the sniffing and grubbing, we could make out a final clue that told me it was a mature bear, and on the larger side. That clue was the proportion of its neck to the body. A younger bear, or a leaner bear will show a lot of neck. An older, heavier bear will look like its head is sewed onto its massive shoulder muscles. It had all the markings of a boar. I believed it was certainly over an eight footer, and it may even go nine foot, but no bigger.

It was somewhat leggy, and it's unusual to kill a bear that looks very leggy and have it go high into the nine foot range. Another clue was simply the ease of movement as it worked its way over the tundra. A young bear has quicker and more nimble body movements in general. A larger, heavier bear gives an impression that it's doing some real work to move itself along. It's more deliberate in manner, less playful, or at least less wasteful of motion as though it were a commodity to be conserved.

My hunter was patient and wanted to know exactly what my opinions were of the animal. My take on the bear was that it was in the mid to high eight foot range and absolutely a nice trophy. The average size in this part of Alaska, after all the dust settles and all the bullshit walks, is about eight foot, perhaps five to six hundred pounds. Most guides will have a couple of nine footers to brag about, and possibly one or two more that makes ten foot, but they will have mostly a slew of beautiful healthy specimens in the eight foot range.

The bear we all had centered in our field glasses was a really nice example of a healthy Alaska Peninsula boar that any hunter would have been elated to bring home.

The decision was made that it would be the one. The cameraman had been polishing his tools for days now. He was as thrilled as anyone to finally be able to film a stalk and hopefully a kill. Our biggest problem was the bare naked space between us and the bear, 600 yards of short vegetated tundra with a few sprigs of alder here and there. The terrain was of two distinct grades.

It rose evenly and gently at about 15 degrees for half the distance in front of us, then it climbed sharply but evenly at about twice that pitch up to the bear and beyond, turning into grey scree and rock that was mostly hidden by snow.

Luckily, in the latter part of the day, a steady rain had eaten away the skimpy snow that had accumulated at mid and lower elevations so our camo colors would work well for the stalk. There was no covert way to close the gap using terrain cover. That left one option; let's call it the ultra-slow-crawl-when-nothing-is-looking.

Now this is truly one of my favorite stalks, I imagine because it's so blatant, bold and risky. But done correctly, it will work on a bear because they can't see very well at all. Nothing like a sheep, caribou or goat for example. If you tried it on those animals you would have to be almost perfectly matched with the right camo, and you would have to go very, very slowly. I have done it with some success on sheep but in a white suit of camo that they don't associate with danger, and by going so excruciatingly slow they can't detect movement even if they were staring right at you when you were "moving".

But such a stalk here, on this bear would take an hour to cover 400 yards. It would be dark in an hour. In this case I wanted to cover the 400 yards in 15 or 20 minutes, and that was entirely possible because we would belly crawl for a time, and then quickly pop up to shuffle forward on hands and knees every time we saw the bears head drop back down to feed. Danny set up his camera with its long lens at the 600 yard point and got ready to film it all.

With Mike and Randell ready, loaded and chambered, the three of us went prone and began to crawl head to toe, one man snug behind the other, in a tight formation so we appeared from a distance as one dark gash in the sod, if anything was discernable at all. I kept my field glasses out as I crawled on my elbows, stopping often, looking up to confirm the bear's head was down before I called out to the human snake behind me to slither ahead. Each time the bear's head went up and he took a few steps I gave a quick hand signal to halt.

We all got into a rhythm and slowly, slowly, began to chew through the yardage. The soft tundra was poorly drained in some places and when everyone halted on command we had water pooling up deeply in the indentations made by elbows and knees.

After about a third of the way I gave up trying to keep the water out of my sleeves, boots and front zipper. It was just going to be a cold sloppy mess to be suffered. When the bears head came up, we hit the deck. When the bear's head went down or turned away, we rapidly wormed our way through the swampy mattress of dead sedges and grass. As we closed in on the 300 yard mark of the 400 yard minimum crawl that had been our goal, we paused at a couple of different lumps in the tundra that looked like decent locations to shoot from. It was tempting.

The light was getting worse by the minute and there was actually a chance the bear would simply decide at any time to move off. And that can happen fast. Before you know what's happening you could be looking at not only a shot from 300 yards, which is too far, but a shot perhaps only at his big fat ass as he meanders away. So a good solid broadside shot in good light is always tempting...even at 300 yards.

It's all part of the thrill of a good stalk, the constant calculation and recalculation of your very best move at that instant.

Mike Fifer, the designated shooter for this bear, tried to get comfortable at a random, dryer-than-most hump of tundra at about 300 yards from the bear. Mike found the bear in his scope and I heard him pull off the safety.

I braced for the concussion....that never came. Mike didn't like it. I heard him exhale the breath he had pulled in anticipating a final aim and delivery. Actually, Mike was thinking exactly how I was thinking, which is a beautiful thing when it occurs. Communication without speech. Primal telepathy. I didn't like it either. We could do better.

I worry a lot about a shot at 300 yards when you are cold and tired and the light is marginal, when you are strained to find a comfortable position, and when you are so excited your heart beat pulses hard into your neck and face and lips and your balls have disappeared into your guts. This is not a great space, physical or emotional, from which to dispatch a first shot let alone a follow up shot. And you may need one, or you may need several. I like my hunters to be focused on what happens when the bear does not go down.

Without speaking he flips the safety back on and clicks the scope covers shut. I motion that we are once again going to be inching ahead. Just before we begin I put the glasses to my face and make sure the bear is still feeding slightly quartering away.

But just as I get ready to pull the glasses down the bear's head pops clearly into the sparsely lit circular image hitting my eyes. Its head snaps our direction, alert to something. As I begin to loudly whisper the "stop" command I see out of the corner of my eye that one of our guys had already been moving, just beginning his crawl. He was only trying to get back into formation after we had spread out a little to allow the possible shot.

I'm back up to the glasses instantly to try and determine if the bear had us. If he had caught a bit of that odd, blurry, slightly-out-of-place motion in the falling terrain 300 yards below it. The bear had us. His head was dead still, his attention purposeful. He bore down and tried to focus. We tried to not move the smallest muscle.

I kept the glasses glued to my face looking for any clue how things were going to unfold over the next several seconds. The bear would either begin to relax or it would likely bolt. A third possibility that happens once in a while is that they are curious and begin to move toward you. They will come and investigate.

But the highest probability is they will bolt and run and you will never see that bear again anytime that season, period. We waited... motionless. Seconds that felt like minutes, trying to breath shallow to not show large plumes of human condensate billowing up.

The bear was motionless, staring with every bit of his marginal eyesight to make something out of what he thought...he just saw. Each of us was exhaling a white plume of exhaust in the 38 or 40 degree air. Could the bear see that? The light wind dissipated it some, but was it still visible?

The breeze was helping us in other ways, now coming over the top of the mountain and towards us and eliminating any chance the bear would wind us.

I could feel the sweat pouring off my face as I strained to hold an awkward partially prone position on my elbows holding the glasses like a permanent fixture that was growing out of my skull. We did not dare try to prepare for a shot since any movement would be a dead giveaway. It was a standoff. But the bear...finally... blinked.

Slowly I saw him first turn his big coffee colored head to face forward...and then he took a couple steps ahead... then his head sank deliberately back into his business of hunting freshly greening roots. I called a lightly audible "all clear" and we all let the stress pour out of our limbs and tried to regain some level of comfort by changing positions, moving from elbows to palms, and getting ready to inch ahead.

One hundred and fifty yards. That's what I like to have. At one-fifty a bullet has a really nice smack of kick ass that is significantly stronger than it is at three hundred yards. If it loses 20 percent of its energy at one fifty, it's off 40 percent at three hundred. I'm a big fan of an explosive, shock and awe first strike on a big bear. I really like fifty yards with a shot into big chest bones. One can hope.

And a bullet delivered that close hits like a high speed train and dumps its massive amounts of muzzle energy all at once. And the bear still may not go right down. It often takes several. So I wanted to be close. Mike felt the same way. We wanted a clean kill and we needed to get close...so we tried. I gave the signal and we began to close the gap.

We had only covered another 30 yards, which probably took under ten minutes, and I'm back on the glasses, up on one elbow during one of my rhythmic, every-three-yards peeks for current status...of the coffee headed beast. But our luck was apparently over, because the bear is onto us again! The disrupted image in the glasses causes me to blurt a little louder than I should have "Stop"!

The bear is now turned towards us, his eyes have us pinned, and worse, he has alerted strongly enough that he has taken four or five steps in our direction and is searching the air for clues. And here we have the very obvious and ever-present problem with a straight-on stalk with zero cover. Everyone freezes. We wait. We hope. We wait. Perfectly still.

The bear is confused. He alternates between looking at us and looking behind him which appears to be an attempt to search the air again for a missing scent. As the bear takes a few steps away from us and almost seems distracted from us, the two Ruger hunters take their best prone positions, Randell as a backup shooter. Again, it's as though we have all done this before, made the calculation of what's ideal, verses what's possible, divided by the completely unknown factor of what this wild animal will do next...and how rapidly.

We all knew it was time to land some crosshairs on that bear or our chances could thin to nothing in a matter of seconds. We weren't going to get any closer. We all knew a shot from over two hundred sixty yards would be much better on a calm, still bear rather than a running one. You can't hardly shoot anything running from prone.

And it's a long, long fucking poke for a kneeling or (no thank you) an offhand shot. This was the calculation. It was now or never. It was now, or be reduced to telling the lame story from an armchair over beers... and chucking all the film footage already collected.

With the bear almost directly sideways and my guys settled into a reasonably stable firing position, it feels doable. I am about to put my glasses down to plug my ears, because I know what comes next. Kaboom comes next. But I was slow getting my hands to my head and the concussion and noise about detonates my noggin. The barrel was close, like five feet off my right ear cavity. Trying to ignore that painful concussion, I see the bear is hit, first shot, and is accelerating across the face of the hill, left to right, quartering towards us, and the opposite direction he was feeding. Instinctively I'm back on the glasses.

Then the bullets started flying in rapid succession. As they should have. The bear was hit, and probably well, judging by the shock reaction when the round landed. It had been very forward in the chest, almost the brisket, missing vital organs but hitting a lot of bone, and going on through to do its damage to the front leg that faced away from us, but missing bone on that limb. Lots of "Shock", but not quite a full load in the "Awe" department.

A running bear at over 250 yards is not easy to hit in any position. So the guns keep exploding in my ear as I'm trying to get a read through the field glasses if we have a dying bear or a highly motivated bear. I lost count of the rounds but I see two more of the several volleys are clear hits. After running seventy five yards with some real gusto, the big boar is hit better, again in the chest, the round breaking the front shoulder to pulp and travelling on, spraying its splintering and tumbling carnage into the lungs. The bear stumbled hard, picked itself up, stumbled again and then went down. And, if it matters, I was deaf.

The bear was a beauty. It was an 8 foot 10 inch boar, healthy, and with a heavy coat that was perfect in every aspect.

After a couple of hours of skinning by the light of our headlamps, it was black as ink and I knew it would be a chore to make our way down the hill and back to camp given the amount of high brush in the creek bottoms that we had to navigate. I decided it was not a trip I wanted to make with a 90 pound hide slopping around on my back. You stumble plenty with that weight in great visibility on accommodating terrain.

I decided to carry it down to the first bench where the pitch got steeper and then stash it for a return in the morning, which proved to be a smart move. We did have some trouble once in the creek bottom, in brush over our head, in the dark. Imagine that.

The walk was a straightforward affair when made in daylight and there was little chance of getting even the least bit disoriented. It was this fact that caused me to not bother carrying a GPS....which would have been nice to have.

It's a little embarrassing being the guide and stumbling around in the dark for even 10 minutes, looking for the way out of the maze when having a GPS would have eliminated any possibility of mistakes. Unfortunately I relearned that lesson, but thankfully not while sweating my ass off with 90 pounds of bear hide lashed to my back. The master did make it into camp, shortly after we had killed the bear and was waiting for us.

We had found success, and that success felt as much earned as it felt won. The shortness of the available time to hunt made the sum of the feat feel like a miracle. We had only one more day available to hunt before the group needed to return home. What were the chances?

But the determination on everyone's part is what made it feel earned. It was a dispiriting struggle to get there, with roadblocks at every turn, and the relentless press of the weather, both before and during the hunt. But it came together. No one planned to hunt bears in a blizzard in May, but we slugged it out. Getting all of it on commercial film and making a movie of it was, to me, one of the most improbable accomplishments. I'm definitely calling it a win.

Chapter 8

Sheepzilla in the Brooks (2007)

It was the first thin drops of rain that stirred me back to consciousness at 3 AM. This was not the best way to begin the day, the two of us spooning to be able to get cover under a five by seven plastic tarp. My partner Kurt and I were lying in the rocks waiting for light to break so we could continue our overnight stalk. At this point all of our logistical choices had been made and this spike camp above the spike camp would have to do for a couple more hours.

Anyone who has hunted sheep understands how far and how fast you travel is always governed by what you decide to carry up and what you can plan to reasonably carry back down after you include a dressed out sheep. The chance at a monster ram has the tendency to push these decisions toward the "light and fast" end of the spectrum. The weather had been very stable with little indication of radical change and this factored into the decisions about what we had to have verses what would be nice to have. We had decided to undertake this overnight stalk by going ultralight.

Hearing the rain begin to pick up pace, I mentally questioned if the tarp would keep both of us dry and allow a good start in the morning. Beyond that critical piece of equipment we had no overnight gear. The spare tent and sleeping bags had been deemed excess to what was absolutely necessary. A thin roll up pad to lie on was the only luxury and it did a fine job of insulating and smoothing the rocks.

As the wind picked up and the corners of the tarp began flapping loose, I knew there would be no more dozing off and the narrow comfort zone would begin to deteriorate as the water eventually found a way in. With just a couple more hours to go until there was enough light to shoot, I shifted my body to reshuffle the latest sore spots and once again reached to secure the tarp's corners blown loose at my feet and head. The "huddle and cover" arrangement would hold out most of the weather and what water was soaking in from the bottom could be suffered.

With any luck, the next time we stirred it would be light enough to at least move up from the temporary bivouac at the base of the hill to where the rams were last spotted. That would get our legs working again and build back some body heat.

After many years of looking for the fabled monster ram, and many years of coming home with lesser sheep, the thought of finally getting a crack at a really big one made it hard to stay put and even harder to try to get a couple hours of sleep. We had hiked hard all day until just after midnight, until it was too dark to move well or, more importantly, too dark to allow good visual tracking of the animals through a spotting scope. Curling up at the base of the last high pitch was the best way to get close, but not too close, and allow a quick and sure stalk in very early dim light.

It had been eight or nine years since first hearing rumors about an area that had been really productive for a couple of other Alaska hunters who worked the Brooks Range together. In sheep hunting circles there are a lot of rumors.

Rumors are often the fuel that drives the adventure, sometimes with all the intrigue of treasure hunting...the maps, the logistical hurdles, the dead end leads, and intentional misinformation...usually from other sheep hunters. As the story went this specific but still secret area produced a string of heavy rams for these two fellows but access was incredibly difficult. Tales of a couple of damaged airplanes and even broken bones...along with an airstrip strewn with some remnant of one of those broken airplanes, all played into the intrigue.

Legend had it that these two hunters who had located and pioneered the spot initially walked the many miles into it, for the first time, and then brushed out a crude airstrip somewhere near where they could hunt the sheep they were after. They then walked back out and brought their airplanes in.

Understand that if you were a detective trying to solve this riddle, it was for sure a cold case given that these hunters had not used the area for over ten years. And it was over several succeeding years that Kurt and I gathered bits of information any way we could.

We came to learn which Brooks Range fuel stop the fellows had staged out of and about how long their aircraft took to make a round trip when they had been staging and supplying their hunts. We learned that they had banged up a couple of airplanes at different times and that some remnants of one of these was likely left at the site. We heard this duo finally abandoned the area after one of these accidents ended in not only a badly damaged airplane but a broken leg. Who could even know how much of it was true?

That was about the extent of it. It wasn't much. But it did allow us to start drawing radius lines on a map, outward from the lodge, and hopefully get a closer idea. The area was immense. But the big payoffs and high risk sounded alluring. What could possibly be a bigger challenge than finding this spot and then thrashing our equipment trying to access it? Operating with this scant information, for four consecutive years and then again intermittently, my partner Kurt and I looked for this spot.

During those years we found and harvested several decent sheep but all were outside of where the hypothetical radius had fallen on a map. We found nothing within it. We had always been looking primarily for past evidence of a discernable man-made clearing in the chest high brush, a long gash cleared someplace near the bottom of the various hills and mountains within that hypothetical circle.

This gash we knew would be grown over with brush after all these years but should remain visible as evidence of a landing strip. It could be very faint, depending on how well the brush grew back in the brutal Arctic Circle climate.

Even when we were not specifically on a mission searching for this spot we made it a point, every time we flew through or hunted in the Brooks Range, to be aware of the radius we had plotted and take some extra time to look for that one telling visual clue. The hunting in the area in general was mediocre. There simply were not a lot of sheep, nor did they seem all that exceptional in size. But for several years running we managed to scratch out some success, never coming back empty handed, but never finding the secret spot.

Our preparation for the 2007 hunt began like any other year with heaps of physical training, a lot of attention to how to make our kit lighter, how to make our airplanes function at their limits, and much discussion about where to go. Would it be the Brooks again, or the Alaska Range, or the Wrangells?

We both had hyper-capable bush planes and we were both at the pinnacle of our skill when it came to making them perform. Being able to meet almost any physical demand is also a necessity. And when you are in the best physical condition of your life it's a great feeling, a confidence in yourself bordering on swagger but just short of arrogance. Whatever the mountains and the weather could throw at you, you were in it to win it.

Where we usually hunted the terrain demanded that you had the skill of being able to push a bush plane to its absolute limits. Our skills had been sharpened to a knife's edge after thousands of hours of practice flying and landing in the mountains. Together, the physical capacity and the tactical means form a unique and intoxicating capability. Nothing compares to it. Think about it for a moment. You roll out a map of Alaska on your kitchen table and no matter where on it you choose to stick a pin, you have the method, the means and the talent to put yourself there with a pile of gear. How many people get to do that?

Over the endless talks of where to go, Kurt and I kept coming back to how much we loved the mostly good weather in the Brooks, those endless sunny, hot days in early August that many times have you hiking in nothing but your boxer shorts and your pack. There is nothing like getting a sunburn above the Arctic Circle. The opportunity to land a plane high was alluring, something you can more often do in the Brooks. What would have been jagged peaks topping the mountains several million years ago have been eroded away in many cases leaving you with something contoured enough that you can attempt to land an airplane on it.

It sure beats walking from the bottom, if even you can find a suitable place in the bottom to land. Many times you can't. You either land on a rocky spine, at altitude, or you don't hunt it. It had been a couple years since we hunted the Brooks or looked for the secret motherlode. A decision was made after plenty of late night Merlot-infused arm waving and storytelling.

We were going to do our thing in the Brooks.

Our sheep hunting mission began as it almost always did, flying north three or four days before the season opens on the tenth of August. We would fly from Palmer to the deeply interior city of Fairbanks nonstop, refuel, and continued north to the Arctic Circle. Hour after hour we guided the airplanes through the mountains, into the passes beside the legendary Mt. Denali, over the massive Tanana Flats, across the Yukon River following landmarks and our instruments to reach each plotted waypoint. We had launched in good weather which is not something you could often count on in South Central Alaska with its coastal influences.

It is a highly exciting time, finally pushing off, but at the same time it's relaxing; you look forward to a long, steady, methodical day behind the controls. You have it down to a science. The sky is generally clear, the winds spirited but cooperative. You kill the time more often than not by jabbering on the radio between the airplanes, keeping each other company. This eight or ten hour drawn out bullshit session can be technical, strategic or even just the bush pilots' equivalent of barber shop small talk.

SSSClick: "Unit 1 to unit 2....go to private."

Click: "Roger unit 1....frequency change to private."

There is a dead space between us as we both switch our radios to a covert channel.

SSSClick: "Robert, are you there?.... Nice air tonight."

Click: "Yo baby. I got you. For sure it's perfect".

SSSClick: "We are making good time."

Click: "We're killing it!"

SSSClick: "What RPM setting are you running?"

Click: "I'm at 2450."

SSSClick: "I have been at 2400 since we crossed the Yukon River."

Click: "My prop is a little flatter – that must be it."

SSSClick: "How's your temp?"

Click: "I have been holding tight at 190, but jumping up to about 205 in those steep climbs getting through Denali. Running nice and cool".

SSSClick: "Me too. 185 to 195." "I'm indicating 92 airspeed... ground speed is showing 101. Gotta love it."

Click: "I'll take all of that I can get! A nine mile an hour tailwind!"

SSSClick: "Free money."

Click: "Hahaha...we are printing it baby!

Printing...Free...Money!"

SSSClick: "I'm going to climb. At 9,000 it's supposed to be even better."

Click: "I'll hang here at 6500. I'll throttle back some so I don't get too far ahead when you climb."

SSSClick: "Roger that. I'll tell you if there is more tail-wind to be had."

Click: "By the way, how's your burn?"

SSSClick: "Let's see. We are an hour and a half out of Fairbanks and I'm still above three quarters in both tanks."

Click: "Eight gallons an hour probably. I show almost full still. But these sixty gallon tanks always read fat, except when they read skinny. Which means... I can never tell for sure."

SSSClick: "Going up.......Be in touch."

Click: "Turn all your strobes on so I can keep track of you."

SSSClick: "There you go. Merry Christmas."

Click: "I may have to piss before we get all the way there, can't tell for sure. Do you want to come down with me and take a break if I can find a place? Or do you want me to catch up?"

SSSClick: "I'm good, and I don't want to lose all this altitude. Can't you find a Ziploc bag or something to piss in?"

Click: "The coffee pot is somewhere packed right behind my seat. I think I can reach that. But man I get tired of pissing down my leg and spilling all over the seat."

SSSClick: "It's not that bumpy. Don't go down. It's getting dark enough you may not be able to find me again until we both meet at the landing strip."

Click: "Haha....Should have brought a few diapers."

SSSClick: "Use the coffee pot."

Click: "If you don't mind drinking my coffee tomorrow..."

SSSClick: "I'll let you have the first couple pots."

Click: "Where you at?"

SSSClick: "Eighty two hundred."

Click: "Any tailwind up there?"

SSSClick: "Let me level off for a sec. Looks like 104 up here, that's 12 MPH on the tail! Money! Printing it!"

Click: "I'm on my way up."

SSSClick: "OK. Then I'll go on up to ten thousand and hunt for more. See you at ten."

Eventually, but never soon enough, we can see the outlines of the Brooks etching a dark silhouette onto the late evening sky. It's still 100 miles away. That means another hour of squirming around on a tired, sore, sweaty pair of ass cheeks before getting the planes down on the river bar and uncoiling our bodies from the confines of the small cockpit. There is nothing comfortable about the solitary confinement of a Piper Super Cub.

Alaska Raw

By the time we arrive over our usual landing spot, it is just before midnight. But it's clear, the wind is a whisper tugging small ripples into the surface of the deep blue river and there is still enough ambient light in the Arctic sky to read a newspaper.

The river bar is usually plenty long, about 900 feet when the water is low. As we fly over we notice the river is up. It had been raining days earlier, and our normal 900 feet has shrunk to about 600.

This is still plenty but when you are very heavy, as we were, now you have to pay attention.

With trees on the bank at both ends of the strip, and plenty of running water front, back and left, a couple of dead-tired pilots could easily get complacent and make a mistake. It all happens so fast, and it's often when you get lazy.

Flying into base camp you are always heavy. Everything you may possibly need for a week or two in the mountains is only about a quarter of that load. The rest is fuel. Lots and lots of fuel. The long range tanks built into the airplane would still be half full on arrival (from topping off at intermittent fuel stops) but the area that a passenger would normally occupy, the back seat, is removed, and this area is crammed with five gallon jugs of aviation fuel stacked wide and high.

I had come into this strip before with as much as 110 gallons, or 660 pounds. You are one big ass bomb flying along at 100 miles an hour looking for a spark. We were not quite that heavy this time but close. So we were jolted out of a relatively complacent eight hour slog by a stiff whiff of reality. Man and machine had to perform. We had to wake up and slip these airplanes into a narrow gravel bar with barriers on all four sides. It's all part of the experience. Hours and hours of boredom punctuated by a few moments of exhilaration.

It went just fine.

We hastily propped up a two-man mountaineering tent, rolled out our sleeping bags and left the rest for daylight. We were in the zone. Surrounded by mountains and opportunity. For hunters, the zone is a place where the next level of anticipation begins to take over and drive your thoughts, attitude and behavior. There is a refinement of purpose that starts to block absolutely all else out of your head. The mission becomes everything. It's magical.

In the morning we took some time to unload and get organized. The sun was up and building towards a 70 degree afternoon. We split the gear into two piles, one each for main and spike camps. The river bar would be our staging ground and main camp, though we rarely stayed overnight there.

A tent there held extra supplies and gear and the most of the fuel was stacked next to it. Gear for a spike camp and several days food was sorted, repacked and readied to go back into the airplanes after we made some runs to stock up on even more fuel. We had a stash of fuel delivered in advance to a point on the Dalton Highway that we could pick up and fly back to our base camp. If not for that stash we would be stuck paying the Arctic Circle rate up there which was $9 dollars per gallon.

By the time we were done hauling fuel that day we had 200 gallons. That was a good start but we may require even more eventually. With the engines idled way back as we operate them when spotting sheep, the airplanes burn about five gallons an hour each. That was 40 hours total, or 20 per airplane. That's a lot of grinding around in the air but sometimes it takes a lot. We did a little spotting as we were coming and going ferrying fuel but the real hunting would begin the next morning.

And what a morning it was. What a charmed life it was.

Wall to wall blue skies, a manageable north wind of about 20 miles per hour twisting down river to greet us, and a forecast of an ongoing high pressure throughout the Eastern Brooks Range. The airplanes were packed, base camp secured, a quick cup of coffee and some oatmeal and it was game on.

That day we went back to where we had often seen a few decent sheep and where Kurt had once killed a 41 inch beauty. Just finally being in the air and actually hunting was a kick.

We split up and methodically combed mountain after mountain, slope after slope, canyon after canyon, with the keen eye of a predator.

Chattering back and forth on the radio, we compared notes, coordinates and strategy. After half a day of flying we located a string of five rams, four of which were full curl, and one looked especially sweet from the air. We would have to get on the ground and hunt it, get close, and get a spotting scope on it to be sure. Where these animals were, it would require landing on the very top of the mountain on a small, rough flat spot about 500 feet long. Then the hike would be mostly lateral and about two miles, if they stayed put. This was not at all a difficult effort as sheep hunts go.

The next step was to fly back out to base camp to optimize our load considering the high altitude landing that had to happen. Fuel had to be siphoned out of the airplanes and back into five gallon cans until we had the bare minimum weight...but still had enough to get us from the base camp to the spike camp ridge and perhaps three gallons reserve. The airplanes perform exponentially better when empty.

We took just one rifle between us, as we usually did, along with an ultralight tent, pads, sleeping bags, freeze dried food and a small cook stove. All of that packing completed, we shoved off again for the high strip and a chance for at least one nice sheep. The flight was only twenty minutes.

Once there, both of us took several test passes down low over the short flat landing spot, testing the wind direction and how the wave effect of the wind actually bent it in mysterious ways as it flowed like water over the mountain ridge. The landing strip was at 4,700 feet. It was as technical and difficult a spot as we usually attempt just about anywhere.

It was clear. We had to go in upwind, but that direction was also slightly down grade, making the braking more difficult. The wind was at about 20 so it slowed you down well. But the wind was coming over the mountain in a big laminar wave and curling hard downward at the front lip of the approach, which was a steep cliff feature. In a perfect, low, slow approach heading toward the cliff, the wave wanted to suck you down with it unless you added gobs of power right at a critically timed moment. If you carried any more than the minimum speed on the approach you would never get it stopped before shooting off the far edge. If you carried too little speed the wave would suck you down at the last moment and you would not clear the lip of the cliff.

If felt nasty. But we didn't want to keep the sheep waiting. After repeated test approaches, mocking a landing but bailing out at the very last moment, we figured out how to time the burst of power at the threshold to outgun the sinking wave. It was all very delicate. We got the planes in without breaking anything. We set up camp and spent an hour filling gunny sacks with rocks to form dead weight anchors that the wings and tail could be lashed to.

The tent was popping and cracking in the steady wind that would scour the mountaintop most of the night. A bottle of red wine in the cargo had survived the landing nicely and soon Kurt and I were sporting a warm alcohol buzz and relaxing in our sleeping bags. We needed a good night's sleep. You never sleep worth a shit when you are lying in the rocks and your tent is barking like a savage in your ears hour after hour. Stuffing yourself with a meal loaded with fat and lots of red wine helps.

I'll never understand why having a stomach full of red wine which is then floating a thick lump of gooey animal lard is such a great sleep aid. But it is. Like a grenade to the heart.

That morning was opening day of the season. We got up early and began a long side-hill hike into the area the five rams were roaming around in. With luck we would spot them at some distance and be able to spend a bunch of time critiquing their strengths and weaknesses through a spotting scope. By about 3 PM we were closing in on the last bump that separated them from us, or so we thought. But they had actually moved our way without us detecting it.

As we walked along, generally unprepared for any big surprises, Kurt was in front and caught a glimpse of white flashing around a rock pile just 80 yards ahead of us. He alerted me and we instantly guessed we had spooked them. Another 150 yards ahead of us lay the ridge we believed they should have been grazing behind.

The flash of white was the last of the five rams going around a rock pile on the far left hand side of that ridge... and over it. We sprinted the 80 yards to get a peek over the ridge. In an instant we were there, peering over the ridge and watching the five sheep aligned neatly one behind the other and trotting downhill and quartering left. They are in the wide open at just about 100 yards.

We only have one rifle as per plan. Kurt has it and it's chambered and leveled already and he has the string of rams drawn into his scope. I instantly have them in my field glasses. We are both breathless and pouring sweat from the exertion. We both understand the urgency of the next 15 seconds.

Kurt: "Is it the second one back?"   "IS IT!!?"

Me: "I think so, maybe...probably."

The sheep are now at 150 and moving along briskly. Things need to happen very quickly.

Kurt: "FUCK!....PROBABLY?.... PROBABLY?   I think its number two. Is that the big one? CONFIRM!"

Me: "I think so, but the first one has a lot of curl on its left!"

The sheep are now at 200, still going away at 30 degrees off dead ahead. They are startled but not in a full blown panic.

Kurt: "Did you get a good look? CAN YOU SEE?"

Me: "Oh, it turned, no, no.....nooo, IT'S NOT THE FIRST ONE, it's broomed (damaged) on the right horn! I can see it! The big one wasn't broomed! "It's....."

CRACK BOOM

A millisecond after reaching consensus on which in the string was the larger ram an explosion inside Kurt's rifle sent a slim 140 grain bit of copper and lead down the slope and through both lungs of the trotting animal. It was quite a nice shot considering the angle, distance and that it was moving. The fatally wounded ram appeared to barely have noticed the bullet swiftly passing through its soft organs. In my glasses I could see blood misting out of the hole in the ram's ribcage with each big lung full of expelled air. But it kept on going without missing a step.

The entire string, now on high alert, picked up their pace and kept running for another hundred yards until the wounded ram slowed and fell out of formation, stumbled, and then tumbled end over end a good distance down the steep scree slope.

We had ourselves a nice sheep.

After making our way down to it we confirmed it was the right animal. The several passes in the airplane the day before gave us a lasting visual impression that matched what we now saw on the ground. Having made the decision in a big rush after first having blown the stalk, the fact that we got the right one was really fortunate, and a huge relief. It was not as big as we had hoped. It had looked like it could have been a little larger during our overhead spotting, but it was still 38 inch plus and no meat was damaged which was a satisfying result. We took a slug of pictures and just hung out re-narrating the event start to finish a few times and bathing in the hot Arctic sun. We were taking in the moment before getting down to the work. Once the animal was finally dressed out and lashed to pack frames we began the hike backwards to our spike camp.

Getting back to the spike we split up the sheep meat into the two airplanes in a further effort to keep the birds light on takeoff. The little bit of camp we had was broken down and all of it was hauled back to base camp on the lower river bar. After an overnight rest and dosing with oatmeal, cheese and coffee, it was time to find a second sheep. We decided to split up.

I went east to fly more country while Kurt went west and back to areas within the "radius", back to the core location we had always believed held the fabled Sheepzilla rams.

With two airplanes we covered a lot of terrain, each of us selecting a range to start looking about 20 miles apart. I was on four more legal rams within just a couple of hours. They were hard to see well, planted deep in a steep canyon. I was making a few more passes to try to get nearer to them and get a better look when the radio hissed to life.

SSSClick: "Oh Man...."

I heard Kurt's voice coming through my headset clearly. Then...pure silence.

Click:"Kurt? What is it?"

SSSClick: "Oh Man... Ohhh... Man!" "Fuck Oh dear!"

You could hear the surprise, then the disbelief, and then satisfaction all rolled up in those few words.

It was sounding to me like the several years of searching could possibly be headed towards something big.

Click: "What is it?" Kurt? What do you have? How big?..... Kurt? "How Big? KURT?"

SSSClick: "Oh my god!.... I'm going around them again, I don't know yet, but these two sheep are fucking hogs.... Come this way."

Kurt had spotted what turned out to be the largest rams either of us had ever seen in the field, or would ever see in our lifetime. I immediately broke off from eyeballing the group of four very respectable rams I had been surveying and headed his direction. My mind went where it always goes first at a time like this, to thoughts of how tough it would be to find a way in. It's always the same singular calculation once you find something sheep hunting; can you get anywhere near them with an airplane? Within five or six miles is about where we draw the line. That's as far as we want to carry a camp and sheep back from. After you have done that once or twice you are sufficiently humbled.

Sometimes in five or six miles as the crow flies you climb and descend and repeat this many times, so the distance is actually far greater.

As I plotted a GPS course to Kurt's coordinates I pressed for more detail.

Click: "Whaaadya got?" "KURT. TALK TO ME."

SSSClick: "I'm just coming around them again now, a little lower, so maybe I can tell you in a second. The two are just over the edge at the absolute top of a spine, but tucked in tight to the rocks on the lee side. The wind is coming over the spine pretty hard, I can't get close enough to see really well without taking a beating, but I'm going to try coming in upwind, lower, and then climb hard while I try to get a look. Two of us together in one airplane would be the trick."

This terrain avoidance maneuver sounded a lot like our last mountain top landing. There is seldom a dull moment once you are onto some rams.

Thirty seconds pass.

SSSClick: "MY GOD...THESE ARE ABSOLUTE PIGS."

After confirming the two sheep were true monsters, the next step was to put together a winning plan. There was really no sense in my going over there and having two aircraft possibly disturbing the sheep. I was near our main camp location by then, about to pass high over it on the way to the sheep, when we both decided over the radio to meet at that camp and make a plan, so I corkscrewed straight down from altitude and went into base camp. Fifteen minutes later Kurt came quietly gliding in for a river bar landing, the tail trimmed perfectly, flaps down full, power pulled off, quick to find the brakes.

While I was understandably elated to be getting a chance at a big sheep after 15 years of hunting and killing average ones, Kurt had some reservations about me killing this one. Let me explain...it goes like this: Kurt had previously been a big game guide. He was both my neighbor and hunting partner for years and we had known each other for a very long time. Kurt explained that this specific sheep could be worth as much as $200 thousand to the right European oligarch. And Kurt possessed such a Rolodex.

The sheep was that big. As I understood it, the deal to be cut with such a client would likely be a sliding scale trophy fee charged based on how big it actually was once it was in the bag. The fee may start at $50 thousand with some still exceptional sizes established at that price range, and then end up at $200 thousand if it proved to be among-the-largest-in-the-world size. Further, it would have to be brokered through the local guide that held that specific area in his portfolio, another set of long fingers in the pot.

This was all way over my paygrade, but in general terms, in such a scheme I would stay put in the field and Kurt would run back to civilization that very day and find the appropriate guide to book the hunt. That guide would get the Europeans to the site within just a couple of days.

I would get my share, whatever that was, which figure I can't remember probably because I never seriously considered giving it up for money. I knew that the minute I agreed to pimp my ram for cash the entire venture would be spinning out of my control and I would end up, in the end, with a bologna sandwich and a sore ass. To all of that noise I simply said: "I'm eating this sheep." That did not completely end the overtures but tamped them down long enough that we continued planning our moves.

There was a nearby spine we thought we could possibly land on. It was high, short and bumpy, and if we used it, it would be as challenging a location as we had ever landed a bush plane. We prepared so we could land high if it looked good, or low, and hike more, if we thought there was no other way. Several hours were spent debating, sorting, deciding and re-deciding what could be left behind and still accommodate both possible ingress scenarios. Everything was shed from the airplanes but a spike tent and bags, one rifle, provisions and water for two days, optics and gear to anchor the aircraft down.

One hundred percent of the fuel was drained off into spare plastic jugs so we could accurately measure the volume of what we needed to reload and no more. We worked at getting super light, a requirement to land short, or rough, or both, at altitude. If landing somewhere in the bottom proved to be our only option, so be it. We were prepared for either.

It was time for both of us to take an extensive and critical look at the landing spots and see if we could align our respective appetites for risk. Wadding up a one hundred thousand dollar plus airplane is a complete buzz kill.

Dying in one that catches fire while your legs are helplessly pinned in the bent cockpit is never too far from consideration either. Dying happens with some regularity in the sheep hunting business, and when it does, it's usually in an airplane. We launched in the late afternoon, got over to the actual hunt area, and began the most important work that ever takes place, figuring out a safe way in.

As we looked over the possibilities in the brushy bottom drainages that lie on either side of the mountain that the sheep were parked on, something caught my eye. It was so faint a mark in the landscape you had to look hard to see it. But once you did, it was unmistakable.

It was the overgrown remains of a short, crooked airstrip, no more than 350 feet long, right in the very bottom of the brushy creek bed. This was a stunning find. It was 2,500 feet directly below the sheep. It couldn't be a coincidence. After a closer pass I saw in the brush at the far end there was a skeletal framework of rusted tubing, the tail section of what was, years ago, a functioning bush plane.

After these many years of looking, we had finally found the secret spot, having been led there first by stumbling upon the monster sheep! This was of course exactly backwards from how we dreamt we would find it. The strip was too grown up to be useful, and it was short, and it was a lethal looking dog leg affair with about 150 feet running straight down the rough creek bed before it twisted off 20 degrees left for the last 200 feet to avoid some big boulders.

To use it would have required walking in and re-cutting the brush. And even then it would still suck. There was one more option to consider, and that was walking all the way in from a landing out on a main river that these creek tributaries fed. It was eight miles as the crow flew and about eleven on a manageable hiking track. Time was a big consideration.

If we took three days to walk in, brush out the strip, and walk out, then spend another night before flying in, would the sheep wait for us? That was very hard to know, but our karma is just not that good.

By process of elimination it looked like the landing for the Sheepzilla ram would be made at altitude on a high spine, if at all. The high ridge several miles south of the rams that Kurt had spotted had looked promising at first glance.

The potential touchdown location was actually a saddle with sharp inclines on both ends. The inclines trapped a narrow swayback spine that was about 500 feet long. Subtracting rough terrain on both ends, and accounting for an awkward approach, about 300 feet were left to work with.

We both made pass after pass for the better part of 20 minutes testing the wind and surveying each and every bump over and over, trying to catch terrain shadows from every angle possible to allow a true picture of the landing zone to become mentally imprinted. This spot was high, rough, short and had terminal obstructions on both ends. You would tightly slip around the initial obstruction on the way in to land, and plan to get stopped before running into the obstruction at the opposite end. There would be no do-overs or second chances once you chopped the power on final. It's what's known in the business as "land it or lose it." Like putting all your money on red and telling the man to spin the wheel, double or nothing.

To make it all work and miss most of the big bumps on the approach end, and to slip the airplane tightly around the big terrain feature coming in, the landings were made by going about 20 degrees diagonal to the direction of the spine, rather than lining up directly with it. Think of a giant saddle on a horse, but it's a really skinny horse. And you have to clear the back lip of the saddle on the way in and not hit the horn if your run-out is too long.

And the spine, just like a saddle, rolled off at a good sloping pitch on both sides. And since you are landing in the saddle diagonally, you have to target the touchdown point just below the spine, slightly on the left side...which means you were partially side-hill, left wing tilting down on touchdown. Then you roll up and across the ridgeline, momentarily wings level, then rolling on your transition to the right hand side of the spine, and end up with the opposite wing tilting down.

Kurt went in first.

He did a great job, hitting the mark and using up only about 80 percent of the available room. I circled and watched, sweating like a farm animal. After one final look I lined up to come in. With a quartering and intermittent headwind of about 8 MPH, the trick was to use the wind to your advantage, but not get caught in any possible lull of that wind, or behind the wind "shadow" of the steep mountain in front of you....during the final seconds of the approach.

If you did that you could prematurely settle in too short, stuffing it into some of the rougher ground at the landing threshold. This may even kick your ass altogether, leaving the airplane and your panties bunched up in a wad. There was an exceptionally narrow performance window.

I came in ever so slightly under that curve, and was approaching in a momentary ebb of wind flowing over the spine. This resulted in a touch down thirty feet early and in some of the rougher zone. Since my touchdown was short, this gave me more total room to runout, but it was rougher and much, much harder on the airplane. I gritted my teeth once I chopped the power because the bottom instantly fell out of my stomach as it followed the airplane down to impact.

The plane hit, I jammed on the brakes, and listened to the banging of fabulously expensive parts beating a path through nearly every chuckhole, boulder and divot we had been trying to miss. The plane bounced hard a few times, but I kept the stick buried in my lap and the nose up and the prop out of the rocks. It worked.

My bird rolled, skidded, bounced and shimmied to a final stop just 100 feet before becoming a mountaintop slag heap, a permanent monument to how sheep hunting can go really wrong, really fast. "Landing" is really too generous a word to describe what looked and felt a lot like a controlled crash.

Vegas could never be as fun. The odds there are too close to even.

So there we were. We had two planes in the zone and nothing broken. The sun was beating down. The sheep were several miles away and a thousand feet above us. It was mostly a slightly rising lateral hike to get on them. I was washed by a sense of relief. Getting out of the airplane, shaken and sweat soaked from a gut full of stress, I peeled off my shirt and pulled in a few deep breaths. Kurt was able to get it all on video so whenever I get too relaxed at home and want a chest full of anxiety and to practice my panic attacks, I can just pop that landing footage into the DVD player.

With both airplanes down safely we began making quick preparations to anchor them to the ridge. As always, if the wind picked up it could be trouble, the airplanes were completely exposed with no way to get any cover. We repeated the exercise of gathering loose stones and filling up several duffel bags for the wings and tail. This was usually good for forty to fifty miles an hour.

If the wind picked up during the night to more than that, the party would be over. This was a risk we had to take after choosing to bivouac overnight on the exposed spine. In a couple of hours we had everything anchored down; our spike camp was pitched, and we were ready to make a play. Without warning and against the wisdom of our most recent forecast, clouds were now forming overhead. The weather was clearly changing but the wind stayed down.

We set off with the minimum gear, planning to walk carefully until late night toward the place we had last seen the sheep, to get into bivouac position in the dark below them, and make our last move just as soon as light allowed it the next morning.

At various points along the way we were able to find the sheep in the spotting scope. They were laying down right at the pinnacle of the mountain, their shapes easily visible against the darkening blue sky behind them.

As the rain rattled down on the tarp over my head I reflected on how well things had gone so far. Water was running off the edges of the tarp and leaking in from the sides. We were slowly getting wet from the bottom as well with runoff from the scree slope above. There was not much spare heat left in my core and shivering began slowly and intermittently as it always does. I thought to myself, we are so close, it doesn't really matter, we will warm up when we get on our feet again. I couldn't have spent another four or five hours in that shape, getting wetter and losing more and more body heat, but it was almost over.

It was 3:30 AM. There would be no more sleep, just another hour or so of shivering, withdrawn to a fetal ball and staring at the tarp pulled up over my face. Soon we would try to relocate the rams in a spotting scope and begin a final stalk. By 4:30 enough faint light was reflecting off the grey scree to allow us to see the outlines of at least each other. The decision was made to fold up the tarp and strike out.

Moving up the mountain with a slight cross angle would take us up, over, and across several spine ridges that ran top to bottom all along the mountain. Working up to the edge of each one, we paused and carefully scanned each draw in the pale light. It would be easy to stumble into the animals or have them see or hear us before getting within shooting range, blowing it all. That fear felt all too familiar.

We climbed for less than half an hour before catching a hint of something pure white against the dark grey voids of space, the very top edge of a ram's back was showing, just as we crested another of the several ridges. Two rams, both on their feet, showed themselves at 250 yards, slightly uphill, their heads down grazing.

Slowly backing down, retracing our steps behind the ridge to stay out of view, we were able to pick a path in the next draw over to continue our upward stalk and close the vertical distance. Picking an outcropping above us that could be used as cover and eventually a shooting nest, we carefully moved for it in complete silence.

The cover provided by the draw became ever more shallow as we crept up it, so shallow that we needed to eventually belly crawl to reach the outcropping. Our final position at that point was just above two big rams and 150 yards.

It would be another twenty minutes to get enough light out of the heavily overcast sky to determine positively if they were the same sheep spotted the day before, and then which of the two was actually Sheepzilla. We lay quietly in the drizzle and watched the blurry, shadowy outlines formed by the feeding animals. In this low light, with a river of endorphins running through your brain, you have to be extra careful. In the shadows your eyes can begin to see what your brain wants them to see. Both rams were very big. One was the bigger.

Minute after minute ticked by as we strained to catch any light reflecting off the ram's horns which would settle it for sure. Was it the one in the lead, or the one behind it? (Here we go again) From the several times we were able to view them in the spotting scope we knew they were very close to the same size, probably within two inches. But in the sniper's perch we had time to wait.

The animals were moving ever so slowly left to right, heads down still, feeding in the calm. We could finally tell the big ram was the one leading. The second one, very nearly its clone, fell slightly short of his companion's total mass. The sheer volume of horn on either of the sheep was nothing short of gob smacking. These two animals were at the very top of their class.

I centered the scope's crosshairs in a generous broadside of the sheep's chest. It always seems out of place to hear the thundering crack of a high powered rifle after hours upon hours of tranquility. The first shot split the still air with an outrageous bark that reported off the canyon walls and reverberated throughout the close valley. Anything loitering around in the dusk was now fully awake. A large and visible patch of white hair flew up from the bullet's impact and disappeared over the back of the ram. The visible flying fur was a little odd but it reinforced that the sheep was hit.

The bigger sheep and its near clone lunged forward at full speed across the steep mountain slope. I was so rested during the shot and before it, and so completely relaxed, having spent so much time waiting for enough light to gauge the animals, that I was one hundred percent confident the bullet went through the ribs as intended.

I knew it. I was 150 yards and slightly above the ram when I slowly squeezed off the shot, and from a prone position, with a solid rest. The sheep was dead on its feet. Period. You just know these things if you are a hunter. It was all over.

I calmly waited for it to bleed out and then topple over. But...it kept going.

Kurt: "Did you hit it?"

Me: "Oh yea. Square."

Instinctively I had already jacked another round in but there was no need. It was going down, any second now. But then again... it was looking pretty damn healthy for a mortally wounded animal, a thought I tucked away in the back of my otherwise confident head. I kept the animal in my scope to follow its progress...so I could watch it fall.

Kurt: "Shoot him again!? Did you hit him!!?"

Me: "He is hit! I hate to ruin any more meat. Did you see all that hide flying? He's done...........A goner."

Both sheep were still running; seconds had passed. Now, I was having some doubts. I followed the ram with my crosshairs and took aim as it moved swiftly over the rocks. THE RAM LOOKED FRESH! What the hell! They were both approaching a ridge feature that they would soon disappear behind.

Kurt: "Shoot! SHOOT.... AGAIN!"

As it happened, the two sheep slowed from a full run, but only for just three to four seconds. They stood almost still at about 250 yards, allowing me one more brief chance to get it done. In that split second pause the ram turned its body slightly sideways and its head backward to look back at us. My crosshairs were already locked onto its ribcage.

I took a deep breath, exhaled half, held on point, and squeezed. The explosion sent another lethal payload down the barrel and on its long flight across the mountain slope. One quarter of a second after leaving the barrel the bullet struck hide and flesh. The sheep instantly fell and tumbled down the slope. I thought it strange that all four of its legs kept up a flat out running movement as it rolled and tumbled to a stop 500 yards lower downslope. This motion looked unnatural, like a windup toy.

On its side now, its fall arrested by a narrow ledge, the legs kept up the mock run like it was having a bad dream. It was vigorous, and the vigorousness alone made it seem out of place. I waited for it to stop, sure that it was now hit mortally. The running legs continued for way too long. It then tried to get up, seemingly getting a second wind. In disbelief, I chambered a third round. It would be an even longer shot since it had rolled downhill, if I had to take it.

I was just about to shoot but finally it fell onto its back again, and then the running-leg-spasm slowed, and then it stopped. It's not unusual to have some amount of involuntary reaction from an animal when it's being killed violently, but this went on too long, and I have seen a lot of animals die. I was interested in seeing where and how badly the sheep was hit. We gathered up our optics and our packs and started the side-hill hike over to the ram. As we exposed ourselves the second sheep finally ran off beyond view. When we got to the ram it was still moving! I hesitated to shoot again or cut its throat because either action makes its own kind of mess. It was very close to dead so we just held tight and waited a few minutes. The autopsy was enlightening.

The first shot had almost missed. It nicked down just to the bone of a vertebra high in the hump between its shoulders, blowing out a two inch round patch of only hide and hair. The wound was not deep enough to really bleed much but instead just left a bald, reddish pink hole on its backbone the size of a golf ball. So that shot was fifteen inches high and directly above my intended mark.

Round number two, when I was again aiming for the lungs, had grazed the very top of the ram's neck, largely a superficial wound, and then travelled into the very edge of the jaw under its ear, and then down through its lower rear jaw, on the other side, shattering it. That round was also 15 inches high and barely, barely hit the animal. I came extremely close to missing with both shots. That's why the ram was so stunned, its legs spending so long running in an unconscious fit of death throes. It was knocked silly by the shot to the back end of the jaw and eventually bled out from those wounds.

The sheep of a lifetime was nearly lost. That took a while to sink in.

Though we knew this was a very big animal, nothing prepared me for what I saw as I approached it. From the front, the grandness of this ram caused a silence between Kurt and me that lasted a while.

No one said a word; we just looked at it in awe. It was broomed on one side but otherwise balanced, symmetric and breathtakingly beautiful. Viewed from the back the horns looked like two enormous baseball bats emerging from the head, holding the mass all the way down to the jaw. One side was broomed at 43 inches, testimony to the many battles it had fought and no doubt won.

The other side ran out to 46 1/ 4 inches. The initial Boone and Crockett score was 177 and 2/8 with a final score after it dried and stabilized at 176 and 3/8.

During the pack back to the airplanes the ceiling kept dropping and the rain picked up. It was a little worrisome because if the ceiling came down another 1,000 feet we would be trapped on the spine, unable to fly off of it due to lack of visibility. We crossed our fingers and trudged on. Within five hours we were back in camp. Unfortunately in that five hours the mist and fog had crept in and settled over our landing strip and unwound any hope of getting back to our main camp. We now had to wait. It could be hours, or days. It was impossible to know.

The overall vibe from taking the big ram was so positive that I could not have cared less. We crawled in the tiny tent and stripped off our wet clothes. Getting into our bags to keep warm and wait it out was all we could do. As tired as we both were, we blinked out within a few minutes, just about as soon as our body temperature rose enough to allow our brains to signal it was OK to stop running all that heat generating machinery at full speed.

I was out for hours and was only pried awake by the sharp, misplaced sound of metal clanking. Really...metal clanking? Here and now, on this mountaintop, where we are all alone, wrapped in a cocoon of fog and mist, with no one for hundreds of miles? Really??? Semiconscious, trapped in a mental fog, I dismissed it, chalking it up to the white noise of an exhausted brain. I faded back into unconsciousness and the comfort of my warm feathered bag.

Clank, CLANK, tic, tic, clankity, click...CLUNK.

There it was again....but I'm mentally submerged in half a coma and I am sure it is a fragment of some dream. I want to ignore it but it is ten feet from my head, just outside a thin layer of nylon tent wall. CLANK, tic...tac, Clunk...

I am waking up now, and putting the full attention of my foggy brain onto the noise. What the hell? Now I know there really is a noise and I thought perhaps one of the planes had come loose in the wind. What else could it have been? Kurt is still out cold. I decide it is worth crawling part way out of my bag so I could unzip the tent flap and peek out. I really did not want to get up, get redressed in wet clothes and have to retie an airplane down in the wind and rain. But I was going to have to do it.

Maybe just the airplane door had flopped open and was banging in the wind...and I could ignore it. Most likely that was it.

With part of my nakedness still in the bottom half of the bag I reach the tent flap near my feet, unzip it and peer out, looking backwards and around towards the airplane fuselage that is eight feet away. We had camped directly under the end of the wing of my airplane. Kurt's was anchored next to that.

The noise was close, like really close, so I suspected it was a problem with my airplane. When I took a peek out the tent flap all I see is a big bent over hulk of brown fur. Shit! It's a brown bear! Somehow a damn bear has found us on top of the mountain! The bear is pawing and chewing on my bloody aluminum pack that is still all roped up with half a sheep in it.

Alaska Raw

The pack is leaning upright against the steel landing gear of my airplane. The noise was the aluminum pack clanking against the gear leg as the bear tugged and fussed with it trying to unpack his meal. By then I'm as awake as you can be without amphetamines. My heart is beating in my throat so hard I want to choke.

The bear had his head down and was concentrating on his good fortune, his rear was facing me just eight feet away. I could have jabbed him in the ass with a walking stick. The wind is blowing well enough to mask a lot of noise and he never heard me unzipping the tent. The status quo was chill for the moment. I did not want to yell out and try to scare him and then have a bigger problem on my hands.

I eased my head back into the tent and woke Kurt, shaking him and trying to whisper with some forcefulness. He did not process it very well in his foggy state, but when he saw me reaching for the rifle he knew something was up. My plan was to try to scare the bear off the meat. The gun was loaded and already chambered. With the safety flipped off I swiftly shuffled halfway out the tent door on my knees and got to where I could stand and shoot the bear if I had to. But he was parked right in between my two expensive airplane tires so I really did not want to take the chance of shooting up my own equipment, or Kurt's rig right next to it.

I raised the gun upright and fired a shot in the air while at the same time belting out my loudest Kurdistani battle cry...while jacking another cartridge into the chamber. I'm not sure what the yelling was supposed to do that the gun-fire would not, but I think it made me feel like I was on the offense instead of the defense. I'm in a crouch, barefooted and wearing nothing but my underwear, so I could have used some self-confidence.

The bear was understandably freaked out. It bolted, jumping and stumbling over one of my tundra tires and trying to disappear into the fog. What a buzz that all was, trying to go from snoozing in the sleeping bag to combat ready in an instant. My face was flush, my heart rate still pegged. It seemed that all of it had worked out just fine. But then that would be too simple.

Kurt had been spectating, peeking out of the tent and not knowing if all hell was going to break loose when I challenged the bear or not. We only had one gun. Neither of us ever carry a pistol on a sheep hunt. So Kurt had only a knife to participate with if things went sideways. That's when a deep background in kung fu would come in handy.

But the bear was gone. I relaxed a little and flipped the safety back on the rifle and squeezed back into the tiny tent.

Kurt: "He's not going away".

Me: "What? Bullshit, he was hauling ass. Did you see him running? I think he will stay gone. That scared the shit out of him."

Kurt: "He'll never stay away. He'll keep coming back. Watch."

Me: "Well it only needs to stay gone until we can get off this mountain".

I started to have my doubts also, after I gave it some thought. We were in a tough spot, not being able to leave until the fog lifted and not wanting another bear hide to add to the stack. Interestingly the bear was not a grizzly at all. It was a relatively rare brown phase black bear, and not very big, about six foot and two fifty to three hundred pounds. We could tell it was a black bear because it was missing the big hump over its shoulders, despite its chocolate color. It's unmistakable.

I got dressed and thought it best to stand guard for a while to see what was going to happen. There was a new sense of urgency to get off the spine before we had to fight the bear over who was getting to keep the sheep meat.

Visibility in any direction was about 100 feet. We were thick in the paste. It was eerily damp and quiet except for the wind that propelled the fog in ever-shifting shapes as it swept it up and over the saddle and down the other side. I was awake, like really awake, and I strained to see outward inside the mountain top cloud, watching and waiting. The fog could not lift soon enough. It felt like it was time to get off that spine.

But all morning it continued fog to the ground. There was no way we were moving. We sat around until two in the afternoon before some holes started to appear in the cover. It was not until almost 8 in the evening that it lifted enough to risk launching. And then we had another problem. Since noon, the wind had shifted westerly and was blowing directly 90 degrees across the saddle instead of aligning with our runway.

We were screwed unless we wanted to try the sole option left which was simply lining up into the wind and punching the throttle...and just driving off the cliff edge of the saddle, but before we actually had enough airspeed to fly. The airplanes should drop smoothly over the edge if all went swimmingly, and then begin to fly shortly thereafter. We thought about it...

It felt like we needed to make a move. If we stayed and waited, then the wind came up to 50 or 60 or more, and it easily can do that in the fall, the airplanes would be blown off the saddle.

There was risk in staying, and risk in going. We decided to do the cliff shot and we loaded the planes and warmed them up thoroughly. With the eighteen to twenty mile an hour wind we would not need to roll very far to get airborne, but there was only about 60 feet available and that would not get you enough airspeed to enable flight. We would depend on the sharp drop off to build that last bit of airspeed. I drew the short straw, mostly because Kurt went in first when we landed we decided it was my turn on point.

We both pushed to position my airplane by rolling it backwards down the side of the saddle. That would give the best running room ahead. In this position, when I pushed the throttle to its stop the plane would have to climb the hill some, but that extra room gave the engine a head start to be all spun up for the next 50 feet of run...to the crest of the spine and then off the other side.

With the plane warmed up and in place, the brakes jammed on to keep it from rolling backwards into oblivion, I began my checks: mags, fuel, carb heat, flaps. Deep Breath....full throttle, release brakes, deep breath, and go. The airplane gathered speed slowly as it labored a little going uphill, then it hit the top of the spine and gathered another ten miles an hour. Feeling hopeful but seriously anxious it would work, it accelerated another 30 feet and staggered off the cliff nose down. But it flew.

Kurt then followed each of the same preparations I had stepped through. I watched from the air as he pushed his airplane backwards until he had to jump into the cockpit and catch the brakes to keep it from going too far. That move in itself was highly risky. When I backed my airplane down he was there to help and I was in the cockpit manning the brakes so it could not get away from us. He went through his preflight check and then took off just as I had, while I circled above watching the action. It all worked. We were two for two on the sheep project and one sheep was a lifetime achievement award.

I have a lot of stories as you may imagine, and many of them will never be told. I chose to share this one mostly because it ended with such a prize, because it was so personally satisfying, the culmination of years and years of sheep hunting. To even find such an animal is a mix of dogged perseverance coupled with a lot of luck. I'll never be able to repeat it. The high, misplaced shots still nag me to this day.

Test firing the gun later showed it was in fact about 15 to 16 inches high which is way, way off. The rifle had been sighted in before the hunt to hit dead-on at 200. It worked just fine for Kurt when he shot his ram. Funny thing is neither of us remembers dropping it in the rocks or any other explanation as to how it came to be off so far. How it happened will always be a mystery. And yes, the meat was fantastic.

Chapter 9

The Wrong Side of the Edge (2010)

Curtis Spencer may as well have laid down and spent the last few seconds of his life reflecting on whatever one reflects on when taking their final several breaths; children, spouse, parents and all those about to be pried away. Sudden death is quick and deliberate but full of loose ends. Where would your mind begin, after recognizing that you had perhaps ten seconds to reconcile it all? There would be no time for the long list of regrets. It must come in flashes, in pictures, of those few you love and who love you, if it comes at all, if you can push aside the horror in those few seconds.

There was no way to know in advance that a 300 yard by 600 yard section of heavy wet snow, four feet thick and directly up slope, was held in place only by the barest of margins. You couldn't know that every force was balanced on a knife's edge but still held perfectly in check against gravity, that the smallest of disturbances could set it into motion, or that perhaps a train in the distance announced by its horn could immediately awaken a 4 million pound slab of compressed snow.

On that fateful day, the train rumbling towards us sent vibrations that radiated out toward every mountain face in the closely framed valley. Either from the train's disturbance or from some other trigger, the unstable snow pack above us overcame the friction anchoring its base and began to move. It moved quite slowly at first, like water beginning to breach the top of a full pail, creeping out of its containment, compounding bits of energy while relentlessly building speed.

Four of us were riding in a close group along the base of the hill, a hundred odd yards scattered between us, each of us directly in the avalanche path, each of us having more or less time to react depending on when, or if, we noticed the event unfolding. Five more of our party were just a little bit further back and narrowly out of harm's way.

Several million pounds of tumbling, accelerating wet snow makes some vibrations and noises that are unlike anything else in nature. Even to people who spend a lot of time in the mountains, it's a noise that is oddly out of place and causes a quick and sober focus in its direction.

The fracture line of this mass had first broken loose two hundred yards above and a couple of hundred yards laterally down the ridge from me, but this was directly above another of my friends, Jim Bowles. Jim was unaware of it. As I glanced up at the odd movement I could see what was happening and that the tear was quickly advancing the short lateral distance toward me with the upper edge separating like a sideways parting zipper.

Just as quickly as I recognized it for what it was, it was coming down directly above me also, and coming down on all of us. As best I can describe it, it I felt like I was in a slow motion movie, the special effects rolling the camera speed back so that a couple seconds of carnage can be absorbed at a pace the brain can handle.

In fact the avalanche looked slow because it was slow... at least at its beginning. The instant I noticed the movement it was at the pace of a man walking, appearing something like a gentle mud slide would look coming off a rain soaked hill, oozing like lava over the forms in its path, pushing down and crushing the alder and willows and anything else standing in its way.

Curtis Spencer had that very moment driven directly into the coming path of the avalanche, but it was still high above him, and he was still unaware. He was going to lend a hand to Jim who was struggling to get his snowmobile unstuck from the waist deep fresh snow.

Curtis came to a stop on his snowmobile and shut it down next to Jim. At some point Curtis heard the faint rumble and felt the unfamiliar vibration. Looking up, he recognized instantly that he was in a fight for his life. He had at most five seconds to escape. There were no good options and those that existed were being devoured as the snow mass accelerated. No longer moving like an oozing mud slide, it was half way down the mountain to us and rushing at about 20 miles an hour, soon to be 50 or better.

I am certain I saw the mountain fail before any of my three friends. I just happened to glimpse a bit of movement in peripheral vision way up and right. I had a more broad view than they, having been one hundred yards behind Curtis and Jim, and seventy five yards behind and to the right of another of our friends, Al Gage.

As Jim was struggling and digging in the deep powder snow trying to free his snowmobile and Curtis was pulling up alongside him, I was also on my way over to lend a hand. Al was just slightly down the gentle slope from all of us where the long steep mountain gave way to a near flat bench directly ahead.

It was clear to me that Al was unaware of what was developing above him as he rode straight ahead further into the path of the developing slide. Shot through with adrenalin, I reacted by yelling out a warning through my face mask at my friends who had helmets on, some with their snowmobiles running. Calling out was a panicked, futile and muffled effort with all hell breaking loose now directly above me. No one could hear anything I yelled. But at some point they heard and then felt the roaring release of energy.

I could now see a massive wall of hurtling snow slabs, tumbling through clouds of explosively charged white mist eating up the distance. My mind struggled to measure it in fractions of seconds and know that it was going to bury me alive. Instinctively, I jerked the snowmobile hard left, downslope, putting all my weight and muscle into the lean and rolling up into a banking, full power turn in the deep powder snow.

I held the wide open throttle, accelerating, and hunkered down waiting and expecting to be hit from behind by the force. It would be my good fortune that the machine obeyed every command. I went a couple hundred yards under full throttle before I glanced back once to see if I was in fact outrunning the wall of snow or if it would consume me like it would the others.

In the same instant I was making an urgent mental map of the terrain across the bench and downhill for the best way clear. I needed to guess which way the snow mass would ultimately flow and try to be anywhere else. Straight down was mostly blocked by a stand of timber. Angling down and away toward an open end of the semi-timbered bench under full power was the best option. But I had to be thinking about all possible exit paths should the wave catch and begin to engulf me.

There were a couple of directions it could flow besides straight down the slope. I looked back in a panic to see if I had chosen the way clear or something much worse. In that single split second look backward, my eyes captured the still unforgettable image of Al being hit broadside with the mass of the slide moving at full speed. He disappeared under ten feet of snow.

Jim was simply in the worst situation one could be in at that moment, his snowmobile stuck in the deep heavy snow eliminating any possibility of mobility. Curtis had just pulled up to him and shut off his machine, stepping off of it to lend Jim a hand.

Within seconds one or both of them noticed the wall of snow accelerating down upon them. It was rushing down the mountain by the time they saw it, having consolidated its energy to nearly full speed and crushing everything in its path.

There was really no way out for either of them. Curtis was one step away from his snowmobile which he had just shut down, and Jim was several steps behind him. Both were in waist deep snow that was nearly impossible to move through. Such snow is best navigated by crawling like an infant on forearms, knees and belly. There is no more awkward or debilitating of a natural medium to attempt to wade through than bottomless powder snow.

Instinct was in command. Reaction was immediate, fluid and decisive. Both Curtis and Jim wanted desperately to live.

Curtis motioned for Jim to jump towards him and onto his (Curtis's) snowmobile as Curtis himself lunged to grab the controls of his machine. Finally throwing himself onto it, Curtis flipped off the kill switch and slammed his hand down on the start button in one desperate motion. The engine fired. Curtis turned his head back to see if Jim was climbing on with him, or had been able to grab the rear bumper.

Then their world went dark.

A wall of snow crushed onto the men. Curtis's body was smashed forward into the handle bars. His form fitting, impact-resistant chest protector that he wore under his clothing was broken by the forces. The handle bars were displaced and bent forward. He broke the small windshield attached to the front of the cowling when his helmet was crushed into the forward bay of the snowmobile. Curtis recalled in that instant, the sound of the engine being drowned out, muffled by the enveloping deluge of snow as though the running snowmobile had been submerged deep in water.

His hands had in fact made it to the controls as the blast hit and the force of the impact that leveled his body also crushed his hands onto the bars as he throttled to full power. The high performance snowmobile exploded with its characteristic rush of energy and shot up and out of the smothering onslaught of snow. Curtis was spit out like a submarine surfacing out of control. Jim had been unable to make that last second lunge to at least grab Curtis's bumper and try to hang on.

There simply were no miracles left for our friend Jim. He was crushed under the massive wall of accelerating snow slabs and ice. On the side of that gorgeous hill that clear February afternoon, Jim Bowles and Al Gage paid the ultimate price for being avid outdoorsmen, for wanting to experience the excitement and freedom that we hunger for in the wilderness.

But against every probability, Curtis Spencer lived.

I was able to outrun and out maneuver all but the very tail of the slide and came through it safely. I remember my entire body being limp from exertion and fear.

As the cloudy mist from millions of pounds of tumbling snow subsided and then settled, I saw Curtis emerge downslope and upright on his running snowmobile. He immediately pulled his machine around in an accelerated turn and tracked back uphill to where the snow first collapsed on him and Jim. Another friend in our group, Eric Spitzer, who had been back just a few hundred yards, had now made his way up to the avalanche site and pulled up parallel to me as we both rode toward Curtis, looking for any sign of Al or Jim. There was no a trace of either of them. Blanketing everything was a massive mound of avalanche rubble that stretched 500 feet wide and 1500 feet downslope.

Eric was for sure the biggest and one of the strongest men among us. An active Alaska State Trooper, Eric was also well trained for emergencies. His past life as a Marine Corps drill sergeant made him a natural leader. His six foot five inch frame added to this imposing stature and, accordingly, everyone's confidence in him. This is a guy you want on your team. I am still amazed at how he took charge, calmed nerves, and helped guide a coordinated effort.

Ed Gohr was just seconds behind Eric. Ed, a long-time hunting partner of mine, is a bull of a man and as capable as anyone you would want to be with in the field. Ed would have been right in the middle of it all, when the avalanche fell, had he not blown a drive belt on his snowmobile moments earlier. Quickly behind Ed came three other of our extended party who had worked their way over to the site once they fully understood what had happened.

We quickly coalesced into a sizable, very capable squad. All of us had carried avalanche equipment, shovels, probes and beacons. Everyone was armed ahead of time for such a rescue and no one wasted any time. We knew seconds mattered and split up into two teams and attempted to find Al and Jim simultaneously.

I felt like I was in shock and trying to process it all and just not believing Jim and Al were not going to pop out from around the stand of spruce trees in the foreground, or the alder bushes just past the avalanche chute. My friends could not possibly be gone. I simply couldn't process the finality of it. The facts of the moment refused to take hold and become my new reality, even though I actually saw Al being consumed with my own eyes.

It's now a...rescue?? Not possible. They must be here somewhere? Should we look farther down the hill?

Part of my shock was no doubt the overdose of adrenaline that still flooded my body as a result of barely outrunning my own death. I found it difficult to breathe and impossible to concentrate.

Eric led us, or at least I can say for sure he led me, and I am thankful for that since I was too rattled to think well. Curtis and Ed instantly took charge as well and put everyone to work.

As part of our group began the search for Al, we were troubled by comments that he had not worn an avalanche beacon, or at least someone recalled Al mentioning that he did not have one. As a couple of us combed the hill below for the last spot I had seen Al, others looked for any sign of Jim or his machine poking up through the snow. There were no signs of either rider on the surface. We swept the spots Al and Jim were last seen with the avalanche beacons. There were no beacon responses from anywhere near where Al went down, and we went over it again and then again.

Alaska Raw

But Jim's beacon was chirping at us from deep within the layers of white jumble. At that point there was a glimmer of hope of finding Jim alive, but only if we worked fast enough.

If Jim had a pocket to breathe in, like inside his helmet and face shield, he could last a half an hour or possibly longer. The snow is dense and hard but still porous. Several men stayed with the search for Al, holding out hope the beacon would start working from some different angle, if there was a beacon at all, or they would hit a clue by probing. They worked the probes in and out of the snow mass quickly and relentlessly in grids.

For the other group, the process now was to try to locate Jim more specifically using feedback from the beacon that he carried on his body and which transmitted up through the depths to any of the many receivers that we carried. The beacons were both transmitters and receivers and are standard avalanche safety gear. Five or six of us fanned out and walked the hard compacted snow straining to hear a signal. Within a minute we had a steady beeping which meant Jim was directly underneath the signal in the snow pack. The beacons do not give a depth.

We all then began to probe the snow with long aluminum wands, the folding, extendable tools made for the purpose. We were hoping to sense the soft resistance of a body as the probe otherwise glided down unobstructed with each thrust. We probed directly down from the most intense beeping, then sideways at angles, until finally after several excruciatingly long minutes one probe hit something hard and deep. It did not feel like frozen sod nor sound like rock. A faint sound transmitted up through the long aluminum pole. The contact clanked like metal. It was Jim's snowmobile.

After much more probing around ten feet down, feeling for that soft feedback of clothing and flesh, we found nothing but more metal.

It was a crushing disappointment at the time, as we knew the beacon should have been on Jim's body but sometimes riders will put them on the snowmobile in a handlebar bag or someplace in a gear compartment but not actually wear them. It's a terrible practice since avalanches often separate the rider from his snowmobile, but it was looking like it was possible Jim had done that. Everyone's anxiety was acute and building. It had been 10 to 15 minutes. We all knew the odds go way down after 25 or 30 minutes.

The other possibility was that Jim was directly underneath his machine and we could not sense him with a probe. We still had a good chance to save him if he was still alive. Everyone began a frenzied effort to dig to the depth of the snowmobile on the chance Jim was under it. But that effort took almost fifty more minutes. Avalanche snow is hard and compact like an impenetrable clay. It's hell to dig.

Progress is made more difficult as you descend into a manmade hole that becomes funnel shaped, narrowed the further you go down making less room available for bodies to work the shovels. Near the very bottom there was only room for two men, so we took turns there, chipping, digging and gouging with every ounce of energy until exhaustion. I knew it was time to hand off the shovel each time when I was exhausted to the point of puking.

Nothing you did was fast enough. No effort expended was good enough. No idea or methodology was productive enough. I have never in my life felt so physically or mentally impotent as during that hour. Nothing you did, or that anyone did that hour, felt anywhere near adequate.

Yet it was absolutely all any of us physically had to give. Nothing you did could make you feel confident you were going to be able to reach your friend who you knew was struggling in his darkest hour for his last breath.

Nothing was good enough. I will never forget that feeling...supreme and overwhelming inadequacy. It haunts me.

We reached Jim's snowmobile, its aluminum tail section coming into view as the shovels and fists cleared it first. After quickly shoveling along its length toward the front, Jim's gloved hand was exposed and emerged from under the front ski. It did not move. The machine was found as it was buried, fully on its side. Before it was completely excavated, Eric thought we had enough manpower to muscle the sled up and out, if enough of us could reach down and grab on to some part of it and heave. He was right and it saved precious digging time. The snowmobile was pried loose from the ten foot deep conical pit exposing Jim.

Jim had been lengthwise underneath the snowmobile. It appeared to me that when he knew the snow was going to bury him, he dove to the deck tightly along the sheltered side of the machine trying to get some protection. The rushing snow flipped the machine up on its side and both were immediately buried.

Three of us pushed Jim's body up from the bottom of the hole while others above received him. I was in the hole lifting Jim's body and once I got squarely underneath him, I placed my hand in the small of his back directly on his spine to lift. It felt severed. I add this here only to share my hope that Jim may not have suffered.

Our believing that Al and Jim's deaths were quick is one of the ways those of us who lived through it can begin in some small way to reconcile the horror of it. Emotionally it is very hard to not continue rerunning in your head the ways it could have been different. And years later I still do.

Crew at the top of the hole immediately removed Jim's helmet. Eric knew CPR well and initiated the mouth to mouth while I kept up chest compressions. We were able to get word out to the Alaska State Troopers that we needed a medical evacuation for at least one and possibly two men. The crew that was working the probes looking for Al continued looking all across the downslope for any sign but the effort was unsuccessful.

Teams of searchers would find him ten days later with cadaver dogs and probe lines during a methodical and emotionally intense recovery effort.

At one point about ten minutes into the CPR I noticed Jim's face began to have some pink replacing the blue. There was some hope from this but still no pulse or heartbeat. After an hour, and beyond the time we really believed Jim could be revived, a helicopter and paramedics arrived to take over. Eric and I were able to hand off the CPR, or at least the decisions to continue life saving measures, to the paramedics.

Of all my experiences in the outdoors this is the event that left permanent scars. I have spent years trying to get my head around the loss of my two friends. I can tell you, and my wife and closest friends can confirm, the event changed me in some lasting ways.

When you see how fast it can all come to an end, and how many people's lives are instantly changed by losing a loved one, it makes you think twice about why and how you are living. As filled with sorrow as I am, I cannot imagine what Jim and Al's wives and families went through. We miss them both.

A Final Word

We all ask ourselves from time to time, what acts of ours should, in the end, accumulate to some satisfactory finish that memorializes the high water mark of our time here. What body of striving or accomplishment or just earned sense of peace will we reflect on when we are all alone and mentally ticking down the list of missed opportunities, hoping to leave here with as few regrets as possible? A summit bagged or some expanse conquered perhaps? Sure. That all works. Big, bright, tangible.

Maybe the mark is no mark at all but only the satisfaction of rejecting a life lived looking through a keyhole constructed by the myths and memes of our time, a keyhole that divines order out of disorder in the minds of those who cannot live without it. Maybe it's not about any high mark but all the white space in between, savoring the moments we live that are scrubbed of all pretense and insincerity. Among such moments are our experiences in the wilderness.

There is something spiritual about looking behind you after just laying a single mark on crystalline untracked snow that reaches upwards through the frozen hills and canyons for thousands of feet. The landscape is your canvas but the picture you drew will soon be gone, as will its artist. It is the canvas that lives on forever, waiting to temporarily accept the handiwork of another spiritual voyager.

Right there among the gods and angels of our vivid imagination, another picture will emerge, laid down a piece at a time like a painter drawing color from his brush, and again it will disappear leaving nothing at all. In a life well lived we should craft many beautiful things, songs from nothing that we sing into the wind without a care if they are ever heard again.